# KICKING
# THROUGH
# THE ASHES

*My Life as a Stand-up in the 1980s Comedy Boom*

## RITCH SHYDNER

MR, MEDIA BOOKS
ST. PETERSBURG, FLORIDA, USA

**Visit us on the web!**
http://www.RitchShydner.com
http://www.MrMediaBooks.com

**Front cover photograph by Rosanne Buemi Jarvis**

**Front and back cover design by Lori Parsells**
http://www.VibranceAndVision.com


Mr. Media® is a registered trademark of Bob Andelman

Manufactured in the United States of America
10 9 8 7 6 5 4 3 2 1

ISBN: 1535565284
ISBN-13: 978-1535565288


Also available as an e-book.

RUSS,
I HOPE YOU ENJOY YOUR JOURNEY
AS MUCH~~AS~~ AS I

*For Vic Anderson*

ENJOYED MINE.
GO HARD + HAVE
FUN.

iii

"*Kicking Through the Ashes* is surely one of the best books ever written about the experience of becoming a stand-up comic and an artist. Ritch Shydner is a fantastic storyteller. It's a hard book not to keep reading. Each chapter is better than the last. Personal and provocative. A thrilling memoir." *Mike Binder, comedian, writer, actor, director, novelist, etc, etc.*

· · ·

"Ritch Shydner's dad told his friends that Ritch had joined a religious cult rather than have to admit that his son was pursuing a career as a stand-up. Though an argument could be made that the two things have more in common than his dad could have imagined. Ritch tells the story of the millions of small battles and ground skirmishes he fought as he morphed from law student into real live working comedian in a compelling way. I enjoyed reading it." *Merrill Markoe, author/humorist*

# Contents

Acknowledgments ............................................................... xii

Introduction by Bill Maher ............................................... xiv

Foreword ........................................................................... xv

1 **"Don't Want Nothin' That Anybody Can Touch"** ............. 1
The source of humor.

2 **"Waiting for Someone or Something to Show You the Way"** ............................................................................ 5
Hard lessons for an amateur comic.

3 **"Each Night Begins a New Day"** .................................... 12
Law school turns funny.

4 **"So Now You See the Light"** .......................................... 17
The first time doing stand-up.

5 **"I Get My Back into My Living"** ................................... 19
The search for an audience.

6 **"There's a World Where I Can Go and Tell My Secrets"** ... 23
El Brookman's bar.

7 **"It's the Classic Contradiction, the Unavoidable Affliction"** ............................................................................. 29
A living-room show.

8 **"He Got Caught in the Spotlight"** ................................. 32
The opening act, lessons in showbiz.

9 **"They Come from the Cities and They Come from the Smaller Towns"** ............................................................. 38
1970s stand-up scenes across America.

10 **"I Rest My Case, You're Out of Reach"** ........................ 45
The Laughing Stock at Garvin's.

11 **"Go Ahead, Bite the Big Apple"** .................................. 51
Move to New York City.

12 **"Open Your Eyes, Look at Your Part, Boy"** .................. 56
Bombing as a booker.

13 **"A Student at the Comedy College"** ............................. 59
The New York City Showcase Clubs.

v

14  **"A Buck Dancer's Choice"**                                      66
Rodney Dangerfield.

15  **"Try to Catch the Deluge in a Paper Cup"**                      70
The temptation of an agent.

16  **"You Gotta Do It Till You're Through It So You Better**         72
**Get to It"**
Funny for money in 1979.

17  **"Don't Need No Rank Beginners When It's Time to Shake**         77
**My Shake"**
Uncle Dirty.

18  **"It's Pretty Human, Make All the People Holler"**               80
A fork in the road, clean or dirty.

19  **"First You Must Learn How to Smile as You Kill"**               84
A lesson for the monkey from the organ grinder.

20  **"The Wind Catches Your Feet, Sends You Flying"**                86
A first tour on a new road.

21  **"Once I Get Started I Go to Town"**                             89
Mike MacDonald.

22  **"To Listen to Your Fears"**                                    94
Canadian immigration and the art of stand-up.

23  **"The Clown ... Does the Trick of Disaster"**                    96
Hitting the stage and the wall.

24  **"Where the Shadows Run from Themselves"**                       97
A good room.

25  **"Something to Make Us All Happy"**                             102
Props.

26  **"Come too Far to Ever Turn Back Now"**                         105
Andy Kaufman.

27  **"Please Allow Me to Introduce Myself"**                        109
Publicity, credits, and then an introduction.

28  **"Consider This, a Slip**                                       114
Heckling.

29  **"Gettin' Had, Gettin' Took, I Tell You Folks, It's Harder**    120
**Than It Looks"**
A bad gig with good friends.

30  **"Looking for a Sign that the Universal Mind Has Written     125
    You into the Passion Play"**
    Ronnie Shakes and Rodney Dangerfield.
31  **"Circumstance Beyond Our Control"**                          127
    The show must go on.
32  **"What You Pay for Your Inches of Fame"**                     131
    Move to Los Angeles.
33  **"Don't Give a Damn for Just the In-Betweens"**              136
    Jay Leno.
34  **"Great Expectations, Everybody's Watching You"**            139
    Robin Williams.
35  **"This Ain't No Disco, This Ain't No Fooling Around"**        144
    The 1980s stand-up comedy boom.
36  **"Saturday Night I Like to Raise a Little Harm"**             154
    Ollie Joe Prater down in Pittsburgh.
37  **"Ease Out Soft and Slow"**                                   158
    A town not ready for comedy.
38  **"The Devil's on the Loose"**                                 161
    Comedy seeks the level of the room.
39  **"Thursday to Saturday, Money's Gone Already"**              164
    John Fox and the white stuff.
40  **"All the Boys There, at the Bar, Began to Sing Along"**      167
    A honeymoon on the road.
41  **"To the Comfort of the Strangers, Slipping Out Before        168
    They Say So Long"**
    The opening act and the rest of the show.
42  **"Funky Little Boat Race"**                                   172
    Career timing trumped joke timing.
43  **"Fight Your Secret War"**                                    174
    Performance under the influence.
44  **"Revel in Your Abandon"**                                    181
    Bumped record holder.
45  **"Nothing to Do, No Way to Go Home"**                         184
    Vic Dunlop up in Alaska.
46  **"I'm the Innocent Bystander"**                               189
    Comic, coke, and convicts.

47  **"If Dreams Were Thunder and Lightning Was Desire"**    191
*The Tonight Show Starring Johnny Carson*

48  **"Cause There's Something in a Sunday That Makes a Body Feel Alone"**    195
Sam Kinison.

49  **"Man, You've Been a Naughty Boy, You Let Your Face Grow Long"**    201
Drunk, disgusted, and unfunny.

50  **"Living Just a Little, Laughing Just a Little"**    205
Getting sober is not a joke.

51  **"Hocked All My Yesterdays, Don't Try and Change My Tune"**    208
The power of letting go.

52  **"I'm Gonna Ride the Serpent"**    212
Phyllis Diller.

53  **"Just This Side of Deranged"**    215
The in and outs of sex and stand-up.

54  **"Heartaches Are Heroes When Their Pockets Are Full"**    222
Changing a reputation, one night at a time.

55  **"Careful What You Say, You'll Give Yourself Away"**    223
A writer and a performer.

56  **"Danced Myself Right Out the Womb"**    229
Bill Hicks.

57  **"I Don't Mind Other Guys Dancing with My Girl"**    235
Never saw them coming.

58  **"We Are Vain and We Are Blind"**    239
An industrial accident.

59  **"Law of Average Plainly States That Chances Go Around"**    241
*Married With Children.*

60  **"I Was Crowned With a Spike Right through My Head"**    246
Heckled by a ghost.

61  **"The Simple Things You See Are All Complicated"**    251
Not another stupid pet trick on *Late Night With David Letterman.*

62  **"They're Only Pretty Lies"**    253
Jokes, Jokes, and Jokes.

63 **"It's the Same Old Tune, Fiddle and Guitar"** 262
Morey Amsterdam and your joke.

64 **"There Must Be Some Kind of Way Out of Here Said the Joker to the Thief"** 266
The joke thief.

65 **"A Connecting Principle ... Almost Imperceptible"** 274
Tim Allen, a related act.

66 **"Tongue-tied and Twisted, Just an Earthbound Misfit"** 277
Forgetting a one-night stand.

67 **"Talking Funny and Looking Funny and Talking About Nobody Judge Me"** 281
What to wear on *Late Night With David Letterman.*

68 **"Got to Find a Way to Bring Some Understanding Here Today"** 285
The comedy condo.

69 **"Nothing to Do and All Day to Do It"** 289
Comics selling merchandise.

70 **"If I Had My Chance, I Could Make Those People Dance"** 293
Comedy club owners.

71 **"A Man Hears What He Wants to Hear and Disregards the Rest"** 299
The Steve Martin movie *Roxanne.*

72 **"Eagle Flew Out of the Night"** 303
Filling in For Howard Stern.

73 **"Turning Cartwheels Across the Floor"** 308
No dancing on *American Bandstand.*

74 **"I'll Try Not to Sing Out of Key"** 311
Ringo's joke.

75 **"You Have You to Complete and There Is No Deal"** 313
Changing the audience.

76 **"I Got a Baby's Brain and an Old Man's Heart"** 318
The why of the laugh.

77 **"Let Me Play Among the Stars"** 324
Carson convinces Dad.

78 **"Everybody Wants a Box of Chocolates"** 327
The Prince and the Prisoner of War.

79 **"Someday You'll Need Someone Like They Do"**     330
Funny and nice.
80 **"Paint-by-Number Dreams"**     335
Stand-up, the one-man show.
81 **"Suspended from a Rope, Inside a Bucket Down a Hole"**     340
Career advice from Sean Penn.
82 **"You're So Afraid of Being Somebody's Fool"**     343
A writers room, not a stage.

Glossary     349

Index     362

About the Author     372

# Acknowledgments

The stories and events recounted in *Kicking Through the Ashes* took place between 20 and 40 years ago, so I have relied on many people for help with memory installation and repair, including: Jeff Abraham, Len Austrevich, Alan Bursky, Kerry Awn, Craig Bell, Joe Bolster, Jordan Brady, Jimmy Brogan, Paul Brookman, Pat Buckles, Tom Cahill, Tony Conaway, Randy Credico, Barry Crimmins, Evan Davis, Lou DiMaggio, Chris DiPetta, Max Dolcelli, Tom Dreesen, Joe Dunckel, Debbe Duperrieu, Dave Edison, Jim Edwards, Bob Fisher, Peter Fogel, Jim Gagan, Bert Haas, Argus Hamilton, Scott Hansen, Will Hartnett, Allan Havey, Craig Hawksley, Jon Hayman, Clay Heery, Andy Huggins, Hiram Kasten, Chou Chou Keel-Smith, Roger Kleiss, Kenny Kramer, Mitch Kutash, James Ladmirault, Howard Lapides, Colleen McGarr, Tim MacAllister, Mike MacDonald, John McDonnell, Bud McLaughlin, Jeff Marder, Camillo Melchiorre, Geno Michelini, Richie Minervini, Steve Mittleman, Harry Monocrusos, Tommy Moore, Joe "Rufus Quigley" Mullin, Roger Mursick, Bob Nickman, Diane Nichols, Joey Novick, Judy Orbach, Rick Overton, Dan Pasternak, John Pate, Steve Pearl, Jeff Penn, Mark Pitta, Bill Rafferty, Tom Rhodes, Mark Ridley, Kelley Rogers, Kevin Rooney, Mike Rowe, Bruno Schirripa, Oxie Scrubb, Rick Siegel, Steve Skrovan, Dwight Slade, Bobby Slayton, Jan Smith, Carrie Snow, Tom Sobel, Jerry Stanley, Tom Stern, David Strassman, Duncan Strauss, Dave Tribble, Tony Vicich, Howard Vine, Howard Wagman, Bob Ward, Steve Young and Ron Zimmerman.

My dear friend Rosanne Buemi Jarvis shot the great cover photograph of me in the mid 1980s. I was delighted to make contact with her again after all these years and so appreciate her permission to share her image here.

Most of the interior pictures and newspaper clips were shared with me by friends over the years, while a few were the result of special requests for this book. I have done my best to remember everyone and give credit where due. *(If I missed a photography credit, please let me know and I will correct it in a future edition.)* Thank you for many of these to: Gladys Anderson, Mark Anderson, Andy Bloom, Arthur Chicchese, Alice Christov, Scott "Bentley" Davis, Michael Finney, Paul Brookman, Rosanne Buemi Jarvis, Debbie Caltan, Debbe DuPerrieu, Bob Fisher, Silver Friedman, Wally Garrison, Lesley Howes, Harry Monocrusos, Joe "Newton Glutton" Mullin, Linda Myers Jackson, Dave Nuttycombe, Judy Orbach, Jeff Penn, Mark Schiff, Estee Seward, Jim Shahin, Christopher Wallis.

My friend Ron Durkin did a wonderful job of editing several photos.

Leah Krinsky, in addition to providing free psychotherapy, was kind enough to read several drafts of this book and offer great advice on organization, themes, and editing, for which I will always be grateful.

Some friends were guilty of general aiding and abetting; thank you Billy Connolly, Robert Tepper, Mike Ulloa, and the guys at the Big Easy Cigar Shop.

My manager, Sheri Rosenberg Kelton, steered my choices for this book and other projects and I am so grateful for her clear-headed guidance.

I had no idea that when I appeared on the Mr. Media Interviews video podcast (mrmedia.com) in January 2016 that it would lead to a book deal, but that's exactly what happened. Many thanks to host/publisher Bob Andelman and his team at Mr. Media Books for a smooth experience in bringing this story to life. My copy editor, Mimi Andelman, impressed me over and over again with her attention to detail and suggestions for storytelling improvements. And cover designer Lori Parsells put in long hours creating a look and feel that was exactly what I envisioned.

I also appreciate the work of indexer Mary Harper in organizing the contents so that my friends and family can go right to the places where they are mentioned by name — although I do hope they will read the entire book!

My emergency contact number and primary caretaker, Ronna Dragon, read every piece first. Her evaluations forced me to rewrite. Her laughter encouraged me to keep going and to write another, soon.

And, of course, no list of thanks would be complete without my parents, James and Frances Shidner, and my children, Van, Sierra and James. I love you all.

# Introduction

As a comedian now for more years than I can believe — 37 — I've encountered all types. But comedy is based on analysis, and so it stands to reason that a fair amount of comics are not only hyper-analytical about everything around them that they're looking to make into a joke ... but also about their profession itself. I like those kind of comics — I can talk to them all day long. And one of the very best analyzers of this crazy business we call show is Ritch Shydner.

Ritch and I met in 1979 at Catch A Rising Star (he says with unfounded confidence — it could have been '80 at the Comic Strip, it's a fuckton of years ago!) .... Anyway, we met, and we must have hit it off because we've been thick as thieves ever since. Of course, it's not hard to be friends with Ritch — funny, great laugher, and a real guy's guy. He was a little older than myself and a few of the other rookies when we met, so he was a good guy to know because he, for example, knew where you could buy mushrooms.

I told a story about Ritch in one of my stand-up specials, although I didn't mention his name. I was making an analogy about the horrible state of America's infrastructure, as one does in a comedy show. What happened was, Ritch and I and another comic went to this drug dealer's house to get, well, mushrooms. It was a very nice, spacious apartment, and I, living in a box on 8th Avenue above a bus stop, was very impressed. Even cooler, the whole place was decked out with candles, from the moment you walked in all the way through to the upscale-hippie living room. After we left, I said to Ritch, "That guy's so cool, with all those candles" and Ritch said, "He's not cool, he put the electric bill up his nose."

And that's why you should buy this book. Ritch Shydner brings that kind of funny, biting and true analysis to stand-up and sitcom writing and every other weird thing he's gone near. Jump on in — the writing's fine!

**Bill Maher**
*July 2016*

*Bill Maher is a stand-up comedian who has hosted the political discussion "Real Time with Bill Maher" on HBO since 2003. In 1993, he created "Politically Incorrect" on Comedy Central; the show moved to ABC four years later and ran until 2002.*

# Foreword

Once this book was completed, it occurred to me what tremendous chutzpah it took to write a memoir. Especially when no one was asking for it. This book could have easily been titled, "Memories From a Comic No One Remembers."

I started and finished this book because of my late mentor, Vic Anderson. When I met Vic in the spring of 2011, I was dead in the water. A year earlier, my stand-up comeback in Jordan Brady's documentary, *I Am Comic*, fizzled like a wet bottle rocket.

Applications to more than a few straight jobs finally led to an interview to be a Hollywood tour van driver. The Chinese owner dismissed me with a wave of her hand and broken English, "You too old."

I came to Vic after a 13-day stint of staring at the ceiling in the UCLA Psychiatric Unit. I thank Alan Bursky for recommending Julian Neil, and Julian for sending me to Vic. At some point Vic asked what I once did to pay my bills. I said stand-up and comedy writing. Vic suggested I do them again, but for fun and for free.

Like with no other person in my life, I did everything Vic suggested. The stand-up path was clear — free local performances soon led to paying out-of-town gigs. I didn't know what to do about the writing. Vic thought the stories I told about my past might be the sort of thing people would enjoy reading on Facebook. No one ever moved me like Vic. His very presence gave me a contact high.

When he was dying of liver cancer in April 2015, Vic was typically thinking of everyone else. One day he said to me, "You're going to finish the book, right?" Right.

The next few bits of inspiration were easy, the beginning and end of me.

I wanted my parents to know what happened to the little boy who wouldn't stay in the yard. James Thomas Shidner gave me a sense of humor. Frances Lois Hartley Shidner nurtured it with her laughter. They wanted a lawyer, but after reading this they might realize why it could not have gone any other way.

I wanted my kids (Savannah Grace, Sierra Rose and James Wesley) to know what I did before they met me, to see me as someone other than the old man snoring on couch.

Initially, the impulsion to write showed up, like a packed second show on a Saturday night. These stories and opinions had to come out of me, like a tumor. Along the way, when facing the blinking cursor became more daunting than a roomful of drunken bachelor parties at a second show Friday night, I used a few more reasons, or rationalizations.

Most of the stories I simply remembered. That may astound some, especially considering what I was feeding my head in the early eighties. The anecdotes were filed in my brain because they were funny. I have forgotten names of old girlfriends, one I even lived with, but the funny stays, always.

I went through my storage and found some old notebooks. My poor penmanship made most of it unreadable, but some forgotten incidents were found in the scribbling. Letters, postcards, and even checkbooks, triggered more memories. A few years ago, my mom gave me a box filled with pictures, reviews, and newspaper ads I sent her in the early years of my stand-up. It was probably an attempt to show her that her Biff had "made good somewheres."

I made every effort to get the events and dates factually correct, contacting people by phone, email and even snail mail. Posting the stories on Facebook prompted witnesses, victims and co-conspirators to post comments or send private messages. Whether they verified or corrected my posts, it all helped greatly.

Two guys read my stories unfolding on Facebook, and realizing their mishaps might be soon chronicled, contacted me and asked for a pass. They were good guys who suffered a momentary lapse of reason so those two stories were left out of the book. I probably could have written the stories without their names, but they asked and that was that. Maybe I did come down a little hard on a couple of comics, but considering the knife fight that stand-up sometimes was thirty years ago, that was unavoidable.

It was a lot of fun reconstructing these memories from the 1980s. Time burned away the pain and humiliation and left a fine residue of gratitude and humor. The grinding ambition to be relevant in stand-up comedy had long since been replaced by an appreciation of the art form. I was left in a perfect situation to chronicle an era. After all, my career shadowed the 1980s Comedy Boom. I was there, dammit.

Attempting a historical account provided a bit of a higher purpose, but also a responsibility to the comics of my generation. The stories had to be mine, but the book wasn't just about me. It didn't matter if we were good friends, or simply co-workers at a temp job posing as a one-nighter. It didn't matter if you were a comic who, as Red Buttons once joked, "Never got a dinner," or one who ended up owning the restaurant. This book is for all those pros who, at one time or another, had sets so pure and so funny that they left the stage convinced that nobody could make an audience laugh any louder or longer. That on that night, in front of that audience, they were as funny as any comic in America.

For comics my age, the battles are over. The lands have been conquered, the banners raised. I am at peace with the fact that I took it as far as I could take it with what I had. I believe everybody gets their shot. Go up there enough times and you will be seen. You may not be happy with how they see you, but you will be seen. Breaks, luck, who you know ... these are just excuses. Everybody ends up where they should. If you came into stand-up for any reason other than hearing that sweet laughter you were most likely doomed before ever grabbing that first microphone.

One of the first showbiz jokes I heard was about an old man who followed the elephants in the circus parade with a shovel and trash can. At the end of the parade a concerned citizen approached the old man, "Sir, why would you humiliate yourself in this way? Surely you can do something better than shovel elephant shit." The old man replied, "And what, quit showbiz?"

Rare is the person who can get by just doing what they did to enter show business. In my mind, that old man in the joke didn't always follow the elephants with a shovel. Once he was a high wire act, a star in the center ring. When he could no longer do that he became the ringmaster, and when he became too old to charm the ringsiders, he became a ticket taker and then finally, the cleanup man for the elephants. Somewhere along the line I became the old man in that joke, doing whatever it takes to stay in the circus.

If I were 30 again, with what I know now ... I'd do it all over again, only with more enthusiasm. I'd make the same mistakes, and find some new ones. Whenever a young comic calls for advice I always end by saying, "Go at it as hard as you can." It's almost a paradox but I then tell them to have fun. After all it's only stand-up, not brain surgery. That is until the audience doesn't laugh at two jokes in a row, then it seems as mysterious as medieval alchemy.

Maybe some young comic might read this book and realize they are part of a continuum, a long tradition in an original American art form. These stories are not intended to show we old guys were better, because I sure don't think we were. My hope is to demonstrate that, despite changes in technology and style, the basic personality of the stand-up never changes. As George Burns once said, "The comic soul is eternal."

In 1984, I was killing time in a Cleveland record store looking for old comedy records when a black guy wearing a watch cap and an old army jacket handed me an Allen Drew album, "You might like this." While I studied the album trying to figure out who Allen Drew was, the man said, "I saw you last night. You're funny." Before I could become the punchline to an old joke by asking him which show he saw he continued, "Yeah, but you need me to be funny." He gave me a little smile and walked away. I was stunned. The truth of his statement was not a revelation — it only takes two minutes in stand-up to realize that without the laughter we are just idiots ranting in the dark — but I had never been confronted with that fundamental rule of law so boldly by an audience member. At that moment I was overwhelmed with a most unusual feeling, a sense of gratitude. So finally I want to thank the Cleveland Truthsayer, and everyone who ever laughed at me. You gave me this life.

# 1. "DON'T WANT NOTHIN' THAT ANYBODY CAN TOUCH"

The first time I made someone laugh was in Mrs. Kent's second-grade classroom. My friend Steve Raleigh was seated next to me, drawing a boat. He pressed the pencil too hard and punctured the paper on the bottom of his boat, below the water line. I said, "Got a leak, Cap?" Steve laughed so hard we both spent time facing the chalkboard.

I believe most comics retain a clear picture of getting their first laugh. In a 2009 interview I asked a then 95-year-old Professor Irwin Corey if he remembered his first laugh. The Professor immediately recited a funny poem that he performed at age 10 for the delight of his classmates in the New York Hebrew Orphan Asylum, a perfectly intact 85-year-old memory.

My parents provided us with a very comfortable middle-class way of life. There was a nice home, with plenty of food and clothing. There was also a lot of alcohol, which brought wild swings in behavior — dreadful silence or frightening yelling, dark secrets or inappropriate disclosures, violent rage or wild laughter. There was no middle in our very fine house.

I suffered panic attacks from an early age, although I didn't have a name for them at the time. Some nights the fear pinned me to the bed, locking my body in place and making each breath a struggle. When it passed, I would go back to my *Mad* magazine.

My dad loved the funny. He went to see comics like Moms Mabley at Jersey nightclubs in Cherry Hill and Atlantic City, and repeated their jokes for days afterward. Nobody dared talk during *The Jackie Gleason*

**1960**

> I locked the boiler door
> crawled underneath the
> thing and the teacher caught
> to me sent to the office and
> I had to right this letter!
>
> signed Ritchie

**1961**

### TEACHER'S COMMENTS

Ritchie has shown an improvement in his conduct during the later part of this report period.

Ritchie needs to learn how to conform to school regulations - such as no unnecessary talking in the classroom and talks. Glad he is to listen and do as he is told when spoken to - rather than to see what he can get away with.

### ATTENDANCE RECORD

**1963**

Grade Six ........ **6** .....................................

### TEACHER'S COMMENTS

1/8 Ritchie is an intelligent boy but has no self control and shows little respect for others. His work is hurriedly done with no regard for neatness or accuracy.

Irritable, Restless and Discontent ... the early years, 1960, 1961 & 1963

*Show* or an appearance by a comedian on *The Ed Sullivan Show*. But when the jokes were flying, the belt wasn't. I learned the power of laughter early in life.

During my parents' boozy parties I sat at the top of the stairs listening to my dad howling at one of his comedy albums. I was amazed at how the laughter transformed my angry and intimidating father. When no one was around, I played them, listening to Bob Newhart over and over, trying to understand the magic behind funny.

My dad gave me a great work ethic, a sense of humor, and the ability to take a punch. Those three were a pretty good foundation for stand-up, but no way was I ready for the stage.

In high school, I wasn't the class clown, but I was his assistant. All of my friends were funny, mostly employing a poking-fun-at-others brand of humor, but the laughter, and who delivered the joke, was important. In no way, shape, or form was I a performer in high school, unless you count getting laughs from my athletic endeavors. I couldn't even deliver a speech when running for student council president. The pressure of following Bill Hoyman's hilarious talk so unnerved me that all I could manage was a tearful, "Vote for me."

In the spring of 1972, my sophomore year at Gettysburg College was looking like its last when Dave "Tiny" Weeks suggested I take Public Speaking 101. Professor Harry Bolich never gave less than a B for anyone who attended class. Most classmates were reciting excerpts from novels or articles from *Sports Illustrated*, but I did a deadpan reading of the lyrics from Changes, a David Bowie song. I didn't know my serious reading with a blank expression was a form of comedy, but it got the laughs I secretly desired. As we left the class Professor Bolich pulled me aside and asked, "Can you do that again?" That was all the encouragement I needed. I spent more time on the next assignment than all my other courses to date in reworking the lyrics to the Rolling Stones song *Sympathy for the Devil* into *Sympathy for the Salesman*. It wasn't a roomful of strangers, but for the first time I wrote something and performed it with the intent to get laughs, and succeeded. "You're funny," Professor Bullock said. That was important. I had heard "crazy" and "nuts" before, but never "funny."

Nothing made me happier than making people laugh, but I knew of no way to take it any further. I played my George Carlin albums endlessly and watched every comic I could on TV, but never considered what they did as a possibility for me. Show business was just words in a song. I had no concept of how it worked, knew of no one who did. My people worked jobs at factories and offices. Those were my two options, and both seemed beyond me, feeling too blue collar for a white-collar career and too white collar for a blue-collar trade. As graduation approached, all my friends landed jobs and prepared to start their careers. I never went for an interview and left college with no more of a plan for my life than when I arrived four years earlier.

## 2. "WAITING FOR SOMEONE OR SOMETHING TO SHOW YOU THE WAY"

After graduating college, I returned without purpose to Pennsville, N.J. I was bartending, living in my parents' house, smoking low-grade shake weed, and leaking potential like a sieve.

I did learn what I couldn't or wouldn't do for my life's employment. I worked days as a high school substitute teacher, thinking a job with summers off might be for me. And, if school had started at 2 in the afternoon, maybe teaching kids the lies of history could have made the cut. The reality was that the 8 a.m. school bell signaled the start of my daily hangover. There was a moment when I thought of becoming a state trooper until someone pointed out that, before they gave you a gun and a badge and set you loose on the general population, there was a drug test.

My low point was the inevitable, taking a job at my father's office. The only problem was we couldn't stand to be in the same room with each other. We had more fistfights than discussions about the insurance business. Despite that, or thinking that tussling with him at the office might work out better than our kitchen knockdowns, I took a life insurance course.

A salesman in my dad's office said to sell to your friends first — those easy sales would build confidence. My first call was to the apartment of my high school friend Donnie Conrad and his new bride, Joanne. I made my pitch while we waited for the Philadelphia Phillies to come on the TV. While Donnie took a long hit off his bong I informed my friend that he would die one day, and this insurance policy would

5

The Animal Bar with a look of daytime innocence, 1970

provide for Joanne and the kids they were sure to have. Donnie exhaled and said, "Yeah, Shide, but I want to get a boat first." I told him that made sense to me, took a hit off the bong, and opened a beer. My career as an insurance salesman was finished before the first pitch.

I also received valuable lessons in stand-up long before I ever set foot on the stage.

The Mariner Restaurant had two bars, on opposite ends of the build-ing. My dad and his cronies drank in the small, wood-paneled lounge. I worked in the other saloon, a large dance hall, with a more proletariat clientele. They tagged our side of the building "the Animal Bar," and we worked hard to earn their disrespect. They listened to Frank Sinatra, played liar's poker and decided how to run the town. We blasted Led Zeppelin, shot pool and borrowed money from each other.

The Animal Bar's clientele was a mix of rough locals and rougher "island workers." The state's first nuclear plant was being constructed on an artificial island 5 miles downriver and local bars were filled with free-spending construction workers from every part of the country.

The bar's bait: 25-cent mugs of beer, dollar-a-dozen steamed clams and waitresses in tube tops. The cheap alcohol and braless waitresses kept the testosterone on a low boil. The entertainment was varied, with something for every drunk: a loud jukebox, live music on the weekends, two pool tables, a shuffle bowling game, a dartboard, and old-fashioned bar fights.

The area behind the bar was the perfect stage for an amateur comic. Every night from 6 till last call, my official job was serving drinks, but my kick was making the ringsiders laugh. I wasn't preparing material; the humor was situational and usually at the expense of someone else. Biting sarcasm and savage mockery were the styles of comedy I favored, and in a local bar they were effective. Every night I mauled somebody and everybody else laughed. My funny was probably elevated by the fact I controlled the flow of liquor. Free beer buys a lot of votes.

The two owners, Mike Isaris and Greg Petsas, paid me $120 a week to run the joint. Impressed with my ability to keep the police calls and bartender thievery to a minimum, they gave me a pay raise: the punch-board concessions.

Running an illegal gambling operation was not a moral dilemma for me. I was already dealing a little, just enough to pay for my drugs. Amphetamines, in the form of "Black Beauties," "Christmas Trees," and "White Crosses," transformed me from a black-out drunk driver to a wide-awake drunk driver. A devil's choice to be sure, but at the time it was a no-brainer. I was going to get drunk and crash my car, with or without the pills. Seeing the accident happening was a decided advantage over coming to in a ditch and not knowing how I got there.

The pep pills were also a hit with island workers who had to spend all day precision welding after staying up all night drinking. Dealing speed could be rationalized as a public service, since it helped build a safe nuclear plant.

The punchboards were very portable and profitable. Each colorful board contained 1,000 holes with a slip of tightly rolled, numbered paper stuffed in every opening. For a quarter, the customer was given a thin metal key to punch out a number. If the number on the paper popping from the hole matched the number written on the top of the board, the customer won fifty dollars. In a time before scratcher cards, big-screen TVs and cellphones, the punchboards proved to be a very popular bar diversion, especially for the man already proved unlucky with the ladies. Mike and Greg soon divulged a way to increase my take. Popping out a number on a brand-new board and writing that number on the top made the board unwinnable . . . pure profit. The trick was to rotate the dead board with the live one and disappear it before the empty holes over-shadowed the filled ones and made it too popular. Greg warned me, "Just don't get too greedy."

I couldn't recite the seven deadly sins in 1974, but they knew me on a first-name basis. If one dead board was good, two was better and three was genius. On any given night I had four or five punchboards floating along the packed bar. In no time I was a 21-year-old with a wad of cash in my pocket, a job where I could drink and eat black beauties, and a bar full of truly tough guys who were sick of my smart mouth. I was kicked back, tubing down the river with a beer in one hand, a joint in the other and the sun on my face. It never occurred to me to ask if there were falls downriver before launching into the water . . . or to place a secret mark on the dead boards for easy identification later.

In the day, the bar was empty except for a couple of shot-and-beer pensioners, unless it rained. With bad weather the Animal Bar filled with island workers, spending the money they weren't making. They certainly didn't want to sit in their rented rooms staring at pictures of their families. The problem was, the bar in the day just wasn't the same fun palace — the slightest bit of daylight exposed the place for the shithole it was. Every splinter in the unvarnished bar top, every stain on the rough wooden floor, and every dusty neon beer sign fed feelings of homesickness. The Allman Brothers' *Melissa* might get five plays in a row on the jukebox. There was less talk and more staring into drinks. Sullen was the special of the day. We always saw more fistfights in the day. The alcohol sent the muscle energy normally exhausted at the worksite into another guy's face. But all that mattered to me was that the punchboards worked nonstop on rainy days.

Helping me to hustle the booze and pills on one such rainy day was the chronically underemployed Slim, a regular who literally jumped over the bar to pour beer on busy rainy days. Slim was a couple years older and a bit of a greaser, wearing his hair like Elvis, slicked back with long sideburns. His dress never varied — blue jeans tucked inside of black motorcycle boots, a black T-shirt, and a long chain attaching his wallet to his belt. Slim popped white crosses like Tic Tacs, chewing them for faster results. A little stoop-shouldered and wiry, he was always twitching and talking, mostly about the Harley he didn't own. He was a real live version of the rabbit from *Fritz the Cat*. Two years later, Slim killed his girlfriend because she wouldn't give him beer money. We were shocked he had a girlfriend.

At some point, a big, bearded cowboy tossed his punchboard at me and barked in a deep Southern drawl, "Ah ain't nevah won shit offen one of these thangs."

From the other side of the bar, a Jersey Yankee found common ground with the Texas Rebel. "Yeah. Nobody ever beats those fuckers."

I tried to distract by pinning a dick joke on the second, and smaller, heckler. "The only thing you can beat is your meat." This was the sort of nasty put-down that normally scored with this crowd, but not this day. Every conversation switched to the punchboard channel.

One voice cut above the bed of grumbling. "Those boards are rigged!"

Suddenly the bar crowd was a liquored-up Baptist congregation, testifying with a chorus of obscenities. "Fucking A!" "Shit!" "Cocksucker!"

I did my best to shout down the fast-forming mob. "Get the fuck out of here! Tweet won last week!"

Slim gladly bit the hand that fed him speed. "No. Tweet was like a month ago."

The Big Bearded Cowboy slammed a bill roll on the bar and signaled for the punchboard tossed to me a minute earlier. "Gimme dat fucker." I did. With an evil grin on his face he handed me a twenty. "Lemme kno-un dat's gawn . . . Ahm gonna play it till ah git dat hunner dollers or stomp yer cheatin' ass."

He punched out numbers, smiling as he tossed them aside. Soon, the pool and dart games stopped. Everyone was focused on that punchboard. We finally had some fresh entertainment.

Fear shot up my spine. I didn't know if the Big Bearded Cowboy's board was a dead one. While continuing to serve drinks, I nonchalantly tried to gather the other boards. The guys holding them weren't playing, but they weren't releasing their grips on them either — probably waiting to see the results of the cowboy's grand experiment. If his board didn't pay off, every one of those boards would end up broken over my head and worth $100.

When the Big Bearded Cowboy's first twenty didn't yield the winning number, he tossed another at me and punched holes a little faster. I stuffed the bill in my pocket with a flourish, laughing and sipping my beer.

He kept punching out losers and tossing me twenties. I kept laughing, a bit too loud, and drinking shots, a bit too fast.

At one point the punchboard became a group effort. The Big Bearded Cowboy punched the numbers out furiously, other guys looked at the numbers while I counted his strokes. The piles of little slips of white paper grew on the bar. The only break in the action was for him to toss me a twenty and knock down a drink. I'd collect the bill off the floor and pour two Jack Daniel's on the rocks: one for him and one for me.

As the number of empty holes in the board overwhelmed the filled ones, the blood lust in the bar became palpable, and I started looking for an escape route.

The bar was in the shape of a long, thin horseshoe that cut the room in two. On one side was the bandstand and dance floor, and on the other the pool tables, dartboards and entrance. I was standing at the end of the bar, in the middle of the room. Men lined the length of the bar, two and three deep, making it impossible to vault the bar and exit to the parking lot where my never-reliable '65 MGB waited. The only way to make a quick getaway in that car was to get it towed. The last possible escape route was to run to the open end of the bar, past the walk-in freezer and out the back door. I eyed that escape route a few too many times because suddenly a big guy stood in front of the walk-in, with an evil grin on his face.

At some point, the Big Bearded Cowboy ran out of money. I probably had $400 of his money, which I knew would soon be ripped out of my soon-to-be bloodstained jeans. There were less than a hundred numbers left in the board. He held that nearly empty board in the air for the whole bar to see. They roared with anticipation. I kept pushing the funny but nobody was buying. I was a dead man joking.

One of his buddies tossed me a couple of twenties.

The Big Bearded Cowboy glared at me. "We gotcha, motherfucker!"

Everyone laughed at that clever line.

He went back to work on the board. The paper slip readers shouted the numbers and the crowd cheered each loser.

Finally, his buddy unrolled a paper and the smile dropped from his face. After checking the number against the winning number on the top of the board a second time, he handed the paper to the Big Bearded Cowboy and headed for the bathroom to beat the rush. The Big Bearded Cowboy checked the number and uttered a word of defeat. "Shiiiit."

Out of nowhere, a last-minute pardon from the governor had arrived for the guilty man. It was my time to rejoice. "We got a winner!"

No one cheered. No one said a word. I was the only happy face in the place. Slim patted me on the back and raised his glass in a toast no one joined, but only because he knew I'd slip him a few more bucks than usual. A cue ball pounding into a fresh rack on the pool table broke the silence. A lynch party without a lynching is one sad gathering.

I tried to hand the Big Bearded Cowboy his winnings, but his head was down and both his hands gripped the bar. After dropping the five twenties in front of him, I calmly walked out the back door and puked my guts out.

I returned, lit a cigarette, and quietly gathered the other punchboards sitting unattended on the bar. No one protested. No one wanted to challenge my luck and for once, neither did I. That night, after closing the bar, I tossed all the punchboards into the Dumpster.

Soon after, someone tagged me with a new nickname, "the Pirate." It didn't bother me. I liked any attention short of a punch to the head. And if that got a laugh, then I would take that.

There were a couple of lessons here:

1) Outside of the comedy club setting, an amateur comic is just another asshole.

2) You can't keep just attacking everyone, no matter how funny, night after night, without ever taking the pie in the face yourself. The regulars got tired of all the funny being directed at them. When they saw a chance to turn against me, they rooted for the heckler.

3) Oh, and gambling is bad.

# 3. "EACH NIGHT BEGINS A NEW DAY"

Strangely, my vague dreams of a law career were revived at the Animal Bar when I met Basil D. Beck, a charismatic defense attorney from nearby Bridgeton. He had a long beard, shoulder-length hair ringing his balding head, and he wore a leather suit into court. Whenever Basil entered the bar he received a hero's welcome from a roomful of clients. Basil was loud, funny, and tipped like a rock star. His legend was built when he got an acquittal for a man who was clearly guilty of murder. When I asked him about it one night, Basil winked and said, "No one ever made a name freeing an innocent man." We became friends, once entertaining the bar with dueling impressions of John Cleese's Minister of Silly Walks. Basil and I were probably the only two that night who didn't think we made the routine up on the spot. When I told him I was considering law school, he said there was a job for me in his office. I saw an escape route from 25-cent beer nights and took the law boards.

In the fall of 1975 I moved to Washington, D.C., to attend the International School of Law and Screen Door Repair. That was my joke to lessen the sting of my only option being an unaccredited law school.

Nevertheless, I was so intent on succeeding and so frightened by the movie *Paper Chase* that I swore off alcohol during that first year. The only break I allowed myself from constant studying was Saturday night. After finishing my shift at the switchboard of the Gralyn Hotel, I would go to my fourth-floor room, smoke pot, and play guitar until the start of *Saturday Night Live*. My guitar playing never got past three mangled chords, but in hindsight, the real lessons were learned from *SNL*. Seeing funny young people on TV was inspirational. That show was my church, and I never missed a service. Still, my focus was law school, and my efforts were rewarded that first year with a 3.50 GPA.

The summer of 1976, I returned to South Jersey to work for Basil. My dad had a clerking position lined up for me with his buddy, Craig Bernstein, the Salem County prosecutor, but I was already signed up to sail with Basil's skull and crossbones.

There was no need for advertising or ambulance chasing. Basil's reputation as a criminal defense lawyer was solid. The clients came to avoid jail time and gave him all their business after that: the divorces, bankruptcies, and of course, personal-injury lawsuits. That was where the big money was, a one-third cut of anything a client got from a car crash, falling off a ladder, or tripping in a supermarket entrance. I once observed that a lot of his clients drugged a lot. Basil shot back, "That's who you want. They tend to be accident-prone."

Basil D. Beck, attorney-at-law, at rest, 1976

My job was to interview clients and research points of law. Every day was an adventure, some new case, a puzzle to be solved and a fresh lesson from Basil, whom I idolized. I let my hair grow and dressed for the office as he did, in blue jeans, concert T-shirt and sport jacket.

Early in the summer, I earned Basil's respect and trust. Two gentlemen from North Jersey were sitting in the office when I came to work one morning. They wore leather jackets and a lot of gold, and each held a full paper bag. Basil invited me to join him for the interview. Two young friends of the gentlemen had been busted by the New Jersey State Police with a trunk full of marijuana, cocaine, and untaxed cigarettes. It was a large '70s Cadillac, with a very big trunk, so they were in very big trouble. The gentlemen placed a paper bag on Basil's desk as a retainer and left to post bail for their two friends. Basil opened the bag, saw it was filled with cash and promptly sent me to interview his new clients.

The interview was conducted in the parking lot of the Salem County jail. The guys were my age and dressed like their older rescuers. The older guys helped me by constantly smacking their charges and saying things like, "No fucking around," and "Don't bullshit him."

Interstate 95 from Miami to Maine was a major corridor for drugs

13

making their way north. Once the two guys crossed the Delaware Memorial Bridge and entered New Jersey they figured they were home free and lit a celebratory joint. What they didn't realize was there were powerful cameras atop the bridge. The police monitored the bridge traffic for suspicious vehicles, like a Cadillac riding low in the rear from a trunk loaded with contraband. The two guys assured me that all that was left of the joint was a tiny bit of rolling paper clamped in the alligator roach's teeth. Didn't matter. That's all the police needed to search the car, including the trunk full of treasure. This was the "plain view doctrine," one of the exceptions to the U.S. Constitution's prohibition against unreasonable search and seizure. A police officer spotting something illegal in plain view was justified in searching the entire house, or vehicle.

When defending most drug cases, the first thing to examine was the search. If it was illegal, then all evidence obtained was the "fruit of a poisonous tree" and not admissible in a court of law. No evidence, case dismissed.

If the search was good, and this was looking like a clean search, then it pretty much became a matter of Basil bargaining with the prosecutor's office over prison time. Basil knew the gentlemen from North Jersey didn't give him a bag of cash to shave years off their protégés' sentences. Basil was not looking forward to that phone call. It was the first time I had ever seen him nervous and quiet.

When the police report came, I noticed something: They hadn't tested the tiny bit of rolling paper for the presence of marijuana. There was not even a mention of it. Someone had probably figured it was just a bit of unnecessary paper and trashed it. The alligator clip was not even tested for residue. I sensed an opening and started researching cases in Basil's law library. Nothing. Just for the heck of it I went to the University of Delaware's law library. There I found a precedent-setting Colorado case where a police officer used a bent spoon sitting on an open windowsill as reason to search an apartment for heroin. The Colorado Supreme Court ruled that if an object had a legal use, then illegal use can't be assumed. I wrote a motion to suppress the evidence, applying this "innocent use doctrine" to our case, arguing that the alligator clip was used to hold stereo wires together, a perfectly legal activity. The judge granted the motion and the case was dismissed. Basil was ecstatic, dancing around the courtroom while the police and prosecutors fumed. Nothing made Basil and I happier than tweaking the status quo.

We had one more visitor from North Jersey. Another gentlemen, dressed pretty much the same as the first four, placed a paper bag on the desk, shook Basil's hand and left. No receipt was requested. None was necessary. Basil reached into the bag of cash and handed me a bonus.

From that moment on, Basil told everyone I was his future law partner.

Basil and I worked long hours and we partied hard. I went back to law school, but made a lot of trips back to New Jersey during the school year to work and hang with Basil.

*"Life is lived in the quiet of the ordinary." St. Francis of Assisi.*

I was a 23-year-old knucklehead from New Jersey. I wanted to live in the broader arcs of the spectacular. I wasn't doing stand-up, not even thinking about it, but I loved making people laugh. Most of my performances were while standing at a bar, and at weddings. A lot of my friends were taking that big step. If I wasn't officially asked before the wedding, once the reception started and the alcohol flowed, somehow I found a microphone in my hand.

One day at a pretrial hearing for one of Basil's clients, the judge read off the charges, twenty counts of passing bad checks. When the judge finally finished reading the last indictment, he set bail at $5,000 and asked the defendant how he wanted to post bond. I said, loudly, "Check." Everyone laughed, even the judge and defendant. I didn't come down for days.

I circled the microphone for a couple of years.

Looking for validation that I was funny, I wrote stories and sent them to the *National Lampoon* and *Mad* magazine. My submissions were returned, unopened.

A lot of my friends were getting married. I put effort into writing funny wedding toasts. The laughter eased my cravings, but didn't satisfy the need.

In the early summer of 1976, I heard about a place in Philadelphia that allowed comics onstage. I dragged my college friend Camillo Melchiorre to Grandma Minnie's talent contest and entered as the Scat Players. We did sketches previously performed at our fraternity and won. They invited us back the next week. We panicked, not knowing it was permissible to do the same material. We wrote new material and decided to bring back our old closer, an organ-grinder act featuring another college classmate, Craig Belle, a little person, as the monkey. Cam wondered how we were going to convince Craig to once again put on the monkey tail and ears. I said, "We're going to get him drunk." Craig was on a ladder, painting his mother's house and wearing an army helmet when I put a case of beer on the picnic table. A few hours later, Craig, dressed as a monkey, humped my leg, while Cam played his accordion. We were booed off the stage. Cam and Craig intensified their law school studies. I seethed.

On July 4, 1976, the night of our country's 200th birthday, my friends goaded me into entering a talent contest at the Ocean Drive Inn in Wildwood, N.J. Two guys from my hometown, Dave Townshend and Dave "Waddo" Waddington, hosted a talent night. I had no act or any jokes. Not a clue as to what I might do when I hit the stage. My drunken plan was to drink some more and be funny.

The guy before me sang *You're a Grand Old Flag* and *Yankee Doodle Dandy*. The crowd was in a patriotic fever. People sang along, waved flags and danced on tables. The singer took bow after bow before leaving. I walked onto the stage and headed for Waddo. The crowd was still cheering for the singer as Waddo told them the next act was a comedian. In unison the whole bar screamed, "Noooo!!" Waddo wisely pulled the microphone back from my reach and called for the singer to return. The crowd roared its approval. The singer led everyone in a rousing reprise of *Yankee Doodle Dandy*. I made the long walk from the stage to my buddies at the bar who were howling at me. "We didn't even have time to heckle you." Later that night Waddo invited me to come back anytime. It never happened. That audience screaming "No" at me was enough to keep me away from even the thought of performing. I returned to my hit-and-run comedy, the same old clowning in diners and bars. Stuck between a set-up and a punchline, I was too old to be a movie theater comic, and clueless how to go legit.

# 4. "SO NOW YOU SEE THE LIGHT"

In January 1977, after wisecracking around law school for a year and a half, my classmate Howard Vine declared that he was taking me to a place where I was to perform comedy. We didn't even know it was called stand-up. Howard thought I was funny. I thought I was funny. We needed a third opinion.

For the first time, I wrote something with the intent of making complete strangers laugh.

The Iguana Coffee House was in the basement of the Luther Place Memorial Church, near St. Thomas Circle in D.C. In the 1960s it was a happening place, spawning artists such as Roberta Flack. I entered a bunker filled with hippies trying to wait out disco. Howard brought a big cassette tape recorder. It was an open talent night that lived up to its billing, with singer-songwriters, puppeteers and an interpretive dancer. I followed a poet whose last line was, "… like a mango we are ripe for the revolution."

The long-haired host gave my first show business introduction when he said in a laid-back FM DJ voice, "Okay, this guy is going to try something funny … Ritch?"

It was more of a warning than an introduction. "Watch your purses and wallets. This guy might try something funny."

During my seven minutes of stand-up the audience responded twice.

Moments after I started speaking came my first heckle. A guy playing chess with his back to the stage turned around and angrily shushed me.

I continued my little memorized presentation, to silent indifference and puzzled looks.

Finally, I did this line: "I wrestled in high school and just like in

17

First time on stage — remembered sword, forgot lines, 1962

professional wrestling, you can tell who's going to win the match just by the introduction. "Wrestling in the 130-pound class from Oakcrest Regional High School, two-time Christmas Tournament champion, two-time New Jersey state champion, undefeated senior captain, Bob Ciarrochi. His opponent, from Pennsville Memorial High School, former student council treasurer Ritch Shydner."

One guy let out with a single, solitary "ha." That was it. Not a full laugh. Just a man starting his laugh, realizing no one was following and then strangling the laugh before it caused him further embarrassment. Later, in my room, I played and replayed that one particular spot on the tape for an hour, regarding that single "ha" as if a message from God.

That reaction was enough to get me to try it again.

# 5. "I GET MY BACK INTO MY LIVING"

Shortly after my Iguana Coffee House debut, Howard, my un-official agent, found another talent night, at the Gay Cabaret. He told me it was a gay nightclub. This was 1977, and the closet was packed. The only people openly gay were forced out by overcrowding. I knew nothing about the gay culture but needed an audience.

When we arrived, the manager informed us that it was the monthly change of pace, "Ladies Night." We were fine with that. We liked women. We were dense.

Suddenly I found myself trying to force a laugh from a roomful of lesbians who thought they had found a refuge from dicks like me. After a minute I longed for the indifference of the Iguana Coffee House crowd. These women glared at me hard enough that my breath frosted. Only my second time on stage, and I experienced the worst bombing of my career. I expected to hear a woman shout, "Someone get a rope." Finally I blurted, "I guess I'm your worst nightmare." They laughed.

I wasn't savvy enough to realize this inadvertent laugh was the best I could possibly get and to use it as an exit line. Instead I returned to my script and blathered on until one lady had enough. Without saying a word she left her seat, walked onto the stage, took the microphone from my hand, returned it to the mic stand and led me by my arm off the stage. It didn't matter. Listening to the tape, I was pleased that the ad-libbed laugh was bigger than my first show's single "ha." Accidental or not, I counted that laugh as an improvement over my first show. That was enough to send me up there again.

A friend had a band playing regularly in the Jailhouse, a bar in

Stand-up... Gettysburg College version, 1972

Georgetown. They let me go on during their breaks, where I largely traded insults with drunken patrons. I was that most-desperate creature, a comic searching for an audience.

Nearly every pub and bar in D.C. had singer-songwriter nights. Soon they had a young guy begging for five minutes of stage time to do stand-up comedy.

A local pizza shop owner, whom I made laugh as a customer, let me do comedy in front of the three tables of his shop. I had no microphone, stage or special lighting. Without any of those three, or something funny to say, I scared people. Customers hastily tossed whole pizza pies into go boxes and fled the shop. The owner must have gotten a perverse kick out of watching his customers run into the street because he let me do it two more times.

One night, I did what I read Lenny Bruce did and asked for stage time at a 14th Street strip joint. Moments after I launched into my little prepared set, a ringsider shouted to the bartender, "What the fuck is he doing up there?" The man's words made total sense to me. I walked off the stage, straight out the door and never tried another strip joint.

No one ever had to tell me that growth was a direct function of stage time. I continued to go anywhere that allowed me to perform; no group was too small, no setting too awkward. I'm surprised I didn't try doing stand-up for people waiting at a bus stop. The infant comic waddled to whoever opened their arms.

I didn't know what I was doing and the only place to learn was in front of groups of people surprised to see me doing what I didn't know how to do. I knew of no one doing what I was doing, and told no one I was doing it.

My time spent wrestling in high school and college sort of prepared me for stand-up. It wasn't just the solo nature of the performance. I had experienced fighting off my back while 500 people chanted "Pin! Pin! Pin!" So an audience's disappointment after a failed joke wasn't something that stopped me from trying another.

The fact that the audience didn't expect to see a stand-up, or probably had never seen one live, worked for me as much as against me. Once the audience got over the shock of someone trying to make them laugh instead of singing them a song, they generally were receptive. They had no preconceived notions or expectations. Youthful energy helped me, as did my obvious desire to get a laugh. As long as I was interesting (and thinking you're interesting can sometimes pass as interesting), the audience at least indulged my antics.

I was obsessed even before I knew what a roomful of laughter felt like. I was terrible. The laughs were scattered. My performances were mostly baffling in their inconsistency — a joke that dazzled one night, fizzled the next. I was clueless as to how to connect to an audience. My friend Joe Mullin said this was my "seriously unfunny era." What I did have was a desperate drive to succeed, to hear those laughs, so I went out night after night.

I was making the transition that every professional comic made — from making friends laugh off the cuff to making a room full of strangers laugh on cue. A lifetime of getting laughs from friends and a deep need to hear fresh laughter powered me through this birth.

The lessons were coming from all angles. Some were obvious — open strong and close stronger. Some were surprising — a smaller crowd can be more difficult. The first few times on stage I was so terrible that facing an audience of two was actually preferable to a crowd of two hundred, as there were fewer witnesses to the crime. Once I became more skillful it became apparent that a large, packed room was easier to make laugh, and keep laughing, than a few scattered souls. About ten years later, I was in the crowd for a French stand-up comic at the Just For Laughs Festival in Montreal. The whole performance was in French, of which I can't speak a word. At some point I noticed I was laughing, because everyone around me was laughing. Laughter is indeed contagious. Clichés are usually clichés for a reason.

Most important, I started to get scraps of encouragement, and to a starving comic those provided essential nutrition. Some of the singer-songwriters vouched for me with bar owners. A few people started looking for me. If I didn't show, a singer or manager or bartender might say, "Where were you last week? We missed you." The managers put me on earlier in the line-up. My usual introduction was, "Here's a little something different."

I was experiencing R&R. The repetition was gaining me a reputation.

# 6. "THERE'S A WORLD WHERE I CAN GO AND TELL MY SECRETS"

In June of 1977, six months after I first took the stage as a stand-up, a friend showed me a classified ad in the *Washington Post*. A bar in southeast D.C. was looking for comedians. It was very exciting. I was about to meet my tribe.

El Brookman's was in the poor black neighborhood of Anacostia. A neon sign of a boxer throwing an uppercut, a tribute to the proprietor's former career, hung above the front door. The small bar was an anachronism — a 1950s shot-and-a-beer joint with a few white pensioners playing scratchy Conway Twitty songs on the jukebox surrounded by Superfly wanna-bes, sipping Courvoisier and bopping to Funkadelic on the boombox.

Paul Brookman, the owners' 21-year-old son, was a huge comedy fan with an idea to save his parents' dying business. Like a hunter firing his shotgun in a cornfield, Paul was shocked by the number of comics his little ad flushed into the open.

There were many clean, prosperous black neighborhoods in our nation's capital, a.k.a. Chocolate City, but Anacostia wasn't one of them. The streets were filled with boarded-up businesses, cars on blocks, and trouble. Comic Bill Thomas once said, "To get to El Brookman's, just drive down Pennsylvania Avenue until you get scared."

Personal safety didn't stop the horde of wannabes from crossing the Sousa Bridge to test their funny. Lewis Black was one of the first to arrive, soon joined by Dan Knapp, Paula Johnson and David Cohen. When TP Mulrooney and I arrived, Paul Brookman was able to retire as the MC. Over the next few months Jon Hayman, Bill Masters, Kevin

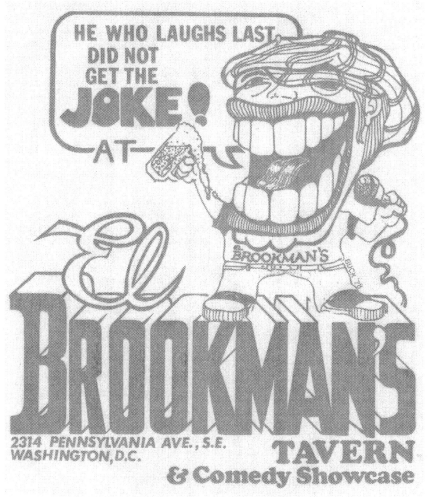

El Brookman's poster by Tim MacAllister, 1978

Rooney, Jim Tam, Howard Manetti, Bob Grainey, Ed Wolinsky, Bill Thomas, and Ron Zimmerman made El Brookman's their proving ground. For some, it was their first steps into a showbiz career, for others it reaffirmed their original career choices. Tom Rhodes, today a highly decorated professional, caught the bug when his uncle took him to El Brookman's at age 12. It also attracted the one-and-dones — guys so unfunny, we wondered where they got the idea they were funny, who ever laughed with them ... not at them, with them.

The official seating of the rectangular-shaped room was 95 people. Hard wooden booths lined the walls. Tables filled the center. The sightlines were clear. The space was tight with a low ceiling, causing the laughter to ricochet nicely. It was a kill room. The front door was right next to the stage. Every person who entered was subject to comedic attack. The comics had every advantage.

At first, the shows were lightly attended by a strange mix of Paul's enthusiastic young friends and disinterested pensioners hunkered over their shots and beers along the bar. The comics shared the stage with an unnamed three-piece country band featuring a 400-pound singer and lead guitarist nicknamed Tiny.

Word-of-mouth and Paul's push in local media quickly revealed a hunger for live stand-up. The place was crammed nightly. Med students from Georgetown. Midshipmen from Annapolis. Staffers from Capitol Hill. The draw was wide and the mix electric.

Newly hired waitresses had to step over people sitting in the aisles. Lines snaked down the sidewalk. Local kids were paid to watch the parked BMWs, Mercedes-Benzes and limos with embassy plates. The fire marshal looked at the jam-packed room, ordered the back door be kept unlocked, had a beer and stayed for the show. Uniformed police officers spent their breaks watching the comedy, never checking identification or the funny cigarettes. Everyone was supportive of this little miracle happening in the Southeast.

In August, Paul hired new musical entertainment, the Original Fetish. They were a humorous punk band whose members performed in pajamas and bathrobes. When they opened with *I'm Glad Elvis Is Dead* only days after the King left the building for the final time, the last few old-timers left in disgust. The comic infestation was total and complete.

Both management and comics were so new to show business, none of us knew we were in it. Paul went with two shows a night on Fridays and Saturdays, but despite the crowd waiting outside, didn't turn over the room. If someone left the bar, the line just got shorter.

It was months of full houses before anyone thought of charging a cover; for whatever reason, $3 became the figure till the place closed in 1982. Paul gave it all to the comics to split. I felt like a professional. I was too new to understand that professional status couldn't be claimed until a person made their living as a stand-up.

The comics built their acts from scratch, one joke at a time. Even without knowing anything, we knew stealing was forbidden. Still, some comics propped up their young, shaky sets with old jokes and classic comedy album cuts. The search for new material became the prime directive. After the first show, panicked comedians gathered in the rear parking lot, searching for something new to do for the same crowd in the second show. Out came the notebooks and pot. The comic mantra was,

"Do you think this is funny?"

The comics mirrored the enthusiastic and rowdy crowds perfectly. None of us knew what we were doing, but we did it hard. There were no rules, boundaries, or language restrictions. Bob Grainey closed with the immortal non sequitur, "I'd like to talk about pussy, but the kitchen's closed."

We enjoyed a supportive atmosphere at El Brookman's. We laughed generously at each other. It was a friendly competition, where each new bit by another comic spurred me to try harder for something fresh.

I experimented with every technique available. Rodney Dangerfield was on *The Tonight Show* every couple of weeks, so one night I became a one-line comic. "My hometown was so small, the ice cream truck doubled as the ambulance." Out at first. I was a fan of Martin Mull and Steve Martin, so I added a guitar to my act, singing two song parodies. Bruce Springsteen's *Born to Run* became *Born to Bowl* and Jackson Browne's *Running on Empty* titled *Running on Money*. I couldn't play guitar, and I couldn't sing, and I certainly couldn't do them at the same time in front of strangers. I gave the song parodies to a guitar act and for the first time felt the jealousy-tinged thrill of watching someone score with something I wrote.

Lenny Bruce said, "Hey, if I say something that sounds familiar, I'm screwed. I speak the English language. I heard. I pick up." Initially, my performance reflected my favorite comics. I loved Richard Pryor, Robert Klein and George Carlin, so my act came off like an urban black Jewish Irishman from South Jersey. Fortunately, the desire to be original was as strong as the instinct to get the laugh. If I caught myself copying a vocal inflection, facial expression or even hand gesture of one of my heroes, I vowed not to do it again. It was a slow process to chip away the influences to find whatever initially pulled me to the mic, to get at my funny.

I also experimented with a stage name.

By the time El Brookman's opened, my legal name, Ritchie Shidner, was presenting problems with my introductions. My last name was mangled every single time. First solution was a fictitious name. I tried on Bud Lunch, Lenny Burg, and Elvis DeGroot. Since the usual mistake was the person using the short "i" instead of the long, I decided to just replace the "i" in my last name with a "y." It didn't help much. The dominant mispronunciation became Schneider, which coincidentally was the original family name before some drunk ancestor copped a resentment against some other drunk ancestor and flipped some letters. Not going with a fake name was a mistake for all sorts of reasons. I might have done more self-promotion, worked harder to support the career of Lenny Burg, but sure as hell wasn't going to lift a finger for that Shidner asshole.

Some comics settled on a name and style quickly.

TP Mulrooney did impressions, closing with a dead-on Dustin Hoffman from *The Graduate*, "Mrs. Robinson, I think you're trying to seduce me." He became the club's first star.

From day one, Jon Hayman had the same sardonic delivery he used when years later he played "The Bubble Boy" on *Seinfeld*.

But Lewis Black struggled. His style then was the same as the one that later brought well-deserved fame and success. Lewis wore a leather jacket and spouted angry, profanity laden, well-written bits in his signature, hand-shaking, apoplectic style, but it just didn't pop the way it did 20 years later on *The Daily Show*. Maybe the aging process turned the unsettling into the hilarious as it did for that other late bloomer, Rodney Dangerfield. Maybe Generation X saw in his poodle-barking-at-a-freight-train rants a hilarious parody of their boomer parents' impotent raging, much as my generation saw in Rodney Dangerfield's loser persona a parody of our parents' devotion to a dimming American Dream. For whatever reason, it just wasn't his time. Lewis soon left for New York City to be a playwright.

Not every funny person at Brookman's took to stand-up immediately. In one of his first times on stage, Kevin Rooney, who later appeared on *The Tonight Show* and won Emmys for his writing, was heckled by a group eager to hear a friend of theirs try comedy for the first time. Kevin discovered they were government workers, and went on a rant about their incompetence and laziness. For the first of a thousand times, Rooney had me and every other comic laughing until we were gasping for air. Exasperated and beaten, a woman from the group tossed her beer on our hero. Kevin didn't perform for the Brookman's crowd much after that night. Instead he found an audience he liked better, spritzing for the comics in the parking lot. We scrambled for the premises and jokes he tossed off like so many nickels. In retrospect, Rooney was our Joe Ancis, Lenny Bruce's legendary muse. It was a huge loss when Kevin went back to U Mass to become a teacher. I didn't see him again until the winter of '79 in New York City.

At El Brookman's, for the first time I experienced getting on a roll. I surfed on waves of laughter and felt the power of killing. With the audience bathing me in approving laughter, suddenly I felt a connection to people that I never got anywhere else. Their laughter put me completely in the moment, without regret of the past or fear of the future. It shut off that critical, nagging voice in my head. Even beyond that, stand-up was turning my darkest, craziest thoughts into joyful laughter.

Of all my insecurities, fear of rejection was the biggest, yet I was diving head first into a job where failure and success take turns having their way with you. Once I got a big dose of those laughs, my biggest concern became not doing stand-up. For those precious minutes on stage all my insecurities disappeared behind the drive for more laughter. This was a drug worth killing for.

The three most important things for the growth of a stand-up were stage time, stage time, and stage time. I was still in law school but hit the stage every possible night. Bartending part-time at a bluegrass bar, Rocky Raccoon's, enabled me to weasel the hosting position for their singer-songwriter night. I hustled opening act work at the Cellar Door, the Childe Harold and the Blues Alley. No audience was too small. No pay was too low.

People occasionally recognized me on the street. The gigs were paying more money. The beautiful daughter of an Italian Embassy official saw me at Brookman's and became my live-in girlfriend. I had a bounce to my step, a few dollars in my pocket and a woman in my bed. There was no other place I wanted to be doing anything else but stand-up comedy in Washington, D.C. I was the big fish in a small pond, unaware there even were any other ponds.

# 7. "IT'S THE CLASSIC CONTRADICTION, THE UNAVOIDABLE AFFLICTION"

One night after a show at El Brookman's, a well-dressed man approached me with a job offer. He offered me $200 to do comedy at his home in Chevy Chase, Md. That was a lot of money in 1978, twice my biggest pay to that date.

I parked my 1969 Dodge Dart with the Grateful Dead "Steal Your Face" sticker two blocks from a big, fancy house packed with people. I found the guy, who was much drunker than when he hired me, and he must have been pretty drunk that night. I asked where I was to do the show. He took me into a dimly lit living room where couples huddled intimately. My host cranked up the volume on the stereo to get everyone's attention before shutting it off completely and yelling, "Hey everybody! Everybody, listen up! Everybody I've got the comedian I was telling you about! Here he is!" He then stepped back and pointed for me to get on the coffee table.

The guests, suffering from severe party interruption, gave me stares that ranged from confused to hateful. To be fair, a few were too drunk to see me. At an unconscious level, they knew a definitely good time was stopped for a potentially bad time. As soon as I jumped onto the coffee table and launched into my act, my employer's wife entered the living room. "What are you doing on my goddamn coffee table?" The husband picked up the cue to begin a dance they had probably done for years. He jumped between us and snapped at her, "He's my goddamn comedian."

As soon as the husband noticed people slipping from the room and me stepping off the coffee table, he went ballistic. "Get up there and tell some fucking jokes!"

29

El Brookman's Bar, circa 1964

I tried to be a good employee, but three women, probably the wife's friends, assaulted me as I tried to retake my little stage. In what was probably a practiced move for all of the husband's new friends, I was pushed through the front door. Not wanting to go back inside or leave without my money, I stood on the front lawn, listening to the continued fighting inside. Exiting guests just shook their heads at me as they passed.

Finally the husband came outside and handed me the cash. These people knew each other well, because no sooner did he finish whispering, "Tell her it's fifty," then his wife burst from the house and into my face.

"How much did he pay you?!"

"Fifty dollars," I said, and made for my car. The wife stayed on me.

"Let me see it. Show me what he gave you." The husband stayed between us until I made my escape.

I liked to think they had great sex that night.

The Dart instinctively took me straight to El Brookman's in time to get onstage in front of a group of people still looking for something funny. It was another valuable lesson — the only way to get a bad show out of your head was to push it out with a good one.

# 8. "HE GOT CAUGHT IN THE SPOTLIGHT"

There were no paying comedy clubs, there was no "road," when I began performing stand-up in January 1977 in Washington, D.C., but there was a demand for inexpensive crowd fodder to open for headlining musical acts. I was as desperate for stage time as any local band and much cheaper. An added bonus to hiring me instead of a band was that no equipment change was required when I left. A soundman telling me which mic to use was the extent of my stage prep.

The audience was there to hear music and was only willing to experiment with drugs, not different forms of entertainment. Forget standing ovations, Bic lighters waving in the air and groupies, most nights it was all I could do to avoid becoming a piece of stage kill. The early beatings I took as an opening act were great preparation for a life in show business.

My first paying job was opening for the Ramones at Bill Heard's bar, the Childe Harold on DuPont Circle, as chronicled in the book *I Killed — Stories of the Road from America's Top Comedians*. I did two more shows for that beautiful maniac — the first club owner to hire me, get me high and then heckle me — before I got a job opening for somebody at Blues Alley. That got me into the Cellar Door, the 300-seat, entry-level room of the area's biggest concert company, Cellar Door Productions.

One of the first things the late, great Dave Williams of Cellar Door Productions said to me was, "If you're early, you're on time. If you're on time you're late. If you're late, you're fired."

It took me no time to learn that those rules didn't apply to headliners. One night, I opened for a D.C. area favorite, Root Boy Slim and the Sex Change Band. Root Boy was a former Yale student who was one acid

The Bayou - Courtesy of Metro Teleproductions

The Bayou, their view and ours
(courtesy of Metro Teleproductions)

trip over the line with songs like *Boogie Till You Puke*. I did my time for the packed house, and then some, as Dude, the soundman, kept giving me the signal to "stretch": do more time. Finally Dude waved me off and the Sex Change Band took the stage, minus Root Boy. The band and the Rootettes, two 300-pound, lingerie-wearing back-up singers, vamped for the audience while Dude pulled me outside. I had been enlisted to help him retrieve Root Boy from the bar across the street. As Dude and I approached, the bar's front door flew open and out stumbled Root Boy, who immediately vomited a few hundred dollars of booze onto the sidewalk. He then stood, wiped off his mouth with his sleeve, and announced to us, "Looks like I puked before I boogied." We led him to the stage, someone handed him a beer, and the show began.

The value of a good opening line that showed you were aware of the situation went a long way towards establishing goodwill with the audience. Quite a few of my first jobs were opening for jazz or blues acts. The audiences were predominantly black. I was predominantly white at that time. A black law school classmate saw me struggling to crank-start a black crowd and afterward said, "The whole time you were up there I kept thinking, 'There goes the neighborhood.'" We laughed. The next time I faced a black audience, I opened with: "I know what you're thinking ... there goes the neighborhood." They howled and the rest of my act was suddenly funnier.

The first professional entertainers who acknowledged me as funny and made me feel like I might have a place in this business were not comedians but musicians. I opened for Mose Allison, his name familiar to me because it was burned into my brain from listening to Pete Townshend say it on the Who's *Live at Leeds* album. After my set, Mose took the stage and acknowledged the job I did opening for him. It was my first time a performer had done so. Between shows I naively asked if he liked the Who's version of his song *Young Man's Blues*. He said he sure did, and liked it even more when he got those big checks. The next show, he talked of our conversation, and dedicated that song to "the funny young man you all just enjoyed." That meant so much to me. When you feel like you're crashing a party, every friendly greeting matters. Thank you, Mr. Mose Allison.

Waddy Wachtel, touring with his group, Ronin, invited me to hang out in their dressing room. Marveling at my non-stop battle with hecklers, Waddy underlined a fundamental principle for me. "Man, if they yell at us, we just turn up the amps, and play for each other. But you can't ignore 'em, man. You gotta have 'em."

I made friends and learned more lessons. There were always more lessons.

Around 1978 I opened for the Robbin Thompson Band out of Richmond Va. About a year later, I opened for Joe Grushecky & The Iron City Houserockers. I became friends with both bands, working with them well past the time when I had to go over the barbed wire for rock crowds. Both groups were powerhouse regional acts, anointed by *Rolling Stone* magazine to make the jump to national stardom. It didn't happen, but both Joe and Robbin never lost their enthusiasm for putting out the best music possible. That was both lesson and inspiration.

One night backstage, someone brought up the fact that Robbin's former bandmate, Bruce Springsteen, was a rock superstar. Maybe the guy expected Robbin to drop his head in defeat or go into a bitter rant about the injustices of the business. Robbin's face lit up at the thought of Bruce. He smiled and talked about how much he loved Springsteen's music and well-deserved success. Later I bitched about the guy's thoughtless remark and again Robbin never dropped his smile. "Awww, it's okay. They don't know. We do it for love. It's all about the music. The rest of the stuff is just stuff." Those words resonated with me but I somehow forgot them a few years later when comics began blowing past me. Robbin had the do-the-footwork-and-let-the-results-go formula down before I even knew it existed.

Sometimes I was more memorable for things other than my performance. One night, after a 1978 show at the Cellar Door, I shared some homegrown weed with the lyricist for the Grateful Dead, Robert Hunter. About 10 years later, I was covering the Dylan/Dead tour for MTV and encountered Hunter backstage. I asked if he remembered me. He hardly hesitated. "You roll a shitty joint, man." He had a good memory for such an old pothead.

Most nights, it was not a matter of getting laughs, but of simply surviving. I defined my success the same as a Civil War general might: If at the end of the battle I still held the stage, the night was mine.

In 1978, after battling/performing for rock crowds for more than a year, I took the stage of the Ontario in the Adams Morgan neighborhood of D.C. to open up for the punk band the Plasmatics. Wendy O. Williams, the lead singer, performed topless with just two strips of electrical tape covering her nipples. She assaulted TV sets with chainsaws and shot live ammo into the ceiling. I was getting paid the ungodly sum of $100, so I didn't care if she came after me with a chainsaw. By this time I was accustomed to rock crowds, and felt confident that I had more clever ways to say "Fuck off" than they did. This crowd just loved screaming "Fuck you." I was facing a Phil Spector Wall of Fuck. In no time I just snapped. "You assholes can kill me and they're still not coming out. You can watch my dead corpse rot on stage for the next 15 minutes; I don't give a shit." This got a decent laugh and a cheer from the crowd. When I came offstage, Wendy handed me a beer and said, "I'll get those fuckers." She took the stage and did exactly that. She cursed them like an underpaid dominatrix. Of course they responded with squeals of delight and orgasmic cheers.

Around that time, I opened for Chicago before about 8,000 at the Merriweather Post Pavilion. I learned the difference between working a big room and a small room. You can't go off into dealing with hecklers with that many people. Momentum is everything with a crowd that size. A small room is a sports car; you can start and stop quickly and easily, move off in any direction, lose them and get them back just as fast. A big room is a bus, everything is straight ahead with wide turns. The weirdest thing was the pacing, waiting for the laughs to finish rolling in from hundreds of yards away before starting the next joke.

When it did work, when a theater full of the disinterested and doubtful were suddenly laughing to my rhythm, the boost to my confidence was immeasurable. I became more confident, even improvising and trying new jokes in front of a thousand people.

One of my greatest showbiz lessons was learned opening for Rick Danko at the Bayou, a large bar/concert venue in Washington, D.C., around 1978. It was more than the fifty dollars, free beer and chance to test my nerves against 500 rabid rock fans. This was Rick Danko of the Band. I loved their music and their farewell concert movie, *The Last Waltz*.

Danko arrived more than an hour late. The promoter, Dave Williams, looked over the standing-room-only audience and gave me a choice — do my act while the equipment was being set or perform after the roadies finished their work. I was fresh in the business but knew that once the stage was set, the only thing the audience wanted to hear was Rick Danko play.

Most of the audience probably never heard my introduction as I drifted onstage with the roadies. I grabbed the mic and narrated the process; the guys tuning the guitars and the fans standing in front of the stage. All the while I was sneaking in bits from my act and references to the Band. Eventually, the crowd came around to what I was doing. They were laughing, applauding and bringing me shots. When the stage was finally set, the soundman, Mitch, signaled for me to leave, which I did to a huge ovation. I thought I was the funniest stand-up in the world. The audience thought I was the funniest roadie. There was a difference, which I was about to learn.

People cheered, hugged and kissed me as I made my way to the dressing rooms in the back of the club. Rick and his group passed me on their way to the stage. They shook my hand and laughed.

His manager grabbed me. "The only other guy I ever saw take over a crowd like that was Steve Martin. You're going on tour with us."

I was led into the dressing room and encouraged to enjoy the spoils of stardom.

Applause, accolades and an altered state ... This was showbiz, and I was in it up to my nostrils.

The first guitar chords prompted us to leave the dressing room just in time to see Danko drop his pants, moon the crowd, and tell them, "You guys suck. I'll be back when you're ready to rock 'n' roll."

He left the stage. At first the audience laughed and cheered as if it was part of the show. Danko's back-up band kept playing, waiting for him to return and complete the joke. Instead, Danko zipped past me and disappeared into the dressing room, followed closely by his manager.

A moment later the manager came out and stuffed a hundred-dollar bill in my hand. "Go up there and hold that crowd for a little bit." I probably took a drag on my cigarette, crushed it under my boot and said something like, "You got it."

I was drunk, high and invincible. It occurred to me that I had used all my material in my first appearance, but that wasn't important. These were my people. They loved me. I didn't need material ... and I was right. The last words I heard were, "Please welcome back to the stage..." I had to push through a wall of boos just to reach the microphone. I couldn't hear myself speak. Then the audience started throwing things. I started hopping around like a chicken on a hotplate, at one point taking refuge behind the drum kit, narrating as if it were a war: "Incoming! Incoming!"

The stage was being pelted with lit cigarettes, beer and iced drinks. There were sparks from equipment short-circuiting. I kept trying jokes, too drunk and high to know the situation was 30 seconds from riot police and 30 years from funny.

Finally, I saw Mitch frantically waving me to leave. As soon as I stepped offstage, Dave Williams grabbed me, kicked open a metal emergency door and shoved me into a dirty, rain-soaked alley. "You got a lot of balls but you best not go back through that crowd." It was pretty much the same thing Bill Heard told me after I opened for the Ramones a few months earlier. It took awhile to notice any improvement in my comedy career.

The door closing behind me and the first raindrops hitting my head signaled the end of my association with the Rick Danko Tour.

In the course of one hour I experienced the best ride showbiz had to offer, the meteoric rise and sudden crash. I chased that high for years.

# 9. "THEY COME FROM THE CITIES AND THEY COME FROM THE SMALLER TOWNS"

At some point in 1978, a law school classmate shocked me with the news that there were comedy clubs in New York City. Clubs. Plural. The Big Apple was only 200 miles away, a straight shot up the 95. This I had to investigate. My classmate took me to her parents' Manhattan apartment the next weekend. We were turned away from the sold-out Improvisation on 44th and Ninth, and Catch a Rising Star on First Avenue between 77th and 78th, but managed to get into the Comic Strip on Second, between 78th and 79th. My discomfort was not just from being packed into a comedy club crowd bigger than I had ever seen, but also from the fact that for the first Saturday night in months, I was not performing.

The show started and class was in session. So intent was my focus that I didn't laugh or hear the laughter around me. After each comic left the stage I soothed myself with the thought, "I'm as funny as this guy." Then the last comic hit the stage, a thin guy with glasses. His material was so sharp and his delivery so tight, I stopped judging and started laughing. I never forgot his bit about amusement parks and "the helpless father-and-son bumper car team." Of course, it was Jerry Seinfeld. That 20 minutes in front of Seinfeld right-sized my ego. The big fish's little pond drained into a lake.

Soon thereafter I was the MC at a Friday night show back at El Bookman's, when a guy introduced himself as a comic who was in town visiting relatives and looking for some stage time. Tony DePaul offered to return the favor: "I run a club like this in San Francisco, the Holy City

On my way to not getting on at The Comedy Store, 1978

Zoo. We got a ton of comics out there. You ever come out there, I can get you on." He also spoke of the most powerful and wondrous club of all, the Comedy Store in Los Angeles. The lake drained into an ocean.

Besides the big hubs of New York City and LA, by the late '70s several major cities boasted small underground comedy scenes. The idea for the local club usually came from a visit to showcase clubs in New York or LA, but the number of hopefuls who immediately materialized when a place for stand-up opened was remarkable. Everywhere it was: "If you build it, they will joke."

The one unifying inspiration for young comics might have been *Saturday Night Live*, which premiered in 1975 with stand-up icon George Carlin as its first guest host. Quite simply, the groundbreaking series showed young people being funny. It showcased other great young stand-ups such as Billy Crystal, Albert Brooks, Richard Pryor, Andy Kaufman and Steve Martin.

There were a lot of other shows presenting young comics that inspired local acts to find a stage — *The Tonight Show, Merv Griffin, Mike Douglas, The Gong Show, Make Me Laugh,* Norm Crosby's *The Comedy Shop*.

As kids, we read *Mad* magazine before graduating to *National Lampoon*. Our comedy albums by George Carlin got as much play as our

Rolling Stones records. By the early '70s, the boomer generation was coming of age and our independent personalities were ideal for an occupation like stand-up, which combined elements of philosophy and preaching. Some books, like Going Too Far and Generations, suggest our generation was forged for stand-up in the same way our parents were built to beat the Nazis. We might not have been able to get the big jobs done like our GI-generation elders, but boomers excelled in occupations calling for creative independence. Nothing calls for creative independence more than stand-up comedy.

These little rooms from Boston to San Francisco were a breeding ground for the new generation of stand-ups that emerged in the 1980s, an era that firmly established stand-up as a saleable commodity and viable profession. Every generation needs places for aspiring comics to be bad. These makeshift comedy rooms provided havens for wild experimentation while enabling many future professionals to learn the craft. There was tremendous camaraderie among the stand-ups — lifelong friendships were formed. By the time stand-up swept across the country in the early '80s, many of the comics from these outposts joined the N.Y. and L.A. comics in manning the microphones.

The scenes in San Francisco, Boston and Chicago were so vibrant that it was no surprise that when comedy exploded in 1980, local comics were able to have "tank-of-gas careers": enough paying gigs within driving distance of his or her city for a comic to make a decent living without ever venturing into the deeper waters of LA or New York. And those who did only to be rejected by the Big Top were able to return home, lick their wounds and live out their comedic lives as local heroes.

Since Lenny Bruce and Mort Sahl led a revolution in the late '50s, making stand-up a respected art form, **San Francisco** was always fertile stand-up territory. In the '70s, the main room was not the hungry i, but a soon-to-be equally legendary venue, the Holy City Zoo in San Francisco's Richmond District. The tiny, 78-seat club got its name from a sign the first owner, Robert Steger, picked up for free at a going-out-of-business sale at the local zoo in Holy City, Calif.

Initially, the Zoo was a folk music club. Jim Giovanni, an impressionist, played there first, followed closely by musician/comedian Jose Simon and stand-up Bill Rafferty. Tony DePaul started around 1973 and ran an open mic on Sundays with Lorenzo Matawaran (Buzz Belmondo), Lou Felder, Jimmy Giovanni, Joe Sharkey, and Robin Williams. Carrie Snow, Dana Carvey and Kevin Pollak came in a short time later. A. Whitney Brown and Michael Davis were two street performers who also started working at the Zoo. *Playboy* magazine did an article on the S.F. scene, thus attracting stand-ups from other cities, such as Bobby Slayton from New York, and Will Durst from Wisconsin.

Gradually, comedy at The Zoo expanded to seven nights a week. The comics pushed the musical acts out of the club, an event that occurred all over the country. Once the stand-up plague hit a room, other acts just disappeared.

In 1976-77, John and Ann Fox opened the Punchline in the Embarcadero, which was later bought out by legendary rock promoter Bill Graham, who also promoted Lenny Bruce's last shows. In 1976, Bob Ayers' the Other Café in the Haight started booking comics. There was the Great Gatsby's in Sausalito's Old Town, where an ordinance designed to keep out rock acts prohibited amplification. The comics got $10, a pizza, and a chance to test their vocal range.

**Chicago** native Tom Dreesen had been to New York City and experienced the Improvisation in 1970. Dreesen saw that by performing every night, the New York comics were able to develop their acts much more quickly. He wanted to find a place in Chicago where he could work out every night like the New York comics did. So Tom went to Henry Norton at the Pub in Chicago. He hustled every radio and newspaper contact he knew to plug the place, so from the opening night there were lines around the block. The problem was he only had a couple of reliable comics — Marsha Warfield, Jimmy Aleck, and Brad Sanders, who at the time was in a duo with a comedian named Bohannon. As happened often in those early comedy venues, Dreesen moved his show several times, first to the Pickle Barrel and then in 1974 to Big Ed's in Rosemont.

The scene in Chicago really began to percolate in the late '70s with rooms like the Comedy Cottage in Rosemont, the Comedy Womb in Lyons, and the Barrel of Laughs on the South Side in Senese's Winery. The comics swarming these rooms were Danny Storts, Dee Staley, Larry Reeb, Ted Holum, John Caponera, David Orion, Kenny Rogerson (before relocating to Boston), Bill Brady, Ken Severa, Roger Reitzel, Dailey Pike, John McDonnell, Steve Rudnick, Leo Benvenuti, Emo Phillips (a.k.a. Phil Soltanek), Judy Tenuta, Arsenio Hall, Paul Kelly, Jerry Dye, Ed Fiala, Jeff Allen, and Orlando Reyes.

As an indication of how Wild West the whole stand-up experience was at the time, Reyes was shot in the throat by a heckler in 1976 at 3G's nightclub. It was a sign of how desperate Orlando was for that sweet laughter that he was back on stage two days after being shot.

Meanwhile, in **Boston** a street juggler named Sean Morey was also inspired by a visit to New York. This time it was Catch a Rising Star in '76, where he got a dose of legendary MC Richard Belzer. Morey returned to Boston and opened Sean Morey's Comedy School. Two of his students, Paul Barkley and Bill Downes, decided to start a floating comedy showcase at the Charles Playhouse on Wednesday nights. They called it the Comedy Connection and it became Boston's first comedy club. They didn't think they could get audiences for comedy on the weekends in Boston, so they stuck to weekdays.

On Oct. 3, 1979, Barry Crimmins, after initiating a comedy night in his hometown of Skaneateles, N.Y., and checking out the scenes in New York City and San Francisco, started weekend comedy at the Ding Ho, a restaurant featuring live music. Within a month, the Ding Ho added Wednesday and Thursday nights. The comics were getting $25 a set and $75 to host the show and the cover was $3. The Ding Ho was soon doing shows in the restaurant, which held 140 people, as well as the lounge, which jammed in 200. Once again, the musicians were muscled out by the packed crowds hungering for comedy.

The Ding Ho regulars were Don Gavin, Chance Langton, Lenny Clark, Mike McDonald, Bill Campbell, Steve Sweeney, Teddy Bergeron, Mike Donovan, and Jack Gallagher. Kenny Rogerson, Kevin Meaney, Bob Nickman, and Bob Goldthwait later came from out of town.

The Ding Ho closed in 1983, as did the Holy City Zoo, casualties of the tidal wave of bigger, better-paying clubs they helped create.

In 1976, in the Old City area of **Philadelphia**, the 150-seat Grandma Minnies's on Chestnut, between Second and Third, ran an open mic of mostly folksingers, poets, jugglers, and a few comics such as Rich Hall, Clay Heery, Grover Silcox, Andy Cowan, and Ben Kurland. The nomadic Hall quickly moved on, but the other four Philly natives moved to a 30-seat room above the London restaurant at 23rd and Fairmont and charged a dollar a head. The sound system was a little Pignose amplifier set on the fireplace with a short cord to the microphone. Other comics there at the time were Ken Lynch, Sam Hollis, Barney Weiss, Frank Daugherty, Bob Myers and Bob Young, Steve Young, Judy Toll, and Tom Wilson.

As with the regional scenes elsewhere around the country, exposure was provided by the local TV news. Philadelphia's NBC affiliate did a piece about the young comics on *Evening Magazine* in 1977. The next week, 200 people showed up in a snowstorm to watch comedy. The Philly comics quickly moved nearby to a place called the Jailhouse for Saturday nights and crowded in 120 people at the same dollar cover.

**Long Island** started developing stand-up comics not physically far from New York City, but a world apart from its more sophisticated showcase clubs. Impressionist Richard M. Dixon, a Richard Nixon impersonator, opened his club, the White House, in 1977 and Richie Minervini got $5 a set or $10 to MC. Here again, the room advertised in the paper for singers, magicians, and comedians, but soon the popularity of the stand-ups gave them the run of the room.

Minervini would ask a bar for their worst night, and soon had four shows in different bars, starting with the Hungry Bear in Huntington. Musician Jackie Martling asked Minervini how to become a comedian. Minervini told Martling to print up cards that said "comedian." Martling got a sound system to go with his business cards and was soon adding other one-nighters to the Long Island circuit. The local comics called themselves the Magnificent Seven: Martling, Minervini, Bob Nelson, Bob Woods, Dave Hawthorne, Rob Bartlett, Jim Myers — and magician John Ferrentino, who the guys let into the group as the eighth Magnificent Seven.

After a trip to LA, where he visited the packed Improvisation and Comedy Store, **Detroit** native Mark Ridley returned home to open the Comedy Castle on Jan. 4, 1979. It was a small room, seating 90. Potential comedians showed up, including Bill Thomas, Tony Hayes, Leo Dufor (who later opened a comedy club in Windsor, Ontario, called Leo's Komedy Korner), Tim Allen, and Dave Coulier. Later the club turned pro and Mike Binder, a Detroit native, was the first headliner from Los Angeles. In no time there were 500 people trying to get in every Thursday, Friday and Saturday.

In **Houston**, the Comedy Workshop was started as a sketch showcase in 1978 by Paul and Sharon Menzel. The comics had Tuesday nights and one spot on the weekend sketch shows. Then the Menzels opened the Annex in July 1979, which was the first full-time stand-up club in Texas. Wednesday night was open mic and Thursday was showcase night, featuring the best of Houston. The weekends were a four-or five-person show. The regulars were Mike Vance, Sam Kinison, Gary Richardson, Fred Greenlee, Jack Mayberry, Andy Huggins, Jimmy Pineapple (Ladmirault), Ron Crick, Bill Silva, Riley Barber, Ron Roberston, Rick Johnson, Don Ware, John Farneti, Steve Moore, Steve Epstein, Steve McGrew, and Bill Hicks. People like Janeane Garofalo, Brett Butler, Rushion McDonald, Ron Shock, Carl Faulkenberry, Jim Patterson, Carl Labove, and Thea Vidale came a little later.

Mickey Finn's, a union bar in **Minneapolis,** enabled Scott Hansen to start shows with fellow comics Alex Cole, Jeff Gerbino and Bill Bower in 1977. A year later, they were joined by Louie Anderson, Jeff Cesario, Joel Madison and Sid Youngers.

Stand-up comedy started in **Pittsburgh** at the Portfolio lounge in September 1979. Every Tuesday night, Bill Elmer hosted a show that included Dennis Miller, Billy Martin, Bill Elmer, Rick Rockwell, Tom Anzalone, Jim Krenn, Bruce Dobler, Randy Lubas, and Chris Zito. These comics did shows at La Cantina in McKees Rocks, Our Joint in Bethel

Park, Price's Tavern in Canonsburg, and "The Dove and Rabbit" in Mt. Oliver before the Pittsburgh Comedy Club opened a year later.

The first comic open mics in **Seattle** were at a club called the Brooklyn Bridge in 1979. It was a biker bar near the University District and attracted comics Evan Davis, Arnold Mukai, Peggy Platt, and Rick Ducommon.

There was a stand-up scene in **Portland** from the late '70s that included comics J.P. Linde, Dave Anderson, Art Krug, and Rick Reynolds.

The key for all these rooms was that they were small, making them intimate and easy to pack. The comics could kill and get tremendous word of mouth. Stand-up was gaining in popularity at a grassroots level, winning fans one laugh at a time.

It was the summer of 1978. My third and final year of law school was to begin in a month. A decision had to be made. My potential employer, Basil Beck, said, "Go figure it out." I drove my 1969 Dodge Dart to Los Angeles. Someone at the Sunset Comedy Store sent me to the Westwood club. I bribed the doorman with some fine Colombian provided by my now LA-based pot-dealing high school friend and watched the shows for a week. One night, sharing a joint with the doorman, I declared my intention to move to LA to do stand-up. The doorman reacted fiercely. "Don't do it, man. I can't get on stage and I work here."

Once back in D.C., the Big Apple seemed distant and forbidding. I knew I had to get there, but didn't know how. I didn't know it yet, but New York City was coming to me.

# 10. "I REST MY CASE, YOU'RE OUT OF REACH"

In January 1979, Harry Monocrusos and Sandy Kalenik opened the Laughing Stock in Garvin's Restaurant of Washington, D.C., presenting New York and Los Angeles comics. Four comedy clubs paying non-locals clearly predated Garvin's, all in California. Mitzi Shore franchised her Comedy Store in San Diego on Memorial Day 1976. A year later, Michael Callie created the Laff Stop in Newport Beach. In 1978, Mike Lacy opened the Comedy and Magic Club in Hermosa Beach about the same time that Bob Fisher and Jan Smith bought the venerable Ice House in Pasadena and went full-time with comedy.

Garvin's was the first East Coast stop on the budding stand-up road. In the Midwest, Mark Ridley started paying out-of-town acts at Detroit's Comedy Castle, also later in January of 1979. Not long after, Dino Vince opened the Cleveland Comedy Club. Around this time, Bill Graham's Punchline in San Francisco started importing LA comics. The Philadelphia Comedy Factory Outlet booked its first New York comic early in 1980, and the gold rush was on.

Even though I had a good thing at El Brookman's, my eyes were on Garvin's from the moment I heard about it. Stand-up was all about taking the next challenge. I initially went onstage to find out if I could do to strangers what I did to friends. Garvin's presented another test.

In late December of '78, I fixated on a key phrase of the new Laughing Stock sign on the Garvin's roof, "Featuring New York and California Comics." I was the neighborhood fast-draw who just learned Wyatt Earp was coming to town. There was no avoiding the confrontation. My fear was being laughed off the stage by a Big City Jokeslinger and left to die in the street like a mangy hack.

45

The Laughing Stock at Garvin's Restaurant, 1979

Before that happened, I had to experience a couple of hard lessons, about the business and myself. First was the age-old comic predicament of competing comedy clubs. A few weeks before Garvin's opened I told a fellow Brookman's comic that we might be able to get work there too. He went right to the owner, Paul Brookman. My fault for not seeing the stadium scoreboard change from "friendly competition" to "cut-throat." The next Friday, Paul summoned the comics to the bar's basement. He stared at me while speaking of loyalty in the face of a new evil, Garvin's, declaring there was a "traitor in our midst." It got biblical. Paul banished me from the tribe. The only surprise was that the other comics didn't stone me to death with their joke notebooks as I left to wander the desert alone. They understood instinctively that my absence meant everybody got a promotion — a better time slot, more stage time and a bigger cut of the door. I left the club for the last time, realizing that stand-up comedy is a pirate ship. Everyone is dancing arm in arm, singing, "Yo-ho-ho and a bottle of rum" until the prize is within reach and then it's every mother-fucker for themselves.

I felt let down by my friends and quit stand-up. For the next few days I drank and glared at the law books on my shelf mocking the certain return of the prodigal law student.

The next weekend was the opening of the Laughing Stock Comedy

The Laughing Stock at Garvin's Restaurant, 1979

Club at Garvin's.

My girlfriend, Alice, insisted we be there. I was so nervous that I stopped to smoke two cigarettes on the Connecticut Avenue Bridge over Rock Creek. When I lit a third, Alice tossed it off the bridge, grabbed my hand and yanked me forward.

Garvin's was an L-shaped room that seated 220 people. The cover charge for the weekend shows was $4, with a two-drink minimum. A *Washington Post* article helped Garvin's to get a sellout on opening night, and the place stayed packed for a long, long time.

It was a surprise when fellow Brookman's comic Andy Evans took the stage as the MC. Andy also scouted Garvin's, and one day happened across Sandy and Harry surveying the empty room. In broad daylight he auditioned for two people ... old-school, vaudeville-style. Beautiful.

The first show at Garvin's was David Sayh and Richard Belzer. They both killed and their contrasting styles complemented each other perfectly. Sayh was cool, letting his exceptional material do the work. His act was like a rapidly assembled jigsaw puzzle — nothing, nothing and then surprise, a picture. Belzer was hyperkinetic and confrontational — a rebel without a pause. He had a rock star's swagger and a dominating personality. "Right, babe" and "Hey, Sparky" rattled around in my head for days.

At some point, Harry spotted me in the crowd and asked if I wanted to alternate the MC work with Andy for $75 a weekend. I was a stand-up comic again.

Initially, each out-of-town act was paid $300 for the weekend, plus a train ticket and hotel room. For New York showcase comics accustomed to surviving on $5 cab fare, that $300 instantly made Garvin's a coveted gig. It wasn't until later that Garvin's booked higher-priced special events such as Elayne Boosler, Jay Leno, Franklyn Ajaye, and an 80-year-old vaudeville legend, Georgie Jessel.

Over the next few months I worked with the best comics in New York: Jerry Seinfeld, George Wallace, Jimmy Brogan, Larry Miller, Robert Wuhl, Chris Rush, Adrienne Tolsch, Joe Piscopo, Glenn Hirsch, Kelly Rogers, John DeBellis, Ronnie Shakes, Carol Leifer, Keenen Ivory Wayans, Brandt Von Hoffman, Rich Hall, Kenny Kramer, JJ Wall, Paul Reiser, Bill Maher, Steve Mittleman, Joe Bolster, Uncle Dirty, Mark Schiff, Dennis Wolfberg, and Gilbert Gottfried.

Garvin's was quickly on the comedic radar screen. Mort Sahl came, expressed his disdain for young comics, and never returned. Rodney Dangerfield stopped by to warm up for a corporate gig. He paused at the bar long enough to grab a frosted mug of beer, before disappearing into the bathroom. He came out looking like a Georgia mule, wiped the white powder from his nose, grabbed the microphone and rocked the crowd while taking sips of beer. After finishing his short set, Rodney walked straight to an idling Jaguar, mug of beer still in hand, and disappeared into the night.

Wherever alcohol and comedy are served, strange beings appear. One was a neighborhood guy, Tom, who became Garvin's first offstage announcer. Tom, a World War II re-enactor, came drunk to start a Friday night show, dressed in a Nazi officer's uniform. A full house got to witness Harry frog-march Colonel Klink out the front door.

In no time, the Thursday open mic, with a $2 cover and one-drink minimum, became so popular that Harry added another on Sunday. Thursday then became a local "pro night" (invitation only) with one of the New York comics brought down a day early to anchor the show. Sunday was the true open mic. Being the MC for those shows was where I made up for the stage time I lost when I was MC on the weekends.

For whatever reason, Garvin's drew more black patrons and comics than Brookman's. Maybe it was the proximity to Howard University and the upscale black neighborhoods. Andy Evans was soon joined by Butch Burns, Greg Poole, The Fat Doctor, and others. A couple of years later, Martin Lawrence and Dave Chappelle made their debuts at Garvin's.

The format for the weekend shows was an MC followed by a local musical act, such as Karen Goldberg, and then the two out-of-town comedians, who had equal billing. This was before the establishment of the escalating show structure of opener, middle and headliner. Still, everybody knew who should close the shows, and if they didn't, Harry told them.

The co-headliners were supposed to do 30-45 minutes. For some of the comics, accustomed to 20-minute showcase sets, this was a stretch. You could see their engines catch fire at the 25-minute mark. Then it was time to pull the cord on the crowd-work chute, "Where are you from? What do you do for a living?" Those lines were stock act fillers since Frank Fay entertained the Dough Boys at the Palace Theater, but we didn't know them at El Brookman's. I was a young Jedi comic with much to learn.

Then there were the comics who not only covered the 45 but tried a fresh joke, or two, or 10 every show. Here was another lesson — unless it was an audition, I always tried something new.

I audiotaped my first few times on stage in 1977, but was irritated by the rough, idiotic sound of my voice and stopped. So many of the New York comics used cassette recorders that it became obvious this was a vital tool for development. I got over myself and studied my tapes. Harry helped by installing the latest technology: a VHS video camera. One Sat-

urday, Rich Hall and I reviewed our tapes. He helped me with performing tips and tags for my jokes. The only thing I remembered was it was
easier listening to me than watching me.

I was the MC and knew my place — don't go long, get the intro
right, and get out of the way — but these big-time New York stand-ups
respected anyone working hard at the craft and treated me well. Rick
Overton and Glenn Hirsch offered to help get me in the Improvisation. I
was to discover later that getting in and getting on were very different
concepts. New York City had a hundred comics as obsessed with getting
onstage to perform stand-up comedy as I was.

Like all the early club owners, Harry loved stand-up comedy. He was
especially fond of his local crew and found us all sorts of side work.

My confidence grew immensely working at Garvin's with the New
York comics. I wasn't onstage for as long as they were, but I got the
same laughs from the same people.

By early 1979 I had finished my law school requirements. The International School of Law was now George Mason School of Law and ac-
credited. Everyone in my family expected me to return to South Jersey
and practice law. It was time to make a tough decision.

My parents were driving through Washington on their way to Florida. I invited them to watch a show at Garvin's.

Afterward my dad asked me, "Are these guys from New York?'

I told him they were.

He said, "They're too sharp for you. That's no place for you."

Someone once said, "If you want be happy in your career, do something your dad loved but wasn't real good at."

# 11. "GO AHEAD, BITE THE BIG APPLE"

The spring of 1979 I drove my packed car to New York City, stopping in New Jersey to tell all interested parties of my new life's purpose. Basil said, "You're not that funny." He then took me partying and slipped me some cash. My usually stoic mom screamed. My volatile dad sat stunned into silence. I later heard my dad told people I joined a religious cult, rather than trying to explain the unexplainable, a showbiz career. That was understandable. I was giving up a career with a clearly defined income to pursue one without a clue as to how I might make living from it... pretty much the same thing my dad did a little over 20 years earlier when he left a steady job at a newspaper to start a business.

My first apartment in New York City was Apt AA, an illegal basement studio with crumbling walls at 630 E Ninth St., between avenues C and D in Alphabet City. The dump was recently vacated by a high school friend, Joe Mullin, who wanted out of New York City so bad he left everything — his furniture, dishes, and a loaded .22-caliber revolver.

The rent was $175, with $2 off for every rat killed, and nightly access to the rooftop for viewing vacant building fires set by squatters, and the street squabbles between the junkies, and other colorful street characters.

The bed platform was next to the sole window. One night, in a crazed attempt to get air into the hot apartment, I unlocked and opened the protective window gate. Early in the morning, I was awakened by a guy crawling across the bottom of my bed. I pointed the .22 at him. He calmly said, "Sorry, man. Thought it was my place." He quickly backed

The Dungeon at 630 E. 9th Street, NYC, 1979

out the window. It was scary, but not enough to make me move. I was there to become a professional stand-up comedian. My life revolved around the granddaddy of the modern comedy clubs, the Improvisation on 44th and Ninth Avenue.

A couple of established acts, Rick Overton and Glenn Hirsch, introduced me to the club's manager, Chris Albrecht, and his assistant, Howie Klein. After passing the audition, I was an Improv regular, which only meant I was free to take my place at the end of a long line of comics. There were two basic categories of comics at the Improv. The first was the "paid acts," who got the coveted $20 spots on the weekend shows. I was in the second category, the late-night comics who normally didn't sniff the stage until after midnight. The shows lasted until 3 a.m., so stage time was available to those who had the ability to "hang."

The hang was an aggravating, but necessary experience, part of paying your dues. I sat alone in the bar for hours, sipping Coca-Colas. The misery was only heightened by watching comic after comic enter the showroom, and hearing all that laughter. The frustration sent many comics home early. The crucial stage time went to the comics who had the patience and stamina to hang. I was a vulture.

Every night I sat in that bar from the start of the show at 9 till either I got onstage or the place closed. I had no other life, no other friends. My only salvation was to hear Chris or Howie say the words, "You're next."

It didn't matter if my spot was 2:30 in the morning in front of six stragglers. I gave it my best, knowing that the only way up was to make those six drunks laugh.

Some nights, I didn't get any closer to the showroom than using the bathroom, but never took off a night. This went on week after week.

One of the greatest gifts during this period was my friendship with Kenny Kramer. We met at Garvin's when he was a visiting act. He was one of those funny, supportive New York pros. Not long after that he quit stand-up to raise his daughter Melanie when her mother proved incapable to do the job. Kenny lived in the Manhattan Plaza, just a block from the Improv. Many nights after getting shut out at the Improv I visited Kenny. He counseled me on the do's and don'ts, the politics of the showcase clubs. More important, Kenny reminded me that I was funny and had to be ready for my chance. Many nights I left Kramer's ready to go at it again the next night.

In July, my D.C. girlfriend, Alice, decided to spend the rest of the summer with me before returning to graduate school in Bologna, Italy. One night, she called me at the Improv. When I took the phone she screamed, "Ritchie! Come quickly. There are rats! Rats everywhere!" When I entered the apartment, Alice sat on the bed, the covers pulled around her. There were four rats in the kitchen area. I threw a book. They didn't flinch. I grabbed the .22 and started shooting. I was half-drunk, or I never would have thrown the book. Alice screamed. Gunshots in a small apartment are loud. The rats fled into the bathroom and disappeared into a hole above the bathtub. I plugged the hole with a bag of cotton balls, thinking that would block the vermin horde.

Alice and I cracked some beers and fired up the bong to celebrate our territorial victory. A short time later, there was a knock on the door. For the first and only time in my life I heard that classic line, "Open up. It's the police." Thinking it was a neighbor goofing, I used an old movie line I had been waiting a lifetime to use: "You'll never take me alive, copper!"

The pounding and the voice became more insistent. "Open up the goddamn door. It's the police." I didn't know anyone who was that good an actor. I opened the door, still holding the bong, and one of New York's Finest entered. He was investigating a report of gunshots and a woman screaming. Like an idiot I explained what happened, showing them the hole in the wall and the pistol. The officer laughed, "You need something bigger than that to shoot these rats." He was very pleasant, probably thrilled to not be dealing with a murder scene. He left, taking with him my unregistered gun.

A stand-up comic rarely forgets that last straight job. It marks the graduation from amateur to professional. After learning about the rats, the landlord inspected my apartment and, as if he never saw the place before, called it "unlivable." He offered me a lease in a recently renovated building on Sixth Street, between avenues A and B. The rent jumped to $200. Didn't matter if it went down to $100, I was broke. My only income was an occasional night opening for a musical act in Washington, D.C., the pay barely covering the train fare.

My landlord asked if I wanted a job remodeling apartments for $5 an hour, cash, under the table. New York City suffered from "white flight" in the '60s and nearly went bankrupt in 1976. The Lower East Side was littered with empty buildings. The city started selling these properties for pennies, with the condition that they be renovated. The plan was to lure people back into the city and increase the tax base.

Eight o'clock the next morning, I was with a crew gutting and refurbishing a nearby apartment building. It took these guys about five seconds to figure out I didn't know the difference between a hammer and a screwdriver. They made me a go-fer. I spent the rest of the day running for coffee, cigarettes and beer. After spending 10 hours smoking, drinking and bullshitting, I collected my fifty bucks, showered and got back on my perch at the Improv.

The next morning, the landlord intercepted me on my way to the job. "Forget about that other job. I got a new job for you. We need help cleaning out these apartments. Can you do that?" Figuring he meant removing trash and debris, I assured him that was not a problem.

I walked a few blocks and met three young Italian guys standing in front of an abandoned building. Introductions were made, and the leader, a short, stocky guy named Lou, immediately got down to business. "You guys ready to do this thing?"

We were soon in the building, cleaning out apartments, which actually meant throwing squatters into the street. That was the job. Some people went meekly; others had to be convinced a quick and sudden relocation was in their best interests.

Every day I worked for eight to 10 hours with these wild guys, kicking in doors, rousting junkies and tossing belongings out of windows. Then I spent all night at the Improv, waiting for the opportunity to make someone laugh. I was constantly nodding off on subway trains and an Improv barstool. Cue Warren Zevon, "I'll sleep when I'm dead."

One Friday night, I noticed Chris and Howie in a bit of a panic. Gilbert Gottfried was on stage, killing a packed house. Comic Richie Gold was scheduled to follow Gilbert in the last paying spot but wasn't in the club. They looked in the bar. I was the only comic there. Howie called

Catch a Rising Star and the Comic Strip, looking for possible replacements. They looked out the door to see if a cab was arriving with the cavalry. Gilbert was wrapping it up when Chris and Howie finally approached me. "Can you hold this crowd?"

I said I could, and I did. In doing so, I jumped over a few other late-night comics who had been there longer than me. There is no seniority or ladder of success in show business. Everyone waits, face down in an open sewage ditch, until they call your name. And you better be in that ditch when they do.

From that moment on, I was a paid act on the weekends and got better spots on weeknights. It was a small thing, that $20, but it made all the difference in the world to me. I looked at my position as greatly improved, and because of that maybe the universe agreed. For whatever reason, within a week, everything changed. Harry Monocrusos offered me the job of booking Garvin's for $300 a month. Jerry Stanley hired me to do his new Sunday night gig at Freddy's in Bernardsville, N.J., for $55.

I quit my day job.

## 12. "OPEN YOUR EYES, LOOK AT YOUR PART, BOY"

> "A man takes a job and he becomes that job."
> --*Peter Boyle, as "Wizard," mouthed those words from writer Paul Schrader in the movie* Taxi Driver

For a short period in 1979, I was not only a stand-up, but also a club booker. In the worst tradition of the comic turned club owner, both jobs suffered.

A few months after I moved to New York City, Harry Monocrusos, the owner of my former home club, Garvin's in Washington, D.C., called to tell me that he severed his relationship with Sandy Kalenick, who booked the room. I liked Sandy, shared more than a few drinks and laughs with her, but didn't ask why. This was the business we had chosen.

Harry offered me the booking job for $300 a month. My rent was $200. Fried from working too many hours as a daytime people mover and late-night comic, I accepted.

A few hours later, a very upset Sandy called. "If you were my friend, you would never take this job."

I explained that I was broke and tired. "If you were my friend, you'd be happy for me."

The bottom line, I told Sandy, was someone was taking the job. Harry wasn't folding the tent on a sold-out show.

Sandy said she would never forgive me and hung up the phone.

At first, it was easy. Garvin's was one of the only out-of-town jobs and everyone wanted to do it. Sending a Larry Miller or Rich Hall for a

Sandy Kalenick, flanked by Kelley Rogers and John DeBellis, 1979

return visit was a no-brainer. It took five minutes to book a month of comedians.

In no time, the first problem arose. Comics approached me for bookings. It was one thing to sit in the back of a room and silently judge someone's act, but another to tell them face-to-face what you thought. I was barely past late-night spots myself. This made me very self-conscious. As powerful as the need for laughter was, it took a lot of effort to overcome my normal insecurity to get onstage. I didn't need the anxiety bumped up a notch with paranoia.

Then the old dictum, "power corrupts," came into play. Holding the keys to a paying gig probably opened a few doors in the clubs. Using that little bit of power as a shortcut to stage time probably appealed to that side of me that was always looking for an easier, softer way. I was reverting to The Pirate, and my old wheelin' and dealin' ways.

I booked a comic knowing he wasn't ready because he had the key to a few other bookings. He bombed both nights in D.C. I felt them in New

York. Actually, Harry called with a blown-joke-by-blown-joke report. Worrying about another comic's performance was more than I could handle. I gave the job back to Harry, who quickly handed it to a real agent. A young Jeff Penn had the good taste and fortitude to cancel some of my ill-conceived bookings and start afresh. I was relieved to just concentrate on being funny.

The payback took about 10 years, but it came.

There was a period of time when the only comedy club in Washington, D.C., was Dan Harris' Comedy Café. Wanting to play D.C. again, I asked my agent, Bill Gross, to call for a date. He called back with bad news. Dan Harris wanted to give me a week but could not. On her deathbed Sandy Kalenick made Dan promise to never book Ritch Shydner.

Some resentment lasts a lifetime. Showbiz grudges can reach from the grave.

# 13. "A STUDENT AT THE COMEDY COLLEGE"

Every generation of stand-up comedians needed someplace to learn the craft. In vaudeville, it was the small-town theaters. Later it was the resort hotels in the Catskills. After World War II, beginning comics created an ad hoc network of training gyms, grabbing stage time in coffeehouses, neighborhood bars (toilets) and strip joints.

By the early 1970s, for the first time, there were rooms dedicated to developing new comedy talent, known as "showcase clubs," not surprisingly in LA and New York City.

In New York City there were three. There was Budd Friedman's original Improvisation (1963) on the corner of 44th street and Ninth Avenue. When Marvin Braverman went on *The Tonight Show* with guest host Flip Wilson in 1970, he plugged the Improvisation, putting it on the map for the paying customer. Comedians already knew where and what it was. Comics like Steve Landesberg, David Brenner, Robert Klein, Richard Lewis, Rodney Dangerfield, Jay Leno, and Elayne Boosler were Improv regulars during the early to mid 1970s.

The other two top New York City showcase clubs were Rick Newman's Catch a Rising Star (1972) on First Avenue, between 77th and 78th streets, and the Comic Strip (1975) on Second Avenue between 81th and 82th streets, owned by Bob Wachs and Richie Tienken. Silver Friedman took possession of the New York Improv in late 1979.

There were other places to do stand-up in New York City, with varying degrees of difficulty; the Bitter End and Other End in the Village, Al and Dick's Steak House on 54th, the Triple Inn, and Midtown's Good Times.

The first nightclub to be dominated by stand-up comics probably was

Explaining things on stage at The Improvisation, NYC, 1980

Pip's (1962), in the Sheepshead Bay area of Brooklyn, owned by George Schultz, who once performed stand-up under the name Georgie Starr. It featured established comedians like George's friend and contemporary Rodney Dangerfield, while also providing a place for a young David Brenner to cut his teeth. By the mid-'70s, the city showcase clubs were the place for a young comic to develop, and Dangerfield's nightclub was the place to see an established comic, making Pip's irrelevant.

The Big Three New York City showcases operated seven nights a week from 9 p.m. until 3 a.m., with a new comic taking the stage about every 15 minutes. That kind of available stage time attracted a lot of comedians. Some mighty fine singers also came through the New York rooms, including Judy Orbach, Mike Sergio, Richard T. Bear, Brian Gari, and pop star Pat Benatar. By the late '70s, they were a spice in the heavy comic soup.

From 1979 until 1982, if not on the road, I was in those New York showcase clubs. Some comics were leaving to higher levels of show business while others were just arriving, but this was the basic roster from that time period, listed with their likely home club. Even though the best worked all three clubs, every comic had a home club, usually the place where they first passed an audition.

Catch a Rising Star: Richard Belzer, The Funny Boys (Jonathan Schmock and Jim Vallely), Richie Gold, Marjorie Gross, Cathy Ladman, Bill Maher, Maurice Touisaunt, Richard Morris, Nancy Parker, Larry Ragland, Kelley Rogers, Rita Rudner, David Sayh, Lenny Schultz, Ronnie Shakes, Bill Scheft, Adrienne Tolsch, Max Dolcelli, The Untouchables (Buddy Mantia and Bobby Alto), J.J. Wall.

The Improvisation: Max Alexander, Alan Avon, Jimmy Brogan, Michael Cain, Mario Cantone, Mark Centor, Jimmy Charles, Billiam Coronel, Larry David, Ron Darian, John DeBellis, Barry Diamond, Jerry Diner, Lou DiMaggio, Gagen and Fine, Melvin George, Vince Gerardi, Gilbert Gottfried, Sam Greenfield, Rich Hall, Allan Havey, Jon Hayman, Dave Heenan, Glenn Hirsch, Ed Hockstein, Dom Irrera, Mike Ivy, David Kelly, Mike Langworthy, John Mendoza, Steve Mittleman, Mike Moto, Ken Ober, Rick Overton, Joe Piscopo, Paul Provenza, Kevin Rooney, Mike Rowe, Rita Rudner, Bill Rutkowsi, Mark Schiff, Angela Scott, Carol Siskind, Bob Shaw, Steve Skrovan, Jonathan Solomon, David Strassman, Fred Stoller, Stu Trivax, Uncle Dirty, Brant Von Hoffman, Keenen Wayans, Mark Weiner, Anita Weiss, Ron Zimmerman, Charles Zucker.

The Comic Strip: Gabe Abelson, Barry Berry, Jerry Allen, Peter Bales, Scott Blakeman, Joe Bolster, George Calfa, Scott Carter, Alan Colmes, Lois Dengrove, The Comedy Clinic (Mark King, Steve Shaffer and Bruce Pachtman), Dave (Jay) Edison, Wayne Federman, Richie Gold, Hiram Kasten, Bill Keller, Sue Kolinsky, Carol Leifer, Bill McCarty, Mac and Jamie, Bill Masters, Larry Miller, Will Miller, Eddie Murphy, J.J. Ramirez, Paul Reiser, Mike Reynolds, Ron Richards, Jerry Seinfeld, Abby Stein, D.F. Sweedler, Joey Vega, George Wallace, Barry Weintraub, Dennis Wolfberg.

That inventory of comics was remarkable. Most of those people, if not still working comedians, found work in the business in some capacity. The years confirmed these showcase clubs as incredible proving grounds.

We never considered the math, but the odds were daunting. In any given week there were 80 to 100 stand-ups vying for about 300 spots. There was not much growth available in two or three spots a week, and the allocation was never that democratic. The top acts worked all three clubs, sometimes racking up five spots on a weekend "scramble night." Ambitious late-night comics sought the necessary stage time in B rooms like Good Times or the Triple Inn.

Everybody knew everybody. There was competition, but also camaraderie. It seemed like every time you came off stage, three or four comics handed you cocktail napkins with joke suggestions. Comics readily swapped places in the show to enable one or the other to make a crosstown time spot. They shared cab rides and tipped each other when stage time looked to be available at one of the clubs. Money was slid under the table to help a broke friend buy a meal at the Green Kitchen.

It was a small community that easily policed itself. Joke thieves were banished to fringe rooms where bad singers punished them with endless renditions of *Tomorrow*, from the Broadway musical *Annie*.

Most comics were in their 20s, and aging fast. It took a lot of energy to turn all that fear, anger and anxiety into big, rollicking laughter.

Everyone was living on potential. There wasn't any money to be made, but a priceless education was free for the taking. Night after night you watched and were watched by some of the best young comics in the country. The sports cliché was never truer — playing with the best elevated your game.

Other than the $20 weekend spots, the only paying position was the MC at $50 a show. At one time or another every top act took a turn at this crucial job of hosting. The tone and flow of the show depended a great deal on the MC. He or she built a rapport with the audience and understood when a little time was needed between acts or to continue the momentum by quickly bringing up the next act.

Joe Piscopo, Kelly Rogers, Jimmy Brogan, and Hiram Kasten were enthusiastic MCs, affable comics able to suppress their egos for the greater good of the show.

The key talent for an MC was crowd work, and no one was better than Jimmy Brogan. Many "stock" lines originated with Jimmy. Brogan: "You, sir. What do you do for a living?" Audience member: "I'm unemployed." Brogan: "How do you know when you're finished?"

At the Improv and the Comic Strip, the line-ups were set by management and there was always subtle pressure on the MC, from a bar full of surging comics, to bring up the next act as quickly as possible. At Catch, the MC was all-powerful, with complete leeway to not only choose the next act but do as much time as he or she wanted before handing over the mic. All that authority created the best collection of MCs in the city. Richard Belzer forged a template for Kelley Rogers, Bill Maher, Adrianne Tolsch and Bill Scheft.

The comics strove to develop original material, but with that many rats running around such a small maze, there was bound to be a certain amount of crossbreeding. I heard so many ethnic jokes, especially of the "I'm half-this and half-that" variety that one even popped out of my WASP head. "I'm half German and half Irish … which means I get drunk and fight myself."

Catch, the Strip and the Improv favored their homegrown talent, hoping to cash in on the notoriety from launching the career of a star. Maybe hedging their bets was why they so shamelessly used each other's acts. Maybe the clubs just wanted to put on the best show possible. Whatever the reason, the top acts moved freely between all three clubs.

In no way was that to mean the clubs were interchangeable. Each one had a distinct personality based on the owners, location and comics.

The Comic Strip was the newest club with the biggest showroom. There was a two-piece band to play the comics on and off, but no singers. One of the founders, Richie Tienken, previously owned a Bronx bar and knew the liquor business, how to handle people, and fill a joint. The crowds were younger, and more likely to be from areas like Long Island and Queens, as were the comics.

The Improvisation was the venerable flagship of the showcase squadron. There was a piano, but the singers provided their accompaniment. Located near Times Square, it attracted sophisticated theatergoers, but also tourists and the hookers working the Lincoln Tunnel. The renowned Improv housed more comics because a new kid hitting town was more likely to know about it and land there first.

Catch was the elite Upper East Side club, as signified by its velvet rope. There was a kick-ass little three-piece band for the comics and singers. The showroom wasn't as dark as the others, all the better to see the many movie, television and rock stars, in the audience. There weren't as many comics in the Catch stable, so it skimmed the cream from the other two clubs. One theory as to why fewer young comics called Catch home was the pressure of performing in front of a room filled with celebrities. Another factor was probably the intimidating presence of Richard Belzer.

By 1979, "The Belz" was on the road too much to still be considered the house MC at Catch, but when he was in town, it was his show. He owned Catch and always did a minimum of 15 minutes of killer funny before handing over the microphone. No friendly crowd work here, Belzer sliced and diced anyone who dared make eye contact. He was incredibly quick-witted. A heckler once yelled, "You talk too fast." Belzer whipped back, "You listen too slow, Sparky." Even his regular bits sounded off the top of his head. Belzer to ringsider, "Hey, pal. Can I bum a cigarette? I left mine in the machine."

Belzer was the rock star of the comedy scene, in dress and attitude, a direct descendant of vaudeville legend Frank Fay, who created the quick-witted, take-no-prisoners, wise guy stand-up. The Belz was so unique and potent that many young comics, such as Dennis Miller, were Belzerized, just as Fay had influenced a young Bob Hope 50 years earlier.

Gilbert Gottfried was another comic from this period who was as original and mesmerizing as The Belz. Both were favorites with the crowds and comics. Belzer and Gottfried were tidal forces. The room filled with comics when either of them took the stage, and cleared when they left.

Gilbert walked a different tightrope. He didn't confront the audience, but challenged them to a game of hide-and-seek. This was before Gilbert settled into his current style of closing his eyes and shouting his material. In the late '70s Gilbert was a shapeshifter. He did an impression, then a one-liner, then a rant, then a prop gag, then an observation joke, then a characterization of an agent critiquing what Gilbert just did. Gilbert threw every possible style of comedy into his mental blender and let it fly with the lid off.

Gilbert was a comedic iconoclast. If someone from the audience shouted with recognition when Gilbert started one of his famous bits, he shut it down and moved on to something else.

If Gilbert wanted to kill, forget about it, especially if he decided to close with Quadradick followed by Tony from Brooklyn. In Quadradick, Gilbert held a barstool in front of his crotch while doing a parody of the movie *Jaws*. James Mason played Sheriff Brody. Jackie Gleason played Quint. It was a handful of dick jokes wrapped in a pop culture reference slathered with famous movie stars. The audience swallowed it whole. Tony from Brooklyn was Gilbert lampooning stand-up comedy. He put on a cheesy sports jacket, pulled out his shirt collar and spoke in a rough Brooklyn accent. "Why'd da moron trow da clock out da winda? Cuz he's a moron. What are ya an idiot?! Why'd da chicken cross da street? Who da fuck knows. It's a chicken. It's got a brain dis big. Are ya listening ta me? A customer say, 'Waiter, there's a fly in my soup.' The waiter says, 'You fucking sayin' I put it dere. Like ahm gonna risk dis stinkin lousy job for a joke! You fuckin' asshole." Gilbert kept pounding with one fractured joke after another until the audience collapsed.

The line-up for the weekend shows at the Improv was an MC followed by three comics, a singer and then two more comics. Gilbert normally occupied that sweet spot after the singer. The 15 minutes behind Gilbert weren't so sweet, and those were my early paid spots.

Watching Gilbert from the back of the room made me think of Salieri watching Mozart, that I was cursed with ambition but not talent. The most terrifying moments for me were after Gilbert left the stage. The MC usually brought me right up, knowing that after Gilbert's masterful deconstruction of stand-up comedy the audience stared at anything that resembled a normal joke.

My act felt closer to the Catskills comics Gilbert was mocking than the jazz he was laying down. If I didn't want to suffer a steady diet of eating it, I needed to toss my usual material. The first three comics usually worked the typical crowd work angle of, "Where are you from?" and "What do you do for a living?" Desperate to pull the audience together after Gilbert's savaging, I started addressing couples, "How long have you been together?" and "Have either of you said 'I love you' yet?" That led me to a new vein of material about relationships.

That which does not kill us makes us funnier.

# 14. "A BUCK DANCER'S CHOICE"

Besides the showcase clubs featuring a endless offering of young unknowns there was one other New York City nightclub to see stand-up comedy, Dangerfield's, on First Avenue between 61$^{st}$ and 62$^{nd}$ streets. Since 1969, this old-school nightclub (with linens, electric table lamps and red leather booths) booked veteran singers and classic comedians, such as Jackie Mason, Milton Berle and Red Buttons. It was also a great place to see its namesake do a long, X-rated set.

Rodney was one of the biggest stand-up stars of this era, and that rarest of showbiz animals, the late bloomer. He left the business as a young man to raise his kids. Depending on whom you believe he either sold or conned house siding. Nevertheless, returning to stand-up as a weathered, middle-age man, all his nervous tics that worked against him as a young man now helped his comedy. Rodney, by portraying a man beaten down by life, attracted a huge following among my generation. He got our respect by turning our parents' mantra of the American Dream into a joke.

By 1979, Rodney was occasionally paying young comics $75 to entertain midnight shows, usually drunken prom kids. That was a big-pay night for most of us, but closer to gladiator work than comedy. It certainly wasn't an atmosphere to tweak new material, but I had faced worse crowds for less money opening for rock bands. Rodney, wearing his post-show robe, often sat in the back of the room, enjoying a drink and the spectacle. There was a lot of encouragement in hearing his loud laugh, punctuated by an occasional, "Alright."

Laughs were secondary to holding the stage until you could hand off the whip and chair to another comic, usually rushing in from a set at one

Album purchased, tie gifted by Rodney Dangerfield, 1980

of the showcase clubs. One night, a particularly unruly crowd sent two consecutive comics to early showers. Luckily for the show, and unluckily for me, I happened to be early for my spot. The hecklers were emboldened by their success with the two retreating comics. My best strategy for survival in these situations was to identify the loudest heckler and as quickly as possible crucify him as an example. In New York, nothing delighted the mob more than to see someone else thrashed.

When my relief finally showed, I was able to hand the guy an audience. Rodney greeted me in the bar. "Alright, kid. You held the stage. You got a lot of balls." I was getting that a lot, which was fine if it were the rodeo. It was better than hearing, "You're unfunny and cowardly."

Rodney then surprised me. "Hey, kid. You wanna do some blow?" Doing cocaine with Rodney was one of the reasons I got in the business.

The next thing I knew, Rodney was cutting lines on a glass table in his office. I didn't watch too closely as his robe was wide-open, exposing the fact he wore nothing under the robe. The first line was a revelation — celebrities get different drugs than showbiz foot soldiers. The cocaine I had been purchasing, from a reputable dealer, was so cut with baby laxative it kept me more regular than high.

At some point Rodney fished some red ties from a desk drawer. "Here, kid. You like those old suits. I can't wear 'em with this shit on 'em." Rodney always wore a black suit, white shirt and plain red tie. Some of his fans were mistakenly giving him red-patterned ties. I wore old suits then, from the '50's and '60s. Rodney gave me three ties. Still have them.

Finally, I screwed up the courage to ask The Master for advice. Rodney told me in his inimitable way, "Ya gotta listen to 'em. Do you tape?"

I told Rodney I tried taping my show but couldn't stand to listen to my voice, that I sounded like an idiot. "Of course you're an idiot. You're a comedian. They ain't paying to hear a brain surgeon up there.

"Whatever they're laughing at, do more, and if they ain't, drop it. They'll tell you what's funny about you. Individually they may be orangutans, but as a group they're genius."

The only problem was, every time I bent over to snort a line I got an eyeful of Rodney's balls. That was another lesson that night — there was no such thing as free cocaine.

I started taping again, hauling that big, boxy cassette player to the club and setting it up in the back of the room, but Rodney's advice saved me a lot of time and trouble. Listening to my tapes caused me to drop the political jokes and focus on relationship humor. An added bonus was listening to all the comments the other comics put on the tape while you were onstage, both the intentional and accidental.

It was painful to listen to myself. Even hearing the audience laughter on the tape didn't stop that negative voice in my head from barking. Despite all that, I did it to improve. It was always about becoming a better stand-up. Always.

There were a lot of established comics hanging out at Rodney's, dispensing great wisdom. One of the perks of working Rodney's midnight massacres was getting to watch the headliners work the earlier shows.

Just as much fun was watching the headliner hang with his contemporaries in the bar after the place emptied of civilians. One night, the kibitz circle included David Frye, Rodney, legendary spritzer Joe Ancis and pretty much every Jackie in the business, Mason, Gayle, and Vernon. A few of us young comics sat at a respectful distance, but leaned in on every story, caught every word. My only regret was not taping them.

At one point Jackie Mason said to Jackie Vernon, "Did you do that thing I gave you for last Saturday night?

Jackie Vernon replied, "No. They didn't meet my price."

Jackie Mason set a trap. "Oh you had a better thing."

Jackie Vernon stepped in it. "I stayed home. I told you. They didn't meet my price."

Jackie Mason snapped. "You didn't work. You have no price."

I looked at the old men and hoped that I was a lot like they were.

# 15. "TRY TO CATCH THE DELUGE
IN A PAPER CUP"

In 1980 the National Association for Campus Activities (NACA) convention was held at the Sheraton Hotel on Connecticut Avenue in our nation's capital. College and university student representatives from all over the country gathered to buy acts for the following school year. It was a gold rush for performers, but cost a lot of money to showcase for the students, or to even have a booth on the convention floor.

An agent had a plan to score at the NACA convention without risking the costly convention fees. Across the street from the convention was Garvin's Comedy Club. The idea was to showcase young New York stand-ups at Garvin's under the assumption that all those student buyers wouldn't want to spend every second in a lousy hotel.

The prospect of picking up lucrative college gigs easily enticed 20 comics to participate. Comics like Jerry Seinfeld, Elayne Boosler, Larry Miller, Rich Hall, Rick Overton, Steve Mittleman, and Gilbert Gottfried traveled from New York City to D.C., and stayed two nights at a nearby hotel, all out of the comic's pocket.

The shows were in the middle of the week, normally dark days for Garvin's. Our agent didn't factor in all the booze, hookers and drugs provided to the student buyers by the big booking agencies at the convention. Nothing short of a five-alarm fire was getting those kids out of that hotel.

Not one college buyer showed at Garvin's, nor did anyone else for that matter. For two nights, 20 comics performed for each other, the least-desired entertainment for the worst audience possible. We eventually made it fun, heckling, doing impressions of each other's act, and performing bits from our favorite comedy albums.

After the last show, a few comics gathered in a hotel room. Gilbert Gottfried called our agent, posing as the buyer for the State University of New York system. Gilbert enthused about the great comics he saw at Garvin's and offered them bookings for $10,000 a night. We then listened in shock as our agent informed Gilbert that was too much money. He could get us cheaper. It got funny when our agent told Gilbert that he, too, was a comic and could handle most of the dates himself.

We went back to New York City with zero college dates but a fun new line, "The gig was so good my agent took it."

# 16. "YOU GOTTA DO IT TILL YOU'RE THROUGH IT SO YOU BETTER GET TO IT"

In 1979, there were very few paying gigs for the young stand-ups of New York City.

Freddy's in Bernardsville, N.J., held its first comedy night on August 5, 1979, with a $3 cover. The promoter, Jerry Stanley, was inspired when he saw a childhood friend, Brant Von Hoffman, performing at the Improvisation. Upon learning that comics got $5 cab fare at the New York City showcase clubs, Jerry decided to pay $50 more. That is how he came to the odd pay of $55. In a ploy that became Jerry's model for securing new locations, he asked for the bar's off night. That was how the Freddy's shows came to be at 10 p.m. on Sunday night. Freddy's first show sold out and featured John DeBellis, Glenn Hirsch and Peter Bales, who was a last-minute fill-in when Von Hoffman secured tickets to a Yankees game. Each of the acts was responsible for half an hour. Interestingly, Stanley's three-act show presaged the graduated opener-middle-headliner structure.

Around this time, comic Ron Richards began booking a couple of rooms, Mustache Pete's and the Jade Fountain. Ron soon quit the booking business to concentrate on stand-up, handing the ball to Stanley, who ran with it. When comedy clubs exploded across the country in the early '80s, Jerry was in a perfect position to become a powerful booking agent.

Stanley quickly built on Freddy's success. Within a year, he had 12 venues in New Jersey, including six Ground Round restaurants, where barrels of peanuts provided hecklers with ammo. The Penny Arcade in Clark became a weekend gig without the overnight stay, featuring stand-up comedy on Friday, Saturday, and Sunday. Comics liked working for

Jerry Stanley in front of map of his empire, 1982

Jerry, a good laugher who always paid that night, in cash. By 1982, Stanley oversaw an empire of 12 full-time comedy clubs nationwide and 41 one-nighters in the tri-state area. Comics no longer made fun of his plaid pants, at least not to his face.

Jerry soon tired of driving in and out of the city and looked to comics with cars. Reliable transportation became as much a calling card for a comic as a tight 30 minutes. Cars had been getting gigs for their owners since vaudeville. Joan Rivers wrote of her car as the key to getting work in the Catskills in the early '60s.

I possessed reliable transportation for a short while. My 1969 Dodge Dart made the move with me from D.C. There was plenty of available parking on E Ninth Street. I soon discovered why there weren't many cars in Alphabet City. One night, I got in my car without noticing the two wheels on the passenger side were no longer there. I put the car in gear and drove the car off two cinder blocks. The right side of the car landed on the street with a loud, screeching clunk. The predators quickly found the lame animal. That night, before I even had a chance to find replacement wheels, the car battery was stolen. A day after that, the trunk was popped and my spare tire and tools were taken. The two wheels on the driver's side disappeared next. I returned from the clubs one night and noticed the car's doors wide open and windows smashed; the seats and steering wheel were missing. Finally, I emerged from my building one morning to find the carcass of my car gone. All that remained were the cinder blocks. In a slow, steady piece of time-lapse photography, the city completely devoured my car.

The comics met in the Improv bar at 8 o'clock for the drive into Jersey. Located near the Lincoln Tunnel, the Improv was the natural rendezvous for all points west.

In no time, there were so many Jersey gigs that Stanley was forced to look beyond the Manhattan comic pool, presenting the opportunity to work with new comics. One Sunday night, I was picked up by two comics from Long Island, Jackie "The Jokeman" Martling and Bob "Walrus" Woods. Their huge 1970s station wagon was a bar on wheels. I understood the concept of "roadies," but this was another level. They had a thermos filled with a potent mai tai cocktail, a large cooler stocked with beer and half a dozen joints for a 30-minute drive into Jersey. It became a three-hour tour. We were lost halfway through the Lincoln Tunnel. Since the comics always brought the sound system, Jackie never worried. We drove aimlessly around circle after circle but The Jokeman kept cackling, "The show starts when we get there." It became my mantra for years.

Working with comics from outside the Manhattan scene led to other work. The East Side Comedy Club in Huntington, Long Island, used city comics to augment their local acts. An interesting phenomenon occurred. Overall, East Side was a great club with a generous host in Richard Minervini but some tension arose between the home and visiting teams. The word back then was that some Island acts resented the haughty attitude of a few of the city comics. This rising competition between the two camps sometimes caused the shows to run long as some of the Island comics refused to yield the stage to the closing City acts. One Island comic in particular was notorious for his hour-long opening sets of free-form improvisation. Every audience had a life span. Comedy was difficult enough without also having to perform CPR on a spent crowd. This scenario of local comics ambushing out-of-town talent was later re-enacted from time to time in clubs like the Comedy Works in Denver.

Soon there were other weekend gigs west of New York City; the Rainy Night House in Queens, Richard M. Dixon's White House in Massapequa, Governor's in Levittown, and the Brokerage Pub in Bellmore.

Before all these gigs, the only other bar that came close to qualifying as a paying gig was Pip's in the Sheepshead Bay section of Brooklyn. At this time, George Schultz ran Pip's with the help of his two sons, Marty and Seth. Schultz claimed to have given Rodney his hook line, "I don't get no respect." He was a funny and supportive guy. One night, I was invited to his upstairs apartment for a few post-show drinks. Suddenly, George and another old comic noticed the time and quickly turned on the TV to watch an old '60s show, *The Rat Patrol.* They explained why they preferred *Rat Patrol* over the other '60s World War II series, *Combat* and *The Lieutenant* — the Nazi body count was higher. Every time a German was shot, the two Jewish gentlemen drank a shot and said, "L'Chaim."

The $60 given to comics for a four-show weekend at Pip's basically covered the cab fare from Manhattan. As much fun as it was to play and imagine it to be a certified showbiz job, Pip's was really just another showcase club. But comics needed every stage that would have them, especially in the '60s and '70s. For a long time, Pip's was a great place to perform.

Whenever there was a gig where everyone was paid the same, someone inevitably pulled the old "short money" gag, probably originated in vaudeville. One night Peter Bales turned to me as we readied to make the trip back to the city and asked, "Did you get your hundred? He was implying he got $100 instead of the $60, hoping to panic me. I knew the gag and shot back, "What are you talking about? It's been a hundred and a quarter for a month." Proving the con was sometimes the easiest mark, Bales stormed back into Pip's to demand the rest of his pay.

The gigs in the areas surrounding Manhattan at this time proved to be the perfect steppingstone between the non-paying showcase rooms and the high-paying, out-of-town comedy clubs. The comics were forced to stretch their acts from the normal showcase 15-minute sets to 30 minutes. They learned to handle the fear, and adrenaline rush, from entering a strange bar. Performing for audiences outside the City taught the comics the need sometimes to adjust both the delivery and the material. Comics, often working for the first time together, experienced the bonding effect of sharing a road adventure. It was the classic showbiz apprenticeship system, getting paid a little money to learn how to be funny anywhere for anyone.

Usually, these nearby one-nighters, after stretching the onstage time and returning with a little cash in pocket, put an extra spring in my step.

Those early local shows had such an impact on me that they came to define a distinct class of showbiz employment — a short drive to a one-nighter for low pay. When I moved to Los Angeles in 1982, someone offered me a job with this description: "It's a quick shot out to Claremont for a buck." I thought to myself, "a Stanley gig."

# 17. "DON'T NEED NO RANK BEGINNERS WHEN IT'S TIME TO SHAKE MY SHAKE"

I once did a particularly rough Stanley gig with Uncle Dirty. Usually they were a welcome break, a short ride for a little money and a couple of laughs. This one was just a game of whack-a-heckler masquerading as show business.

Two seconds into this particular joint and it was obvious we weren't in Manhattan anymore. It was a sea of T-shirts, jean jackets and fake IDs. These were the guys too drunk and stupid to be part of the bridge-and-tunnel crowd.

The 40-ish Uncle Dirty probably sensed this was not his night, so he turned to me and said, "Listen, kid. If I go short, can you cover for me?"

It probably made me feel like I was in a World War II movie, "Cover me, Sarge, while I go for the joke." I told him no problem.

The MC struggled to get a laugh or even the crowd's attention. He then gave Dirty one of those introductions out of nowhere. There was none of the normal flow, where the comic finished the last joke and said something like, "Thank you, folks. That's my part of the show." The applause meant the end of one act and the approach of another.

Instead, after bombing a couple of jokes in a row, the MC abruptly stopped in the middle of a set-up and said, "All right. Let's bring up the next act." The bulk of the crowd was experiencing their first drink and live show for the first time, so they probably didn't even understand why one guy was leaving the stage and another was walking onto it.

Dirty tried a couple of his regular bits and got nothing. Part of the problem was Dirty's material was as dated as he was. His formative years as a stand-up were in the Village coffeehouses of the '60s.

Robert Altman, aka "Uncle Dirty," 1979

most comics, Dirty's style and comedic voice were set early in his career, and he couldn't really change with the times. He was still playing the lascivious hippie character. That was funny in the '60s but was at this time a bit too real coming from a nearly 50-year-old man. Nightclub audiences stay the same age, 20s and early 30s, while the comic ages. Eventually the older comic has to be careful not to look like an old vampire bent over a young girl.

Dirty's body language was saying he wasn't long for that stage when some kid let loose with a heckle that cut through all the bar noise, "Get off the stage, old man."

All of a sudden, Dirty was like an aged fighter who tasted his own blood one too many times. Maybe he had some sort of PTSD flashback to those early '60s Jersey toilets he trained in until he got to the Village coffeehouses. Suddenly, Dirty came out of the corner swinging. I didn't know this side of Dirty existed. He beat this kid down with a steady stream of nasty. Nothing clever, just the kind of body blows this crowd understood ... lines like, "The best part of you dribbled down your mom's leg." They loved it.

In about five lines, Dirty took about 20 years off his age and was stinging like a bee and floating like a butterfly. He finished strong and decided not to risk handing the reins to the hapless opener. Dirty went into my introduction, "I'm going to bring out our next comic. You're going to love this guy ..."

When I finished the show, Dirty was at the bar surrounded by admirers. He had more free drinks in front of him than a member of the E Street Band. Plus, he even scored the drugs for our ride back to the city. On the way back, I saw Uncle Dirty's driver's license. He was the same age as my dad. For the first time, I saw my future, and it made me laugh. Years later, I realized why I was so eager for a friendship with a man twenty years older than me — to get a connection and approval not then possible with my actual dad.

## 18. "IT'S PRETTY HUMAN, MAKE ALL THE PEOPLE HOLLER"

Clean or dirty comedy was not even a concept for me in 1977. I talked onstage the way I talked offstage. A generous sprinkling of the words "shit" and "fuck" was just the right spice for my early paying gigs, opening for rock bands. I don't remember any of the comics I started with in D.C. at El Brookman's or Garvin's ever discussing our language or whether we were working too blue. We were getting laughs by any means necessary. The phrase "blue material" originated in Shakespearean times when the Queen's Exchequer excised objectionable material from any scripts with a blue pencil. Vaudeville dropped it into the comic lexicon by using blue envelopes to notify performers to drop offensive jokes.

Dirty material predates clean. In ancient Greek theater, two nude male statues flanked the stage. When a woman walked across the stage, a man pushed the lever behind one statue and the prop penis rose. One of the first recorded gags was a dick joke.

I always enjoyed a good dirty joke. The first joke I remember ever hearing was the classic built on the primal male fear of sexual inadequacy, or engulfment ... doesn't matter, it was hilarious to a 12-year-old discovering a use for his dick beyond urination: A guy is having sex with a woman but her pussy is so big he falls in. Crawling around in the dark he bumps into another guy, and asks if the guy has a flashlight. The other guy says, "No, but if you help me find my car keys, I'll drive us out of here." Sigmund Freud, a great fan and student of jokes, said that risqué jokes that permit the concealed expression of forbidden impulses can

**Hiccup's, 207 Rideau St. . . . Rich Shydner** is a comedian who should have stayed in his native New Jersey. But it seems he's been making it big on the North American comedy circuit these days selling comedic contraceptives. You know the kind of guy . . . talks dirty to be funny, but he's not really.

Working dirty, collecting laughs and moving on, 1980

impulses can give great pleasure and laughter. Freud believed in the healing power of the dick joke.

With the major exception of Richard Pryor and George Carlin, none of my comedic heroes cursed much. Robert Klein was clean. Lenny Bruce, by the way, was really persecuted for being a Jewish comic mocking the Catholic and Protestant churches. Plenty of Lenny's contemporaries, like B.S. Pully, cursed in the nightclubs far more than Lenny. The authorities needed the pretext of the obscenity laws to end-run the First Amendment.

The late '70s and early '80s was a different era for language and material offstage because society was different. Kids got their mouths washed out with soap for swearing, and "hell" or "damn" was about the limit for even late-night TV. Today people strut through the airport with a big "Fuck Off" on their T-shirt and Comedy Central's *Daily Show* barely bleeps the "u" in fuck.

When my first ex-wife, Carol Leifer, wanted to add some spice to her act, instead of realistic observations of sex, she closed with this old joke: "A madam answers her door and there on the step is a man with no arms and no legs. She says, 'What are you going to do here?' He says, 'I rang the bell, didn't I?'" An all-innuendo joke, maybe built on the female desire to find a great man who won't run away. *Paging Dr. Freud! Paging Dr. Freud!*

As always, comedy reflected the times perfectly. Sometime in the early '90s I noticed young female comics like Felicia Michaels expressing a bolder, more honest take on sex.

Comedy has the power to take our forbidden impulses, and hold them to the light — in our shared laughter we find relief from our shame. Women were, and still are, widely objectified, judged, and slut-shamed. By owning and exaggerating their sexual behavior in their onstage material, female comics began subverting those cultural norms and making people think about them. In a similar fashion, when Sam Kinison did his bit about starving Africans, nobody thought he was heartless as much as they recognized their own helplessness.

Society shifted and comedy moved with it. Comedy was most effective when "punching up," so maybe the audience response reflected the acknowledgment that a power differential still existed between men and women in the real world.

Whatever the reason, a few female comics in the late '80s started by mocking the old double standard (that men could have sex with multiple partners with no damage to their reputation while women could not). Eventually they inverted the old double standard, at least for the stand-up stage. A male comic could no longer do material about sleeping with a lot of women without facing some audience resistance from outraged women and jealous guys, but a female comic could talk all night long about random sex, even bragging about her "slutitude," and women in the audience seemed to find it empowering. The audience, like society, came to see a man who bedded a lot of women as a predator and a creep and conversely applauded a woman who wasn't ashamed to (figuratively) stick it to The Man. And of course the men in the crowd could listen to a woman talk about blowjobs all night long. Eventually there were so many female comics doing these bits, it became almost a compulsory move — female versions of the dick joke.

In 1979, I did a Jerry Stanley one-nighter with Jerry Seinfeld. Back then I used "fuck" to prop up a lot of lame punchlines. In this sort of Jersey bar gig I doubled up on the fucks, using fuck to prop up the fucks propping up the limp jokes. No doubt I emptied my bag of drug and dick jokes on that crowd and saved the labels "motherfucker" and "cocksucker" as nuclear options for hecklers. Basically I said anything and everything I felt I needed to say to get the response I desired out of that crowd. Jerry did the exact same act he did on a first show Saturday night at Catch a Rising Star in the City: clean, well-crafted material. He didn't get the reaction from the crowd I did, and he didn't care. He sacrificed a little short-term for big long-term. For him it was a $55 payday to rehearse for TV. Two years before his first *Tonight Show*, and Jerry already had his eye on the prize.

On the ride back to the city, Jerry bothered to give me some unsolicited advice. "You're a funny guy. Why do you work so dirty? It will work against you on TV."

*The Tonight Show* was our Holy Grail, and even a thick-headed squire such as myself knew that "none dirty shall pass" a *Tonight Show* booker. A fundamental structural change to my act was needed — slapping some cheap paneling over the shoddy framework wasn't going to do it. I noticed that comics who worked dirty in the clubs and dropped the curse words for TV mostly failed. There was a hiccup in their delivery where the curse word was; the joke timing was off. Switching to a more innocent word than "fucking" before the punchline only exposed bad writing. It took awhile, but the effort improved my joke writing and, eventually, my prospects of getting on TV. I actually came to feel more comfortable onstage not cursing. The audiences didn't complain. It was a different time.

My one pet peeve was when a comic peppered his act with "fuck" but then used "wiener" or "pee-pee" instead of "dick" or "cock." It seems disingenuous to me: Once you broke the "fuck" barrier, it was a little late to start acting coy.

I always had sexual material, but at the end of my club act. I approached an audience like a first date. Opening with sexual material was like knocking on her door for the first time with my dick hanging out. I opened the show/date with a little general chitchat (weather and traffic), then on to personal history (parents and school), and then my thoughts on life (dark and sarcastic). Along the way, certain jokes acted like Geiger counters. How the audience responded to a little sexual innuendo let me know whether to go further or not. If all went well, we got to the zippers. Even when I started talking sex, it was mostly suggestive. When I finally pulled out a word like "dick," the shock value rocketed the laughs. I had no agenda to get to the dick jokes. The laughter was all that mattered. Nobody ever walked out of a show complaining it was too clean.

There were clean acts that killed me, and dirty ones that did. Funny was funny.

## 19. "FIRST YOU MUST LEARN
## HOW TO SMILE AS YOU KILL"

"There are two words, show business ... you better pay attention to the bigger one." — *Vaudeville saying.*

In 1980, a New York City talent agency booked a comedy show at Fairleigh Dickinson University in nearby Teaneck, N.J. The four comedians hired, I believe, were Jerry Allen, Rick Overton, Larry Miller, and myself.

There was no road lined with high-paying comedy clubs. We were young, struggling showcase comics and grateful for the $75.

The show went fine. Afterward, the student in charge of entertainment gave us an unsealed envelope containing a check for the talent agency. Someone opened the envelope and looked at the check. It was for $2,500. Suddenly, we didn't feel so good about our $75 payday.

When confronted with our outrage the agent just smiled and said, "You shouldn't have opened the envelope."

We left with four $75 checks.

If you want applause and adulation, then join The Show. If you want to make real money, go into The Business.

The business doesn't always make you happy, 1981

# 20. "THE WIND CATCHES YOUR FEET, SENDS YOU FLYING"

In early winter 1980, my girlfriend, Carol Leifer, was booked at the new Comic Strip in Fort Lauderdale, Fla., with Kelley Rogers, Joe Bolster and Mark Schiff. Carol asked the owners, Richie Tienken and Bob Wachs, to send me, too. The club was only in its second or third week of operation so they couldn't justify sending an Improv comic to Florida ahead of a whole bunch of Comic Strip regulars. They wanted to please Carol, so they found a solution. They offered me the MC job for $300, half of the others comics' pay. Even though I wasn't doing anything that week but banging around the City, my pride said no, but Jackie Mason's words from a night at Dangerfield's still echoed in my head, "You got no price." Besides, it was a week in the sun with Carol.

Airfare was not included so all five of us happily squeezed into Bolster's tiny Toyota for a 20-hour drive from Manhattan to Florida. By the time we poured out of the clown car, our pockets were stuffed with scraps of paper of new jokes on driving a long distance, including at least one joke on that famous South Carolina pit stop, "South of the Border."

The Comic Strip was the second pro comedy club on the East Coast, after Garvin's in Washington, D.C. It was a big deal to the comics, but not to the locals yet. This was a full year before the stand-up movement hit critical mass. Some shows were decently attended, but there were nights when we performed for four people. A full house was easy. The audience felt like they were in the right place, the energy was positively electric before the first comic took the stage. It was easy to get a roll going — people laughed when hearing laughter. The cliché, "laughter is

Kelley Rogers, Mark Schiff, Joe Bolster, RS and Carol Leifer, Ft Lauderdale Beach, March 1980

contagious," was never truer than in a packed comedy club. Conversely, four people floating in a 300-seat room had to seriously question their choice of entertainment. Each comic directed his or her performance at them, an interrogation disguised as crowd work. After two comics, the only thing left to ask was, "So, where was your great-grandfather from?"

The comedy club was the workplace, but our base of operations was the "comedy condo." Garvin's housed the comics in a hotel, so this was our first experience in communal living. The condo was more like a summer camp barracks than a living space. There was no privacy, very little sleep and relentless laughter. It was a Marx Brothers routine with doors constantly opening and closing, a nonstop parade of strange people entering and leaving.

One night, Kelley Rogers motioned me to the telephone. He covered the receiver and said, "Whatever he asks, say you can do it." A second later I was talking to Andy Windsor in Ottawa, Canada, the owner of a new comedy club. Andy asked me if I could do *two* different 45-minute shows. At this point the only chance I had of making the *first* 45 was with a hot crowd, fast clock, and strong tailwind. I did as Kelley instructed and lied. The call ended with a booking for the next week at $800 Canadian.

The pressure was immediate. I started writing furiously. Nearly every bit of stage time was devoted to trying new jokes. My obsession with fresh material really kicked into gear.

Flo and Eddie's in Ottawa was my first headlining gig. My strategy was simple. I did all my best material in the first show hoping that same crowd remembered how funny I was when I took the stage the second time.

The accommodations were the Beacon Arms Hotel. There was insufficient heating for a Canadian winter, worsened by a broken window, covered by a piece of cardboard. I slept in my coat, hat, and gloves. One night the wind blew out the cardboard and I awoke with a layer of snow on my blanket. I didn't care. Someone was paying me to perform stand-up. They could have housed me in the local jail.

I spent all day long shivering, and either watching French versions of American movies or writing new material about watching American movies dubbed in French while shivering. At night, I tried the new material and managed to put another plank in the road.

An Ottawa newspaper printed my first road review. The reporter suggested I "return south of the border from where he crawled," calling me a "punk version of Eddie Haskell." A comparison to one of the favorite TV characters of my youth didn't bother me. More important, I knew the audience had laughed. I stuffed the clipping into my bag and attacked the stage even harder the next night.

One night after the show, Andy called me into his office. On the telephone was Ernie Butler, the owner of Stitches, a new comedy club in Montreal. Ernie asked if I could play his room the next week.

Montreal was a beautiful city with lovely sights to see, but my routine was the same as it was in the Canadian capital. I wrote all day and stayed onstage as long as I could. At the end of the week, Ernie called me into his office and handed over the phone. Mark Breslin wanted me in his Toronto room, Yuk-Yuk's, the following week.

Just four weeks after leaving New York as an MC, I returned a legitimate headliner, and I had a price.

There was a hunger for stand-up all across the country. By the end of 1980, it was happening everywhere, from Fort Lauderdale to Canada to Cleveland, Atlantic City to La Jolla. In no time the money stacked, the liquor flowed and the comics multiplied.

# 21. "ONCE I GET STARTED I GO TO TOWN"

I generally believed that every comic got to where they were supposed to be. If you went onstage enough times, you got your shot. You might not be happy with the outcome, but the opportunity came. Nonetheless, there were a few comics who I believed didn't get their due, for whatever reason. There were underrated players in stand-up. At the top of my list is Canadian comedian Mike MacDonald.

Mike is far from an unknown. He toured for more than 30 years, performed at nearly every Just for Laughs Comedy Festival gala and did three stand-up specials — *My House My Rules* was a classic. Mike is a legend in Canada, the respected dean of the stand-up community.

It may be difficult to categorize a comic with that kind of outstanding career as underrated, but such is my admiration for Mike's talents. If my objectivity is blinded by friendship, then so be it, but here's my case.

In late 1980, my first headlining road tour was three weeks in Canada.

At the Ottawa and Montreal clubs, people said I reminded them of a Toronto comic, Mike MacDonald. To paraphrase Albert Brooks from his movie *Looking for Comedy in the Muslim World*, "Never talk to a comic about another comic." Comics like to think that what they do is novel and unique. It's part of the mindset necessary to take the microphone and force a roomful of strangers to listen. Learning that I had a Canadian doppelganger was initially not a thrill.

The third week was in Toronto, at Mark Breslin's Yuk-Yuk's. It was a 200-seat club, painted all black, with a low ceiling and phenomenal acoustics; a little kill room constantly packed with young enthusiastic

Mike MacDonald, between smiles in New York City, 1981

audiences. There was also a diverse and creative group of local comics, including future stars such as Norm Macdonald and Jim Carrey.

After the first night's show I entered the bar. Like in a scene from an old Western, the other comics parted and I was suddenly face to face with a tall man in a black suit topped by a head full of thick, short-cropped hair. We locked eyes and smirked. There was no need for an introduction or a handshake. I knew this was that MacDonald guy and we were to be friends.

The next night I saw Mike perform. For the first time as a stand-up, I honestly felt intimidated. It wasn't just that he was killing the crowd. It was the method to his madness.

He mimed his bits with incredible power, precision and fluidity; transitioning seamlessly from a smooth dancer to a herky-jerky marion-ette. It reminded me of James Cagney's dancing in the movie *Yankee Doodle Dandy*.

A sense of danger bubbled throughout Mike's act; struggling to con-trol his rage only added to the hilarity. There was no feigned jocularity or cloying platitudes to win the crowd's favor. His comedy was serious business. Either the laughs came or this man was heading for a tower with a rifle.

He was lost in his performance. Every part of his being was commit-ted to the task. Whether it was contorting his body ridiculously or confid-ing his darkest thoughts, Mike was willing to risk looking like a fool to get the laugh.

Some comics left the stage without a trace, never giving a hint as to who they really were. Their comedy was clever and funny, but too impersonal for me. I watched Mike MacDonald for five minutes and understood him completely. He connected to his audience in a profound, visceral way.

His closer was probably the strongest in the '80s — a five-minute tour-de-force of a young man getting caught playing air guitar in his bedroom.

We hung out every night and day for the next week; performing comedy, watching comedy, and talking comedy.

One day we shared our disgust with fart jokes, decrying them as the cheapest of the cheap. We spent a long time discussing possible reasons for their success and eternal popularity. E.B. White once said, "Analyzing humor is like dissecting a frog. Few people are interested and the frog dies of it." We didn't mind killing this frog. Various theories were floated. Farts were uncontrollable and embarrassing. They were tied to one of the most private acts, defecating. Since the last act of the dying body was to relax the sphincter muscle, fart jokes played on an unconscious fear of death. Of all the many ways to kill time between shows in those days — shopping at a mall, sightseeing or sleeping off the night before — discussing comedy with Mike, even breaking down fart jokes, was the most pleasurable.

Before the next show, another comic opined that Mike and I ridiculed fart jokes only because we didn't have any good ones. As a goof, Mike and I dedicated our next sets to fart jokes, exhausting the subject. I followed Mike on stage. As proof of the power of the fart joke, even when my joke covered the same exact territory as one Mike told, mine still worked. We constantly pushed each other to be better stand-ups, even if it meant doing fart jokes.

One afternoon, we ducked into a theater to see Robert Duvall in *The Great Santini*. This movie rubbed open any and all father wounds. Afterward, Mike and I went to an arcade and played pinball for an hour or so, without saying a word. Didn't need to. We had seen the dad characters in each other's act.

We also shared a taste for drugs. One night, a group of comics did acid, and everyone laughed hard for hours. The next day, we didn't remember any of the details, not one funny line. Naturally we regretted losing all that comedy gold. Mike and I decided everyone must trip again to mine some comedy. This time we decided to tape the hilarity. All night long we popped in tape after tape. We awoke excited to play the tapes and divide a treasure trove of new material. On the first tape someone said, "I can't open the window." The rest of the tape was filled with nothing but uncontrollable laughter. Each tape was like that; an inconsequential statement followed by endless howling. Our expedition had failed to discover the Northern Passage to The New Material.

We didn't agree on everything — Mike favored AC/DC blasting from his ever-present boom box, while I liked Elvis Costello pumping through my Walkman — but our comedic sensibilities were totally in sync.

Right before going on stage one night, just after his name was announced and the applause began, Mike turned to me and said, "Calling all madmen. Calling all madmen." It became our greeting, a signal it was time to get down to it.

When I returned in the summer, Mark Breslin sent us to a new gig, a resort located a few hours north of Toronto. His idea was to send Mike and I to a peaceful retreat where we might write a screenplay. The plan was well-intentioned, but problematic. The first problem was that neither Mike or I ever wrote a screenplay, so a weekend was a tight time frame. Plus, two stage monkeys distracted by the spinning plates of show times were incapable of writing anything longer than a set list.

Then there was the gig itself, in a cavernous banquet hall. Our show was to be book-ended by a band, a little music, a little comedy, a little dancing. Before introducing me, the band established a comedic mood by playing a couple of bawdy songs containing explicit lyrics of wanting to have lots of sex, with both humans and animals. Well, we were in the woods.

When I took the stage, I was instantly barraged with audience requests for "beaver jokes." It wasn't that I was against talking about sex; my kit was filled with enough dick jokes to knock down a crowd of drunken nudists. I wasn't closing and needed to keep the hounds leashed. I knew once the audience's minds were locked on to rutting it was tough to interest them in other jokes. My responsibility was to the next comic, my friend. This was all going through my mind while punching forward, clean bit after clean bit against a crowd with a different agenda. The more I resisted the dirt, the more they begged for it, "Talk about big tits!"

I managed to bull my way past the constant heckling and finished my 45 minutes without flashing a dick joke, but they were still heckling me during the exit applause. "What about blowjobs?" "Yeah, everybody likes blowjobs!"

I launched into Mike's introduction.

"Let me bring up my friend, a very funny comic from Toronto —"

"Toronto sucks!"

Maybe I was wrong to tip the opposition that Mike was my pal. In any case, being heckled before taking the stage wasn't a good sign, but one that my friend read correctly.

I looked to Mike at the bar, shaking his head and waving for me. I had a feeling where this was headed. It made no sense to battle a mob for short money in Nowheresville when fun times and great audiences awaited us in Toronto.

"All right, folks. Hold on a minute ..."

The whole audience watched as I walked from the stage to Mike. By the time I got to him, the bar manager and a couple of other guys joined us. To me, Mike said, "Get the car." He then nodded to the others and added, "I'll hold them off."

I made straight for our cabin to grab our unpacked bags while the group of guys surrounded Mike.

A minute later I sat behind the wheel of our rental car, the engine idling, with my eyes fixed on the banquet hall's front door. I was no longer a comic but a getaway driver. Soon the door burst open and Mike ran out. The angry manager, and a small group of like-minded citizens, were on his heels.

"You gotta finish the show! We got a contract!"

Mike pointed at me as he hopped in the car. "Talk to my lawyer."

I smiled, waved, and floored the accelerator. Mike pulled his boom box onto his lap and began blasting AC/DC's *Dog Eat Dog*. We were laughing, again.

Mike and I reveled in our insanity. Later we supported each other in our attempts to become fully developed humans.

In 1990, Mike and his beloved Bonnie married in Las Vegas. An Elvis Presley impersonator started the ceremony with great sincerity. "We're gathered here to celebrate the wedding of ..." With perfect, unintentional, comedic timing "Elvis" paused to look down at a sheet of paper for their names. I laughed, immediately busting up Mike. His manager and close friend, Howard Lapides, fell over, and then Bonnie. The newly married couple was played off to Elvis' *Suspicious Minds* and more laughs. Mike and Bonnie are still happily married.

Mike was very generous with my kids. He made them laugh and brought them presents.

More than 30 years of friendship and we never had a cross word, not even a squabble over material. I can't say that about any other comic. I love the guy.

Mike's liver failed, and he struggled with the transplant. Finally he got back onstage, taking his comedy to another level. The brass ring is still there for the madman's madman.

# 22. "TO LISTEN TO YOUR FEARS"

In late 1981, I drove from New York City to work at the Toronto Yuk-Yuk's. At the Canadian border I told the immigration officer that there was a temporary work permit in my name. A search of the files failed to produce one.

I called the office of the club owner, Mark Breslin, and waited. Time was tight. I was to perform that night and still had a few hours to drive. I sat in a plastic chair under fluorescent lights, watching a big clock ticking.

After an uncomfortably long time facing each other in silence, the immigration officer brought out a large book of immigration regulations. He leafed through the pages for a while, and then smiled, "There is an exception for the work permit requirement for artists."

I stood. "That's it. Thank you."

Without looking up from the book he froze me. "I don't see stand-up comedy listed here under artists."

He had poked an old wound I didn't know I had. A few weeks earlier, on our honeymoon in Paris, Carol and I visited the Louvre. There I saw a painting by Franz Marc, *The Blue Horse*. As I stared at this blue horse, a long buried memory clawed from the grave. My first-grade teacher once had us draw trees with our crayons. Walking around the class, she stopped at my desk and lifted my paper for the whole class to see. "Leaves are not purple. Ritchie did it wrong." She marked my paper, "US," for unsatisfactory. I never drew again. At about age 9, I was singing in church. A woman walked from the choir, took the hymnal from my hands and said, "You don't have to sing, Ritchie. Jesus knows you love him." I never sang again, sober. I never considered making people laugh to be on the same level as a painting or a song but suddenly felt a tremendous need to put it there ... and not just to get to Toronto.

I invoked every big name I could think of, from Mark Twain to George Carlin to Steve Martin, hoping to hit one of his favorites. He stared at me. I compared humor to paintings, in that it gave people a different view of life. Nothing.

For the first time I tried to describe to someone what I did. Telling him how I made people laugh was like describing a steak to a vegan. I may not have been the funniest comedian, but I could always read an audience. This immigration officer was not an easy laugh, but the big clock on the wall was ticking and I was desperate to get to Toronto. I stood and started to do my act. He stood and sternly pointed to my chair. "No. Hey, sit down. Sit down."

I'm sure my agitation and frustration put a frightening edge to my usual hyperkinetic performance. If the guy had a gun, he would have pulled it on me.

Once I was seated, he offered me another chance. "Just tell me some of your jokes."

Two jokes in, he waved for me to stop. "What you're doing is not art."

All he needed to complete the moment was to stamp my papers with a big, official "Entrance Denied. No Talent."

I slumped in my seat, gut shot. My first-grade teacher was right.

Finally, Mark Breslin's lawyer called and I was allowed to proceed.

Before I left, the immigration officer had me fill out an application for a Canadian social security card to pay taxes on my non-artistic act.

I went after the laughs with a vengeance that night at Yuk-Yuk's.

## 23. "THE CLOWN … DOES THE TRICK OF DISASTER"

In the winter of 1980 I traveled from New York City to play Scott Hanson's club, Mickey Finn's, in Minneapolis, Minnesota. I can't remember who booked the gig, and it probably only netted a hundred bucks, but it was one of my first out-of-town headlining jobs and I was so excited.

When I bopped into the club, under the influence of my Sony Walkman, the back wall was lined with local comics, such as Louie Anderson, Jeff Cesario, Alex Cole and Wild Bill Bower, all there to check out the out-of-town competition.

It was a tiny club, like Zanies in Chicago or Holy City Zoo in San Francisco, with maybe an 80-person capacity. Stand-up comedy was fresh and youthful, with a counterculture, underground feel to it. The energy in these rooms was palpable, electric.

Feeding off that energy and wanting to make a big impression on the local jokeslingers, I ran down the aisle and jumped onto the stage, which was, I soon discovered, simply a sheet of plywood resting on a dozen plastic milk crates.

I surfed on the plywood into a concrete wall, crashing shoulder first and ricocheting onto a table of drinks. The crowd seemed to enjoy this quite a bit. A few comics reassembled the stage and I attempted to follow my killer entrance. X-rays later showed a partially separated shoulder. It didn't affect my shows in Minneapolis; the local medical team of Drs. Cole and Bower kept me distracted and medicated for the entire weekend. Besides, I was young, hungry and invincible. Neither rain, not hail, nor sheet of plywood kept me from delivering those laughs.

# 24. "WHERE THE SHADOWS RUN FROM THEMSELVES"

It quickly became clear that where I performed comedy was as important as who I was trying to make laugh. A stand-up show really needs to be in a room with proper lighting, an adequate sound system, and a sturdy stage.

The first time I realized that the room mattered was when I performed without one. One Friday night at El Bookman's in 1977, an audience member asked me to perform the next day at the annual Manassas (Va.) Fire Department Picnic, for free. The last-minute nature of the offer didn't even register with me, nor did the words "Manassas," "picnic" or "free." The only word that mattered was "perform." The nature of the event, distance to it, or possible compensation were all superfluous. My strategy was a fusion of vaudeville and Nietzsche: As long as it didn't kill me, every effort to make a group of strangers laugh, no matter how painful, made me funnier.

The next day, I traveled the 40 miles to Manassas with the same enthusiasm to put on a good show as the Union Army in 1861. It was a full-blown picnic: a barbecue grill every 20 feet, softball players with a glove in one hand and a beer in the other, and kids crawling all over the two fire trucks flanking the stage, which was a flatbed trailer.

I stood around the front of the flatbed stage like the clueless idiot I was until the guy from El Brookman's approached me. He took me backstage (the other side of the flatbed) for a meeting with the other acts. I was to go first, then a band and then the fireworks show. The bandleader told me to use the center mic but not to touch it, because he was worried that I might drop it and he didn't have another. The fireworks man was setting his charges, a little too close to the stage in my estimation. I relaxed a bit when I saw he wasn't missing any fingers. Our meeting was periodically interrupted by blasts from the sirens of the fire trucks and screams of delight of the kids, and hoots from their drunken relatives.

There was plenty of daylight when I went onstage. The El Brookman's customer that hired me introduced me with, "Here's this funny guy I saw last night." He then waved me onto the stage while jumping off it. He didn't say my name and, in hindsight, it was better that way. I moved behind the mic and started talking, careful to not even touch the mic stand. Nothing changed in the scene. The only people in front of the stage facing me were a few old folks in lawn chairs, just early for the fireworks show. Behind them a decent-sized crowd stood around the barbecue grills, watching the hamburgers sizzle. A Frisbee flew over my head. Screaming kids ran past the front of the stage. The fire siren blasted every few minutes. A car stereo was playing Lynyrd Skynyrd from the nearby parking lot.

None of this stopped me. I just kept banging away. The sound system was loud and eventually a few faces turned in my direction. They squinted and shielded their eyes with their hands. The setting sun was at my back, which is a good lighting arrangement if you're charging a line of Stonewall Jackson's troops, but not really conducive to laughter. The main problem was not the constant visual and aural distractions of the picnic; it was that I couldn't get enough of them laughing loud enough and long enough to form an audience. I would hear one laugh and turn to deliver my next joke in that direction, hoping to build on it, only to notice the guy was now watching a bird fly. I might see someone open their mouth to laugh, but I was too far away to hear it. I spent 15 minutes looking like that old plate-spinner from *The Ed Sullivan Show*, only it was a single laugh I was trying to keep going long enough to join another one.

Finally I jumped off the stage and walked through the scene. Again, nothing changed. I heard one pair of hands clapping but was not of the mind to investigate whether the applause was sincere or sarcastic. Someone yelled, "See ya." That, I was pretty sure, was short for, "We're gonna let you slide this time, but keep walking and definitely don't come back." The booker fell in with me for a couple of steps, only long enough to hand me a six-pack. I gratefully accepted the beers, knowing that it was more than his great-great grandfather offered any of the Yankees retreating from the First Battle of Bull Run.

The Manassas Fire Department Picnic was a roast pig stuffed with lessons. No. 1, daylight is good for softball but not stand-up comedy. No. 2, an outdoor venue dissolves laughter on contact. If you do an outdoor venue in the daytime, there better be cash or charity attached, because it won't be for the laughter.

People laugh longer and louder when they hear other people laugh, outdoors or indoors. In 1982, I played the worst comedy club of my career, in Winston-Salem, N.C. It was a restaurant. Nothing unusual about that; in the early days of The Boom all sorts of rooms were being converted into comedy clubs. The only thing the owner did was write "Comedy Tonight" on the sidewalk chalkboard under the catch of the day.

There was no stage, just a place on the floor at the end of the bar. For some reason the rule was, the higher the stage the more respect given the performer. I looked like a guy waiting for an empty stool.

No stage also meant no stage lighting. I stood under the same ceiling lights as the audience, which doomed me to working in the shadows a lot. The best lighting has the audience in the dark and the comic brightly lit. A lot of a comic's performance is in facial expressions and body language. Good lighting makes the comic available to the audience while setting him apart from them. On the other side, people in the audience are justifiably nervous about what their laughter might reveal. Inhibitions slip away under the cover of darkness.

I was handed a cheap microphone with a 6-foot cord plugged into the wall. It was a crackly intercom system normally used by the hostess to call parties from the bar.

The worst part was the seating arrangement. Nearly all of the patrons sat in booths, with glass partitions rising from the top of the booths to the ceiling. My job was to create an audience out of 20 groups of people trapped in separate cones of silence. I could see them laugh, but could not hear them. They, too, could see other people laugh, but not hear them. They became frustrated, and finally defeated. I don't remember the name of the club, but I heard it was gone fast.

On the opposite end of that spectrum was the airplane hangar I performed in at Edwards Air Force Base in California. It was indoors, technically. The laughter floated a few hundred feet to the ceiling and never returned.

Baltimore had a most difficult time finding a decent room for stand-up. In late 1980, the first comedy club in Baltimore opened in the old Playboy Club. The walls were lined with fake animal skin and covered sound baffles, and the floor had deep, red-colored shag carpeting. The audience sat in big, cushy easy chairs. It might have once been a great room for jazz but it ate laughter. All I could think of was doing stand-up in Elvis' Jungle Room.

The next room to open in Baltimore was the Charm City Comedy Club in the harbor area. The problem with this room was that the comics performed in front of a huge wall of glass overlooking the city. If there was a curtain, no one ever closed it. As if the normal harbor lights weren't enough of a distraction, a passing tugboat could easily destroy 10 minutes of material. There is a story, maybe apocryphal. I could never track down the name of the comic it supposedly happened to. Allegedly, the police pulled a body from the harbor while a comic performed. It would be easier to get laughs with a blender going off during the check spot.

There is one more factor, ignored until it's summer: air-conditioning. It was better to face a chilled audience than a sweating one. Chattering teeth are closer to laughter, a perspiring face closer to tears. In my early years I approached stand-up as if it were an athletic event and didn't mind perspiring a bit onstage. With my intake of alcohol and chemicals, there might not have been anything done to prevent it.

The Richmond Comedy Club opened around 1981 in the basement of Matt's Pub. Like most comedy clubs in the early '80s, the place was packed every night. There was no air-conditioning but they aimed two huge hurricane fans toward the stage. I couldn't stand to see the audience wilt, so I turned the fans on the audience. I left the stage soaked in sweat, not just my shirt, but my pants, underwear and socks, but I heard those laughs. That's all that mattered.

"If I came to this town and they were going to give me five thousand a week to work the Fairmont and they're gonna give me five thousand and fifty dollars to work the Christian Science Reading Room, I will work at the Christian Science Reading Room like that ... rooms don't have any identity." Lenny Bruce from The Palladium.

Normally I agree with the great sage, Lenny, but not fully here. Money can surely plaster over any gig's deficiencies, and if your fans show, the venue doesn't matter too much, but some rooms have identity. Like the bad rooms I described, there are good ones. Some rooms just make it easier to get laughs.

The best physical room I ever played was the Ice House in Pasadena.

Not long after I moved to LA in January of 1982 my late friend Neal Jacobs took me to the Ice House to audition. I was excited, because I knew it had a comedy history dating back to the early 1960s. More than a few comedy albums were recorded there, such as Pat Paulson's and the Smothers Brothers'.

I'm not going to get into the nature of any audiences attracted to any club on any given night, just the physical plant. Comics tend to view any crowd through the prism of their performance. If the comic did well, then that's a hip crowd. If the comic bombed, the crowd was a bunch of squares.

It is a small, dark room holding about 200 people, with a low ceiling, hard walls and a hard floor. A sound booth in the back of the room houses a crystal-clear system, with speakers everywhere. The stage and seating arrangement might be the difference-maker. The comics perform at the bottom of this little indoor amphitheater, with the rows of audience tiered, gradually rising to the back of the room. The seating is a theater/club hybrid, every person faces the stage with a tray to hold foods and drink. It is very unusual and extremely effective at achieving intimacy. The audience is right on top of the comic and all facing the show directly, nobody seated around tables. The stage is well-lit, and the audience is in the shadows. The laughter bounces like a superball and always drenches the comic in the bottom of the room.

It is an absolute kill room, a perfect testing ground. A set in that room can restore a comic's faith in the power of laughter, or provide the proof that it's time to drop the mic for good.

# 25. "SOMETHING TO MAKE US ALL HAPPY"

Some monologists consider prop acts as a lower form of the stand-up species. It didn't matter to me whether the comic got the laugh with a brilliant line, funny face or prop gag. I was always more interested in the reasons why the audience was laughing, who was taking the pie in the face. Respected stand-ups such as Rich Hall, Gilbert Gottfried and Steve Martin created prop gags as funny and clever as any verbal joke.

During the first two years of my career, in '77 and '78, I even utilized a few visual aids. Most of my early paying jobs were opening for musical acts. My inspiration was rockers like Alice Cooper, who brought a guillotine, electric chair, and boa constrictor to the stage. Those props sure got the attention of one stoned 19-year-old.

Mine were very portable, everything fit in one pocket — a light-up yo-yo, a fake joint, and a sheet of flash paper. I used them early in an attempt to grab the crowd.

First out was a big, fat Cheech and Chong sized "joint" actually filled with tobacco. Before the show, I informed the promoter of the bit. Not that it mattered. This was a '70s rock concert. All the security personnel got a contact high 10 seconds after entering the building. Shortly after hitting the stage, I lit the "joint," took a hit, and overacted "holding it," Of course, the crowd roared in approval.

At the height of their cheering, I touched the burning end of the joint to the wad of crumpled flash paper hidden in the palm of my hand. I followed the ball of fire with one or two of the Wicked Witch's lines from *The Wizard of Oz*, "I'll get you my pretty, and your little dog too!" and, "I'm melting," with a little mime of the Witch's final moments. Oh, I was a well-rounded performer. Then I passed the "joint" to a ringsider

The best props are the most familiar, 1979

and said, "Go ahead. We can all get high on that. If Jesus did it with the loaves and the fishes, we can try it tonight." I followed that heady stuff with a slew of drug jokes.

The last prop was a yo-yo with battery-powered lights. All I could manage was a few easy tricks with some even simpler jokes attached. Shooting the yo-yo directly at the audience, I said, "This is for anyone tripping." I performed a "walking the dog," announcing, "This is 'walking the dog.'" Then I dragged the yo-yo across the stage while saying, "This is walking the dead dog." When I twirled the yo-yo in the wide circle I again introduced the trick to the crowd, "This is 'Around the world,' a lot different than they do it down on 14th Street (a prostitute reference)." That was why I never made fun of Gallagher or Carrot Top.

The biggest problem was remembering to bring the props to the show. I was more of a yak-yak-and-go comic. Trips to the magic shop for the flash paper, changing batteries in the yo-yo, and rolling the fake joints were chewing into my off-hours.

One night, after a show at the Cellar Door, I was bar-hopping in Georgetown. I pulled a pack of cigarettes from my jacket pocket and accidentally spilled a couple of the fake joints. A D.C. Metropolitan police officer saw me retrieving the fake joints from the sidewalk. Minutes later I was handcuffed and in the back of a squad car, trying to convince everyone that the joints were stage props. Fortunately another officer showed with a field-testing unit. The arresting officer, when taking off the handcuffs, kept repeating one word. "Stupid." Whether it came from a veteran comic, high-powered manager, or police officer, good advice was good advice. I dropped the props.

The only problem I ever had with a prop act was sharing the stage. One weekend in 1981, at the Comedy Factory Outlet in Philadelphia, the opening act was The Legendary Wid, a very likable guy and energetic performer. His act was a fast-paced string of visual one-liners, grabbing a prop from a large trunk, doing the gag, and grabbing another. The first night, Wid finished his act and left the stage littered with props. With props everywhere, it was difficult to move without tripping on something. Before the second show I asked him to clean up his mess before leaving. He was apologetic and promised to take care of it. Unfortunately, the second show was the same. Maybe Wid was excited by his big ovation and nervous about pronouncing my name correctly. At that time in my life, patience was a rumor. As soon as I got onstage his props became my props. Whether I got a laugh or not, the prop got the Lenny Shultz treatment — thrown against the back wall. That always got a laugh. In no time there was a pile of mangled props in the rear of the stage and the front was clear. The next show, Wid placed all his props back in the trunk, leaving quite a tidy stage. I never really thanked Wid properly. Nine years before my first daughter was born, he gave me a valuable lesson in parenting.

# 26. "COME TOO FAR TO EVER TURN BACK NOW"

"Oh, I don't believe what went on out there! ... Now look, son. I don't mind these boys. They come out and start with the same word every night. They finish with the same word. Perhaps they're not too creative or funny maybe. But Goddamn, son! You've got a knack of making people vicious. There's a difference between not getting laughs and changing the architecture of the theater!" — From Lenny Bruce's classic bit, *The Palladium*

Andy Kaufman entered the New York Improvisation showroom one night in 1981 in the company of some very large and rough-looking men. I grew up a fan of professional wrestling and easily recognized two members of his entourage as "Captain" Lou Albano and Freddie Blassie.

I approached the two ex-wrestlers, and told them what a fan I was. Andy was surprised I knew who they were.

A few minutes later, Andy, dressed in sweat clothes and sneakers, introduced himself to me. "Hi, I'm Andy Kaufman." He was earnest, as if it were necessary. I couldn't tell if he was yanking my chain or not. In a very serious and thoughtful way he explained a new bit he wanted to try. He was going to challenge a woman from the audience to wrestle him onstage and needed someone to play the manager of

The New York Improv stage begged for a wrestling match, 1981

the female wrestler. The manager job entailed a lot of yelling and maybe a shove or two, and someone suggested I might be right. It was flattering not only to be asked by Andy, but to know at least one of my peers understood my true nature.

The Improv was packed with a hot crowd, the usual in those days. It was a weekday, so this wasn't a bridge-and-tunnel crowd, but a bunch of local hipsters and knowledgeable tourists.

The comics had to walk through the crowd. By the time Andy reached the stage, the whole audience was standing, applauding and cheering. When the crowd did finally settle, they immediately dropped into a reverential state. Silent and attentive, as they were safe in the hands of a certified comedy star and good times lay ahead.

He paced the tiny stage for a few moments. The audience laughed.

Then he started in on them. "I love women." The audience cheered.

"I love to see them in the kitchen. Cooking my meals. That's right. Cooking my meals." The audience let out a few strangled laughs, quickly covered with silence. Confusion crept into the room.

"That's right. Women belong in the home. Cleaning and cooking." A few women booed and yelled in protest.

"No woman is the equal of a man." The boos increased in number and intensity.

Andy continued his rant against women's equality until the booing was unanimous. Professionally dressed women were cursing and shaking their fists at Andy.

"Oh, yeah. I'll prove to you women aren't my equal. I challenge any woman in this room to a wrestling match. If you can pin me, then you can have five hundred dollars."

Andy pulled five $100 bills out of pocket and slapped them on top of the piano at the back of the stage.

"Come on ladies. Or are you afraid to face a real man?!"

Several young women rushed the stage. Prancing about on the balls of his feet with great theatricality, Andy waved them to the side.

Andy roiled the whole crowd. Everyone, men and women, seriously booed him.

"Okay. Okay. But I'm a trained wrestler. To make this fair, some man should help the poor little girl. Who wants to help the women?" He said the word "women" so dismissively, and with such venom, that women in the audience hopped from their seats and cursed him.

I quickly moved to the side of the stage where the women stood, yelling that I was happy to help the women kick his butt. The crowd cheered me. Andy so knew what he was doing.

He looked over the prospective female wrestlers as if it were a slave audience, finally choosing one who was "pretty enough for me to wrestle." The audience booed him as the other women reluctantly left the stage area.

I talked to the chosen wrestler, telling her to remove her heels and earrings, while Andy did muscle poses and strutted about the little stage. The audience was yelling at him. Suddenly he was yelling in my face, before expertly giving me a fake shove. I did the same to him. The crowd was insane, on their feet, screaming and cursing at Andy. He quieted them long enough to announce the beginning of the match, "Let the best MAN win!"

Before I even had a chance to advise the woman wrestler on executing a single leg take- down, she rushed Andy and grabbed him. There really wasn't any room to wrestle on that little stage. When they went to the floor, the crowd stood, en masse, straining to see the action. Andy maneuvered under the woman. She sat on his chest, pinning his back to the stage. I pounded the stage three times and the crowd went wild.

The woman wrestler leapt to her feet as her new fans wildly cheered. She was still jumping about, thrusting her arms in the air, when Andy scrambled to his feet behind her. He snatched the hundred-dollar bills and waved them in the air before kicking open the metal door by the side of the stage. Before anyone could react, Andy disappeared into the night and into a limo parked on 44th Street. Instantly, the crowd went from celebratory cheering to screams of horror. The whole audience seemed to surge toward the side door. In a wild effort to get Andy, people overturned tables and chairs, and comically tried to squeeze through the door, like an old Three Stooges gag. One frustrated person threw a chair at the stage. The limo drove down the block, chased by a couple of people.

When the MC took the stage, tables and chairs were overturned and scattered. The crowd was still enraged, bubbling with noisy conversations and blocking the aisles. It took several minutes just to get them back in their seats. The next few comics died miserable deaths.

In a few short moments, a beloved funny man purposely turned a rollicking comedy audience into an angry mob. Some people wonder why he did it. Maybe he was looking for an excuse to wrestle women. More likely he was looking to take the joke to the next level.

Comedy was always a mind-fuck. It's all about surprising the audience, fooling them into looking in one direction while bringing the punchline in from another. Probably every one of those people had previously seen, and laughed at, Andy's shocking transition from the goofy Foreign Man to an earnest Elvis Presley. This night, Andy Kaufman played on their fears and prejudices in such a masterful way that they never saw the punchline approach, land, and exit the building. It was the most powerful comedic performance I ever witnessed.

Over the years I saw hundreds of comics kill a crowd with laughter, but only one erased their sense of humor and rearranged the club's furniture, with a bit that made me laugh for years.

## 27. "PLEASE ALLOW ME TO INTRODUCE MYSELF"

Since most of my earliest work was opening for rock bands, it didn't take long to realize the importance of an introduction, of affecting an audience before they ever saw me. Stand-up comics were not ubiquitous in the late '70s and audiences certainly didn't expect a comic to open a rock show. Most of the guys making my introduction didn't bother to warn them, either. Over a cacophony of conversations would come, "Please welcome Ritch Shydner." Of course the booing started at that moment because what most of them heard was, "Please welcome, not-the-band-you-came-to-see." The catcalls only intensified when they saw a guy walk to the mic without a musical instrument.

I started impressing upon the soundman or local DJ giving me the introduction, the importance of including the word "comedian." Some did, and some didn't. A few opted out of any responsibility for what I was about to do: "This guy says he's a comedian, please welcome ..."

Actually, unless the gig was in a comedy club, where the audience rightfully expected you to be doing comedy, including the word "comedian" in the intro was always a good idea. In 1989, I went to London to perform on a couple of British television shows. One was a talk show hosted by the British version of Merv Griffin, Des O'Connor, who finished chatting with a gardening expert, turned to the camera, and said, "Please welcome our next guest, Ritch Shydner." I'm sure some of the audience thought I was going to continue the discussion of mulch, weeds, and ladybugs, and my set was a slow build, the audience caught in an impromptu game of "What's My Line?" I could hear people saying

Taking blame for the credit, 1984

things like, "Oh, I see. He's funny."

Once I settled on using my real name, Ritch Shidner, my lifelong battle with the pronunciation of my last name followed me into show business. Growing up, the most common mispronunciation was using a short "i." I thought I'd solve that problem by swapping the "i" for a "y." It didn't work, but I actually got some sort of perverse fun hearing the various ways my last name was mangled, or maybe it matched my low self-esteem.

Even if the MC/opener bothered to ask for the correct pronunciation before the show, what they said on stage was usually "Schneider." That was my family's original name before one of my drunken ancestors no longer wanted to be associated with the rest of the drunken clan and moved the "n" behind the "d."

My favorite was Long Island comedian Jackie Martling, who went all the way by always introducing me as "Itchy Schneider." At least that had the benefit of putting a rare smile on my face when I took the microphone.

The variations of my name in the newspaper ads from those early years were actually pretty fun too. Some of my favorites were "Shneder," "Shoedner," and "Shydiver." Just as often there was another comic's picture with my name. It didn't matter. The clubs were packed. Everyone laughed. We got paid.

Credits included in the introduction usually followed a tried and true, if generic, format. At El Bookman's it was "He's one of our favorites here." At Garvin's, most of the New York acts used "He's a regular at (Catch a Rising Star, the Improvisation, or the Comic Strip)."

When I got to the New York showcase clubs, most intros were a vague catchall: "He/she plays clubs and colleges all across the country, and is one of our favorites here." Of course, if the comic had any kind of television credit that was a must, from the gold-plated *The Tonight Show Starring Johnny Carson* to its used takeout-container counterpart: *The Joe Franklin Show*. But most of the New York City showcase comics weren't too concerned with the intro, and had the attitude: "Give the credit, say my name, and get out of the way as fast as possible."

There were some introductions that could start you in the negative before you even set foot onstage. The most egregious was the Kiss of Death intro: "This next comic is the funniest guy you will ever see." This was a set-up for failure — a tough straitjacket of expectations to wiggle out of — and you could almost hear audience members' jaws locking shut. There were rookie MCs who used that intro with naive sincerity, but usually it was done as a malicious attempt to mess up someone's set, or as a prank intro between two friends.

I never liked it when the MC said anything about my act. "This next guy does really funny stuff on relationships." Why not hand them a set list so they can follow along, and let me know if I forget anything. We all know it's an act but don't remind them it's in any way scripted. I wasn't Robin Williams, but the laughs always flowed more smoothly if there was at least an illusion I was winging it.

As an MC, I didn't like it when comics gave me 15 credits to use in their introduction. You need two or three credits at the most. If you're not funny in a minute after taking that mic, it won't matter to the audience if you played the Last Supper. I also hated it when the comic gave me a joke to do for their intro. Usually the joke was terrible, and I was the one the audience blamed it on.

In the New York showcase scene of the late '70s and early '80s, the comics effectively policed the credits any comic used, just as they did joke ownership. But there were still plenty of things people used as credits that skirted the truth. Robin Williams popped into the New York Improv one night in 1979 and did a surprise set. The next night, one of the 20 comics who had also been on the show that night had the MC bring him up with the intro, "He just worked with Robin Williams." Afterward, he caught so much grief in the bar from the other comics, he never used that intro again.

But like joke thievery, once the road opened in 1980 and the number of comedians increased tenfold in a year, demanding honesty with intro credits was a lost cause. Everyone eventually learned to tolerate the lies and misrepresentations about careers because it became acceptable standard operating procedure. There are no certificates of authenticity or licensing procedures in stand-up comedy. To paraphrase John Lennon, "Whatever gets you through the set."

However, there were limits. In the early '80s, I worked with an opener whose offstage intro, crafted himself, included "You've seen him on *The Tonight Show*." Since I was the headliner and my best credit was "Evening at the Improv," it was a little strange that a guy with such a lofty credit was the opener, so I asked about his Carson appearance. He explained to me that while attending a *Tonight Show* taping he was caught laughing in an audience reaction shot. With all earnestness he offered to show me the tape, but I declined.

That bit of credit fakery was just a warning of what was to come. By the '90s, it was out of control, with every middle comic alleging that they'd been "seen on HBO and Showtime."

One time in 1984 it was the club owner who falsified credits. My first night at the Cleveland Comedy Club, a waitress proudly showed me the club's ad in the *Cleveland Plain Dealer*. Under my misspelled name were the words, "As seen on *Late Night With David Letterman*." My first Letterman appearance was still two years away, but the club owner, Dino Vince, thought the red-hot *Letterman* show might look good under the misspelled name of a totally unheard-of comic. I was angry and confronted Dino, who dismissed my complaints with, "Nobody's gonna know." Unbeknownst to me, Dino had already doubled down on his deceit by telling the opener to include the lie in my introduction. I walked to the stage angry, but as usual the first wave of laughter washed that away, along with the rest of my useless mind chatter. Oh, blessed relief.

As soon as I finished my set, the anger returned and I went straight for Dino. We argued as the crowd filed past us. One customer leaned into me and asked, "When were you on Letterman?" I replied that I wasn't. He said, "I know. I've watched every show."

Dino picked up the phone and called the *Plain Dealer* to change the weekend advertisement. I got a shot and a beer and tried to spot a coke dealer in the exiting crowd. It would have been more useful to me at the time if Dino had the opener mention that I was a coke addict in my intro.

A smooth pass of the baton was important — when the MC finally finished the introduction, the comic should be able to begin speaking when the audience applause ended.

In 1993 I did a rehearsal show for *The Chevy Chase Show*, the former *SNL* star's fabulous flame-out in late-night television. As part of their effort to reinvent the late-night talk show, Chevy's producer decided not to have the comics enter from behind a stage curtain but from a single door perched atop three flights of stairs. Somebody was a *Twilight Zone* fan. This surreal structure dominated the stage. More of an art piece, The Door in the Sky presented a bit of mystery, as if it was part of a magic act. It did make one stand-up disappear.

I climbed a hidden set of stairs behind The Door in the Sky while Chevy bombed a desk piece. Instead of the usual city skyline behind the host there was a giant fish tank. Fish swam aimlessly behind Chevy's head, a perfect metaphor for the show.

I reached the summit just as Chevy began my introduction. I'm sure if the show had succeeded, the producers would have added an oxygen tank, power bars and a Sherpa guide to the Door in the Sky piece.

Chevy finished my boiler plate intro, "Please welcome, Ritch Shydner."

I opened the door and walked down the steep and narrow stairway. The applause ended three steps into my descent. A bigger name might have gotten two or three more steps of applause, but the audience undoubtedly viewed me as a high-wire act more than a comic and didn't want to be the distraction that caused my 50-foot fall into the aquarium. The music play-on from the band ended with the applause. I kept descending in silence, trying not to use the handrails too much, grinning and waving at the audience like a guy chasing a bus. "Don't leave. I'm coming." When I finally reached the mic stand on the stage, my five minutes were up. The red light on the center camera flashed, signaling for me to wrap it up. I did one joke, collected my laughs and joined Chevy. The audience applauded nicely, not seeming to miss the other four minutes and forty-five seconds of material at all. I missed a great opportunity to separate from the pack. I should have forged a new career — The One and Done Comedy of Ritch Shydner.

Looking back, intros and credits were never that important. If you had opened for Christ on the Sermon on the Mount, you still better be funny in about a minute of taking that stage before the coughs started.

## 28. "CONSIDER THIS, A SLIP"

**H**eckling is part of stand-up. Always was. Always will be. Heckling separates stand-up from every other performance art, as implied by a stock heckler line from the late '70s, "Hey, pal. Do you go to the ballet and heckle Baryshnikov?"

Maybe it is the common nature of stand-up that invites an occasional challenge from the audience. Few people can sing like Streisand or play guitar like Clapton, but everyone likes to think they can tell a joke. Maybe it is the fact that direct audience participation (laughter) is a necessary part of a stand-up show. The comic and the audience form a group to produce the music of laughter. Occasionally one of the group's members might challenge the leader's choice of songs. Or maybe some people can only sit in the dark for so long before crying out for help. Whatever the reason, heckling happens and stand-ups learn to handle it in a variety of ways.

Some comics have a policy of zero tolerance for hecklers, with instructions for the staff to squash any dissent immediately and with extreme prejudice. I understand that attitude. To these comics the risks outweigh the rewards. A bad heckler exchange has the potential to ruin a show, without much possibility of creating material for the ultimate goal, a television shot.

I always felt there was something to be gained from a duel with a heckler. The obvious risk ramped the audience's interest. They delighted in the verbal tar and feathering of one of their own. Crushing your enemies and hearing the lamentation of their women also gave me an immediate and primal stage rush, kicking the show into another gear.

Hecklers inadvertently shaped my act. In my early road shows of

Eyeballing a heckler, 1979

1980, a few hecklers hit me with, "Hey baldy!" It was an obvious refer-ence to my obvious receding hairline. My initial response to these bald-ing heckles was Heckling 101 — strike at the same level attacked. I made fun of their haircut or clothing. Eventually I developed a better tac-tic — to open my show with a few self-deprecating jokes about my fad-ing hair. Not only did the pre-emptive strike on my hair negate the power of any subsequent bald heckles, but vulnerability in acknowledging my faults made the sarcasm that followed easier for the crowd to accept. Vulnerability was a necessary air hose in comedy.

Banging it out with a heckler never frightened me, probably because my early comedy training was trading insults with my high school bud-dies. Take the blow, don't get angry, come back funny ... the same basic tenets of handling a comedy club heckler. The direct heckle was prefera-ble to the audience talking among themselves, ignoring the comedian. Nothing killed a joke as brutally as indifference.

In my eyes, not all hecklers were created evil. Most were simply checking to see if you were a comic present in the here and now, or just another Comic-bot on automatic pilot. This type of heckler just wanted a little proof as to your qualifications to sit in the pilot's seat. One quick retort usually returned this passenger to the main cabin.

Anyone foolish enough to heckle entered a rigged match. The comic stood on an elevated, lighted stage, and was armed with the loudest voice in the room, a barrel full of heckler put-downs, and the crowd's support.

The goodwill from the audience was the comic's biggest advantage. The only judges that mattered rooted for the comic to prevail. Their collective consciousness understood perfectly that a knockout by the heckler meant anarchy, no show, and no laughs.

Bottom line, the public shaming contained in a couple of put-downs from the stage quickly caused most hecklers to beg "no mas." Of course, a drunk was impervious to embarrassment. That's when the staff, either through their diligence or alerted by a code word from the comic, usually removed the cancer before it killed the show. Usually.

In early 1981, I played a weekend at the aptly named Wit's End comedy club in Lansing, Mich. It was a converted biker bar with a new large, elevated stage, union-installed lighting and excellent sound system. However, there were a few possible distractions left over from the club's previous incarnations: the bar, a pool table and two video games were in the showroom.

Stand-up comedy is a delicate soufflé, requiring an audience's complete and total attention. Every word must be heard. Any extraneous noise can flatten a joke. Sporadic, but regular interruptions, like a blender or video game, can become a comedic Sword of Damocles. My main concern was the pool players' noisy kibitzing and the loud crack of the balls. I also knew from personal experience that holding a cue stick gave one a bad case of the Wise-Ass.

The club owner/MC assured me the pool table and video games were always shut down for the show. He was sincere in his efforts, but when I took the stage, the pool players refused to stop their game.

It wasn't long before the noise of a cue ball smashing into a rack dropped one of my jokes. Moments later the crack of another shot sank a second joke.

Simultaneously, I watched the owner/MC pleading with the pool players, delivered a joke, slotted the next three jokes and plotted a strategy to deal with the pool game distraction. I only had that superpower while onstage.

I decided to make a personal plea.

"Hey, guys. Kill the game and when I finish I'll play you for beers."

They just stared at me with a dull look of practiced indifference. The same one they gave every teacher who ever asked them a question. One of the guys said something, the others laughed, and the game continued.

I recognized their behavior as far more insidious than mere heckling. To these guys I was a trespasser, a competitor for the local beauties. Any success on my part was likely to extend their record-breaking streak of going home alone.

As I considered my next move with the pool game and delivered another joke, a woman in the front row heckled.

"Come on."

I heard her, but wasn't sure anyone else had. That was always the first consideration in responding to a heckler. To get into a phantom conversation with a ringsider only served to confuse the audience.

She came back louder and just as unintelligible.

"Hey!"

"I'm sorry, but I don't speak Drunkenese."

The audience laughed loudly, signaling for the heckler to stay down for the count.

I tried to move into material, but she bounced back fast.

"You!"

"Look. I need a noun and a verb." The audience laughed louder, effectively throwing in the towel for her.

"You know!"

"I see you got one brain cell, treading water in a sea of beer."

The audience laughed, but probably also registered the truth of the joke. This was a drunk woman, the most dangerous heckler. It was okay to pound a male heckler until his balls rolled to the stage, but the audience sympathized with the drunken female heckler.

A few months earlier at the Cleveland Comedy Club, a young drunk woman yelled one too many incoherencies. I stepped out of the stage light and addressed her, "I know you. On the night of your senior prom you were lying on your bed crying. And your dad was sitting on the foot of the bed saying, "That's okay honey. I still think you're pretty." The comics howled in the back but it was way too cruel for the crowd and they never really came back to me.

The Cleveland mistake wasn't in my mind when my drunk East Lansing woman spoke to me again. "No. Hey. What are you?!!"

She had exhausted my heckler comebacks so I dipped into the barrel for the one stock line I ever used comfortably. It probably appealed to my mother's Southern heritage.

"All right, folks. I guess this is what happens when first cousins marry."

There were quite a few "ooohhhs" mixed in with the laughter. I remembered the Cleveland mistake, too late.

The pool players saw an opening, the chance to turn the "ooohhhs" of dissent into a full scale rebellion. One of them shouted, "Fuck you!"

No one laughed. Everyone knew those were fighting words.

"Really, asshole? Who wrote that for you?"

It wasn't a clever line but the audience laughed, an expression of the group's conscious desire to avoid where this was heading.

"Fuck you!"

I snapped and went after the guy, with malicious intentions.

"Hey, Nozzlehead! Who'd you blow for that REO Speedwagon T-shirt?! What a fucking limp-dick band! They sucked then. They suck now. And they'll suck when they bury you in that ratty-assed shirt. Cocksucker."

I was about to learn yet another valuable lesson. When dealing with a heckler, mock anger and frustration were funny. If the crowd sensed real anger, and they were amazingly adept at sensing these things, the comic lost.

The pool player tossed his cue stick and rushed the stage.

His first mistake was throwing the cue stick, and then coming after me. The second mistake was expecting me to wait for him to get on the stage before starting the fight. I got in the first few punches as he scrambled onto the stage.

It was no problem to wrestle him to the floor and cast him in the Ned Beatty role for a re-enactment of the movie *Deliverance*.

The audience laughed as I humped him while yelling, "Squeal like a pig!"

I played to the crowd, forgetting there was still an ongoing fight. The guy rallied and put some good hits onto my fat head. Unlike the movies, these things never lasted too long. We both made a few wild swings before I managed to toss him off the stage, to the roar of the crowd.

Jacked up on adrenaline and testosterone, I tried to resume my act.

"My dad smashed mosquitoes against the wall and left them there ..."

The crowd stared at me.

"He treated them like big-game trophies. 'I bagged this one in 1964 ...'"

I pushed for a laugh until I convinced each and every person there of my lunacy — not the ha-ha funny kind of crazy, but the uh-oh scary sort.

As nuts as it was to engage in a fistfight on a comedy stage, it was even more insane to then attempt to be funny.

Their applause didn't signify, "Please, Joke Boy, describe your mis-shapen childhood." It meant, "Fight's over. Now somebody start playing some Seeger."

Most crowds might enjoy a good bar fight on an elevated stage with decent sight lines but a comedian with mussed hair, scuffed face and a torn shirt, not so much.

This was the only time in my career I left the stage early, but nobody complained or asked for a refund. It reminded me of a 1977 Kinks concert I attended at Constitution Hall in Washington, D.C. Near the end of the show, Ray Davies and his brother, Dave, got into fistfight. Roadies finally separated them, but the concert was finished. As the crowd exited, a young woman badgered a man in a suit standing by the ticket offices to return her money. He dismissed her with a wave of his hand, "You got your show."

Saturday night's shows at the Wit's End were packed. I'm sure a few patrons were disappointed that all they got were a lot of laughs and not a bar fight on an elevated stage. Anyway, they got their show.

## 29. "GETTIN' HAD, GETTIN' TOOK, I TELL YOU FOLKS, IT'S HARDER THAN IT LOOKS"

The stand-up community is a pack of lone wolves. The job description calls for soloists. Yet despite our eccentricity and individualism, we form close relationships with each other.

I met some incredible people in stand-up, and became close friends with a few. Working on the road with a buddy was always a bonus, but never more so than when the engagement went sour. A few days in a nightmarish job strengthened old bonds and sometimes turned new acquaintances into lifelong friends. Anybody can turn a hell gig into a funny story down the road, but the ones who wrung laughs out of the accident in progress were special.

In the winter of 1981, Kevin Rooney and I finished working at Giggles Comedy Club in Columbus, Ohio. Our MC that week was a very funny local guy, Will Hartnett. The three of us got along so well that we were thrilled when the owner, John Cochran, sent us straight to a new club in Toledo.

Will was a rangy, energetic young guy with a quick wit and a hair-trigger mouth. Even though he was only a few weeks into stand-up, everyone saw him as a natural.

Rooney was, and is, one of the funniest people I ever met. He has made me laugh ridiculously hard ever since I first met him in 1977.

Our transportation was Will's rusted, 10-year-old Pontiac. In no time we were overcome with fumes from an unknown source inside the car. At the time we thought a faulty exhaust system caused the bad smell and lightheadedness. Looking back, the culprit could just as easily have been the mixture of stale beer and decomposing fast food emanating from the

The cavalry arrives in LA, Kevin Rooney, 1983

knee-deep pile of trash in the back seat. Either way, we drove for two and a half hours with the windows down in the dead of winter. Wearing our coats, hats and gloves, we chain-smoked to stay warm.

We discovered that the gig was not in Toledo, but in a nearby town, Perrysburg. Actually it wasn't in Perrysburg, but in a gigantic disco in the middle of a cornfield a few miles outside of town. The comedy club wasn't in the huge disco, but in a tiny attached building in the rear ... a pimple on the backside of a rhino.

The disco, formerly a barn, was a conversion that perfectly reflected America's economy of the '80s. The small, attached shed, which housed the comedy club, was probably last used as a slaughterhouse. Ronald Reagan's Morning in America morphed into John Cochran's Showtime in the Cow Pasture.

This was a time when many a freshly minted comedy club was previously a bowling alley lounge, hotel conference room, or doughnut shop. Most of the conversions were adequate to the job. Perrysburg was done by Our Gang Productions. A couple of plant lights pointed to a sheet of carpeted plywood nailed to a half-dozen two-by-sixes, with a sound system last used by the local VFW for their Bingo Nights.

The disco's manager, whose pear-shaped body and long hair surrounding a bald head looked to be drawn by *Mad* magazine's Don Martin, greeted us with our survival kit; three motel room keys, three stacks of meal vouchers and three vials of cocaine. The Pear Man held the vials of coke before us and said, "If you run out, see me Friday." This was indeed a John Cochran gig.

The Barn Disco was packed with hundreds of Footloose Fanatics every night. The Joke Slaughterhouse only seated 90, but there were never more than 40 people for any of our shows. It was understandably difficult to get the Perrysburg comedy fans out of the house when sitcoms like *The Jeffersons* or *One Day at a Time* were on the air.

Drinks for the comedy club were brought from the Barn Disco, so every time a waitress opened the door, music blared, knocking the hell out of any potential comedy. *Working for the Weekend* by Loverboy was on a continuous loop that week.

Midway through my set the sound system started receiving radio transmissions, specifically a University of Toledo basketball game. I was suddenly interrupted by a sports announcer's voice, "The Rockets inbound the ball ..."

A moment later the radio interference stopped and I got in a few jokes before the announcer again cut in, "That basket brings the Rockets within two."

Another joke attempt was crushed by the door opening and "Everybody's working for the weekend ..." My act suffered from what was scientifically known as *comicus interruptus*.

A few of the audience members became more interested in sports than comedy. When the game again came over the system, they yelled, "Turn it up."

No one was running the room. The Pear Man was Nowhere Man.

Rooney and Will fiddled with the system for a while before signaling to me it was hopeless. I alternated with the game the rest of the set and didn't care whether my exit applause was for a good show or the Rockets victory.

The comedy club exited into the Barn Disco, like a Disney ride dumping the passengers into the gift shop. We followed the audience into the cavernous bar, where a DJ in a headband announced another playing of *Working for the Weekend* over an expensive sound system.

We found The Pear Man in the DJ booth, listening to Loverboy's masterpiece on the headphones, to get the full benefit of those cowbells. He took the headphones off only long enough to promise to fix the sound system.

We escaped through the surging sea of spandex to the sanctuary of our eight-unit roadside motel. Rooney called for an 8 a.m. wake-up call but was told, "We don't get up that early." He jokingly tried to jump out of the ground floor window, but it was sealed. Apparently there had been previous suicide attempts in the Perrysburg Motor Court.

The next night, two minutes into Will's set, the sound cut off completely. Will was unperturbed. "I don't need a microphone. I took theater."

The Pear Man got the system working again but soon a new problem arose. Whenever one of us reached for the microphone a blue arc of electricity leapt from the mic to our hands. So we left the mic in the stand and maneuvered carefully around it, afraid to even get our mouths too close.

Then the radio broadcast returned. This time it was the radio station's normal Top 40 format. *Working for the Weekend* filled the room.

That's the way the sound system worked all week, alternating between working, not working, shock treatment, and disembodied voices from the great beyond.

Every night we went next door to have a beer, only to be chased out by *Working for the Weekend*. It became our "Niagara Falls ... slowly I turned."

Back at the Motel we watched *The Tonight Show*, a distant and dreamlike vision of actual show business. After that we goofed on the bad late-night programming, making each other laugh until the broadcasting ended in the early morning. There was a time when dinosaurs roamed the Earth and the TV stations shut down.

In the daytime we wrote new material and drove around town looking for things to mock on stage that night. The shows became a challenge to make each other laugh as much as the audience.

One evening before the show we sat in the Barn Disco's little restaurant, eating our pre-game meal and enduring, once again, *Working for the Weekend*, on the jukebox.

Four local nozzleheads, each wearing the same flannel shirt, entered. They were half-past drunk and closing on trouble, immediately eye-balling us for the strangers we were. One of them tried to woo the waitress with a version of the classic going-off-to-war line, "Be nice to me, baby, because we're driving to Florida!" He then loudly asked if she had any black beauties. She ignored him. He quickly redirected the anger from his rejection to us. "What are you looking at?"

Just then The Pear Man entered, and greeted the four drunks as friends.

"Hey, before you guys go, come to the comedy show. My treat."

So, that night, four of the 15 people in our audience were designated hecklers. The Pear Man surely shared his cocaine with his buddies because although they didn't have anything creative to yell at us, they yelled it a lot. The three of us snapped back at the heckling — the two guys offstage, covering the guy with the mic. We caught them in a triangular crossfire.

The Pear Man punctuated the week perfectly. The last night he handed us sealed envelopes containing our pay, and quickly turned on his heels in an attempt at a quick getaway. We stopped him and tore into the envelopes to count our cash. Each one of us was shorted a hundred. He didn't say a word, but simply pulled three $100 bills from his pocket.

On the frozen ride back to Columbus we scanned the radio dial, looking to find Working for the Weekend. We wanted one more chuckle.

Almost embarrassingly, Rooney, Will and I played the same Perrysburg comedy club the following summer. Sure part of it was filling a free week with cash, but mostly it was about us working together. Comics like to laugh as much as anyone else.

# 30. "LOOKING FOR A SIGN THAT THE UNIVERSAL MIND HAS WRITTEN YOU INTO THE PASSION PLAY"

One night in the early 1980s I was MCing at the New York Improvisation when the club manager, Pat Buckles, called me to the phone. Rodney Dangerfield was on the line. It seemed a young "writer" tried selling Rodney a batch of jokes. They were terrible except for one, which was so far superior to the others that Rodney suspected it to be stolen. Any comic knows how unusual it is for any comic, let alone a big-time stand-up star pressed for new material, to look a killer joke in the mouth. Stolen material has been fenced in this way since the days of vaudeville. Jokes don't have serial numbers. If confronted, the star can always claim the joke was bought in good faith. You saying my writer could not have written that joke? You have any proof my writer took that joke? Tough luck, kid. Find a new bicycle to ride.

Rodney told me the joke in question.

I told Rodney the joke belonged to the prolific and hilarious Ronnie Shakes. I can't remember the joke, but Shakes had so many brilliant one-liners like, "I'm not suicidal. I'm semi-suicidal. I just kill people who look like me." And, "After 12 years of therapy, my psychiatrist said something that brought tears to my eyes. He said, 'No hablo Ingles.'"

Rodney asked for Shakes' phone number.

Shakes later told me of their conversation. Rodney wanted to include the joke in his upcoming *Tonight Show* shot. He normally paid $50 a joke but because he did the joke on stage once, Dangerfield offered Shakes $250. In no way did Dangerfield press for the joke. Quite the

Ronnie Shakes, 1981

opposite, he apologized for already doing the joke and completely under-stood if Shakes wanted to keep the gem. Shakes thought it'd be a kick to see his idol do one of his jokes on TV, and probably knew in his heart there were a thousand more where that came from.

In due time Ronnie began a string of *Tonight Show* appearances, with Carson becoming a big fan. In 1987, Ronnie Shakes suffered a fatal heart attack while jogging at a Cleveland gig. He was admired and loved by the comedy community.

There were a lot of stories about the Rodney Dangerfield, his shady past, and wild man ways — but this incident showed how much Rodney loved the art form and how well he treated younger comics. He was a stand-up guy who gave all the respect he never got.

# 31. "CIRCUMSTANCE BEYOND OUR CONTROL"

One of the most cynical showbiz truisms I heard at the beginning of my career was, "The show must go on ... especially if you want to get paid."

It wasn't just about the pay. My fear was, if I didn't get on that stage and get those laughs, for whatever reason, I might never be handed the mic again. It's a comedic paradox that a man with so many insecurities freely chooses a career that offers so little security.

In 1978 I opened for the band Chicago in Washington, D.C., while suffering from a bad cold. The pay was only $50, but it never occurred to me to call in sick. A friend brought me two bottles of DayQuil. I chugged one to get out of bed, and the other moments before I went onstage. The cold symptoms disappeared, along with any ability to hold a thought for more than five seconds. On the plus side, I was so self-conscious then, it probably helped my performance.

Ten years later I was headlining the Funny Firm in Chicago, and came down with a nasty flu before my first show. My voice was shot, but I only ever used three voices in my act and they all sounded the same. The owner, Len Austervich, put a cot in his office, where I could perspire and vomit in private between shows. Six nights, 14 shows, and hundreds of ringsiders infected, but I got all my pay.

I performed the night after I broke my foot jumping off a speaker at the Limelight in Atlanta in 1983. That cast was half the size of the one I dragged onstage after I broke my leg in a motorcycle accident in front of the Comedy and Magic Club in 1989. Both those accidents taught me I didn't need to move around the stage as much as I thought I did to be funny. And I got bits from both accidents, so there really was no down-

A Walkman won't drown out the sound of a gunshot, 1982

side to those broken bones.

Physical pain was always easier for me to handle than emotional pain.

In January of 1982, Phoenix, Ariz., became part of the boom with its first comedy club, Chuckles. I was supposed to open for Henny Youngman but he canceled and I became the headliner. It wouldn't have mattered if they had booked one of Phyllis Diller's old wigs for that first week, the place was an immediate success, packed with 400 people every night. The club owners were shoveling cocaine at the comics like it was coal into the sinking *Titanic*'s boilers. I befriended one of the young guys working at the club. One night, a very distressed waitress interrupted my post-show reverie. My new young friend was in a motel across the street threatening to kill himself and the only person he said he'd talk to was me. My skill set was limited to making a roomful of strangers laugh on cue, but I went to the phone. The young guy was very upset about a failed romance and a directionless life, the sort of young man blues I'd had a few times, and let him know exactly that. I said if he put the gun outside his door, then I'd bring over Jack Daniel's and Titanic fuel, and we could work it all out. No sooner had he agreed to my stopgap measure he shouted, "Cops! Who called the cops???" Then there was a loud bang in my ear. I ran across the street. A police officer stopped me from going into the room. "You don't want to see this." I probably heard those words in a hundred cop shows, but never delivered with that much sadness. One minute I was talking to the guy, then heard a gunshot. It was all so shocking. I returned to the club and ingested every pill, powder and drink offered me, my normal way to numb and forget. The next night we did a show as if nothing had happened. I remember how disconnected I felt from the laughter I heard. Many times in life I had felt disconnected from what I was doing but never while on stage. I forgot the kid's name but not that feeling.

Most of the time the stage actually provided refuge, a total distraction from break-ups, family arguments, or any sort of bad news. Most of the time.

On Monday, Dec. 6, 1980, Carol Leifer, David Strassman, an unnamed LA comic and I finished our show at the Comic Strip in Fort Lauderdale, Fla., and learned of John Lennon's murder. Everyone retreated to the comedy condo, watched the news, and drank.

The next night was the most difficult show I ever did. Everyone came to the club still in shock, and filled with sadness ... hungover in every way possible. We fully expected that night's show to be canceled. The club owners thought the place would be packed with people looking for a distraction ... and bills had to be paid. The crowd was small. The staff was listless. Everyone was in mourning. The comics gathered in the back of the room. Lenny Bruce faced a similar dilemma when he stepped onstage two days after JFK was assassinated in 1963. Terry Southern and Lenny came up with the now-classic opener: Lenny walking onstage, sadly shaking his head and saying, "Man ... Vaughn Meader." The audience laughed because they knew that Vaughn Meader, whose entire career was based on his JFK impression, was finished. Lenny had addressed the murdered elephant in the room, and had a great show.

Not one of the comics at the Comic Strip wanted to perform, let alone think of a possible joke about the murder of a Beatle. The best idea was to not mention John Lennon, or England, or even the word "walrus." Everyone agreed this was the best strategy. The LA comic was the emcee that night. He got about the laughs expected from the small, depressed audience and finished his set. Carol stood ready for the emcee to introduce her. Instead, this comic drove the clown car off the cliff. "I know this is a comedy club, but can we have a moment of silence for John Lennon." He continued talking about Lennon and the Beatles until everyone in the audience was crying. I looked at Carol. She was crying. I walked to the stage and took the microphone from the idiot. It was the most painful set I've ever done. Never have I felt less funny performing for an audience further from a laugh. The three comics who followed me suffered the same fate. I don't think anyone bothered the emcee much about it. Decades later, I still can't see the show going any other way.

Another line I heard was, "The difference between an amateur and professional comic is the pro is funny every night at 9. "It didn't take me long to get the point there, either. Over the years there have been plenty of days I didn't feel like taking the microphone. No matter what the circumstance or my feelings, I always took the stage to be of service to the audience. The job was to be funny, not to feel funny.

# 32. "WHAT YOU PAY FOR
YOUR INCHES OF FAME"

In the fall of 1981, I flew to LA with a pack of New York comics to tape a new show, *An Evening at the Improv* on a relatively new cable channel, Arts and Entertainment. It was my first TV appear ance. The highlight of the trip was staying at the infamous Tropicana Hotel. We partied so hard that a leather-clad rocker with a spiked mohawk knocked on our door at 5 in the morning and asked us to turn down the music.

After my new wife, Carol Leifer, was cast in a television pilot, *Toast of Manhattan*, we packed up our bags and moved to Hollywood in January of 1982.

At that time, the center of the showbiz universe was clearly Los Angeles. There were very few opportunities for stand-ups in New York — virtually all the TV shows and movies were cast and shot in LA. *Late Night With David Letterman* didn't begin until later that year.

Most important, *The Tonight Show Starring Johnny Carson* was in LA, creating tremendous gravitational pull for ambitious comics. In the New York stand-up community, moving to LA was a mark of graduation. As comic after comic from your class moved west, the pressure to follow intensified.

We drove Carol's '76 Firebird straight from the Pittsburgh Comedy Club to an apartment in West Hollywood, the landing zone for most New York comics. West Hollywood was the location of the two main comedy clubs, the Improvisation on Melrose Avenue and the Comedy Store on Sunset Boulevard.

The Comedy Store on Sunset Boulevard was founded in 1972,

Comedy Store regular, 1982

shortly after Johnny Carson moved his show to LA. Budd Friedman had no choice but to move west, opening the Improvisation on Melrose Avenue in 1979.

Richard Pryor worked out his material at the Comedy Store. This helped the owner, Mitzi Shore, in many ways. There was the prestige of America's No. 1 comedian being in residency at her club. Pryor meant packed houses. Stuffed cash registers meant an expansion beyond the initial Original Room — an adjoining space became the Main Room. Another Comedy Store was opened in the west LA area of Westwood, near the UCLA campus. Mitzi opened a club in the Pacific Beach neighborhood of San Diego, later moving it to La Jolla.

Even comedians can do those numbers, eventually realizing that Mitzi was making millions, the waitresses a few hundred a night, and the engines for all this prosperity, the comics. There was no "road" to hit for cash. There arose a labor movement. The eight-week stand-up strike of the Comedy Store in 1979 marked the end of the fun and the beginning of serious funny business. Some comics crossed the picket line. A suspicious fire closed the Improv. A comic committed suicide. Friendships ended. Resentments began.

There were few other area clubs offering stage time and a little money. The Ice House (Pasadena), the Comedy and Magic Club (Hermosa Beach) and the Laff Stop (Encino) were excellent clubs with appreciative audiences. However, the whole point of living in LA was to be seen by the industry. Those executives saw no reason to drive any further than the Improv and the Store. This was the biggest difference between the New York and LA comedy scenes. If New York was the school, LA was the job interview. Everyone took the stage knowing that a powerful manager, agent or network executive might step into the room at any time. On the downside, the thought of possibly being seen by someone important tended to chill experimentation in those rooms.

The Improv had an optimal 275 seat showroom, with clear sightlines, a piano on the large, elevated stage and, of course, the iconic brick wall. Between the front entrance and showroom was a bar and dining area. Although often crowded, both spots offered a place for the comics to gather and complain about their agents, or lack of agents. Like the New York showcase clubs, the pay at the Improv was minimal. Prime-time acts got $15 a set. The newer comics who opened and closed the shows worked for free drinks and the chance that Budd might notice them by saying, "Stay out of the aisles."

The Comedy Store was a comedy multiplex, offering three venues under one roof. The massive 450-seat Main Room was a precursor to some of the huge comedy clubs of the 21$^{st}$ century. The 235-seat Original Room was intimate, an ideal work-out gym. The upstairs 75-seat Belly Room was initially a noble experiment to expand the numbers of working female stand-ups by creating a women-only room. There was no real place to hang out at the Store, so the comics milled about in the parking lot, or lurked in the pitch-black hallways, scaring patrons, other comics and themselves.

Once the strike was resolved there was far more money to be made at the Store. The Original Room only paid $25, but the Main Room was a goldmine where the comics split the door with Mitzi on Fridays and Saturdays. A top regular could easily net $900 a week, at a time when rent was $400 a month. This money enabled Mitzi's comics to stay in town and concentrate on developing a TV career, and a drug habit.

In 1982, the Comedy Store comics were Kip Addota, Louie Anderson, Dottie Archibald, Freddie Asparagus, Richard Belzer, Teddy Bergeron, Sandra Bernhard, Mike Binder, Ed Bluestone, Irv Burton, Brian Bradley, Lois Bromfield, Joey Camen, Donna Cherry, Blake Clark, Andrew "Dice" Clay, Dave Coulier, Johnny Dark, Tony Delia, Barry Diamond, Vic Dunlop, John Fox, Joey Gaynor, Steven Alan Green, Arsenio Hall, Argus Hamilton, Charlie Hill, Martha Jane, Denny Johnston, Tim Jones, Brent Jordan, Ron Kenney, Sam Kinison, Carl LaBove, Steve

Landesberg, Robert Lord, Etta Mae, Howie Mandel, Bif Maynard, Bill Miller, Paul Mooney, Steve Moore, Gary Mule Deer, Marty Nadler, Diane Nichols, Joe Nipote, Tamayo Otsuki, Valery Pappas, Wild Willy Parson, Harris Peet, Jackson Perdue, Piper & Tucker, Ollie Joe Prater, Richard Pryor, Michael Rapport, Michael Richards, Paul Rodriquez, Bob Saget, Angel Salazar, Lenny Schultz, Bob Shaw, Yakov Smirnoff, Carrie Snow, Allan Stephan, Skip Stevenson, Howard Taylor, Tim Thomerson, David Tyree, Jimmy Walker, Marsha Warfield, Lotus Weinstock, Robin Williams, Carl Wolfson, and Johnny Yume.

The Improvisation comics were Jimmy Aleck, Byron Allen, Joanne Astrow, Larry Beezer, Bruce Baum, Elayne Boosler, Jimmy Brogan, Julie Brown, Dana Carvey, Fritz Coleman, Billy Crystal, JoAnne Dearing, Tom Dreesen, Rick Ducommun, Tony Edwards, Charles Fleischer, Rich Hall, Andy Kaufman, Michael Keaton, Bobby Kelton, Mac and Jamie, Maurice LaMarche, Murray Langston, Carol Leifer, Jay Leno, Richard Lewis, Bill Maher, Bruce Mahler, Barry Marder, Pam Matteson, Larry Miller, Carey Odes, Kevin Nealon, Rick Overton, John Pate, Monica Piper, Paul Reiser, Ron Richards, Jerry Seinfeld, Bobby Slayton, Mark Schiff, Robert Schimmel, Wil Shriner, David Strassman, Greg Travis, Brant Von Hoffman, George Wallace, Keenen Wayans, and Robert Wuhl.

Allegedly, the acts favored by the two club owners were different in style and manner. Budd was said to lean toward monologists while Mitzi was supposedly inclined to characters. Although both impresarios surely had prejudices, they employed all styles. Socio-political commentators Argus Hamilton and Paul Mooney were prime-time comics at the Store. The scattershot antics of Charlie Fleischer, and Greg Travis' punk magician, were key acts at the Improv. Funny was always the bottom line.

Some comics worked both clubs, usually on the QT. This was another difference between the two coasts. A little friendly competition existed among the New York clubs, but it was a more-divisive atmosphere in LA Some of it surely was lingering animosity from the strike. Some of it was because the stakes were higher. Jamie Masada's relatively new club, the Laugh Factory, became a safe haven for the comics from both the Store and Improv to share the stage.

The LA antagonism was all pretty light stuff. The worst a comic suffered was an unreturned greeting, petty remark, or flat stage introduction. None of this was comparable to Prohibition's nightclub scene. In 1927, a 25-year-old Chicago comic, Joe E. Lewis, had his throat cut and skull fractured for playing a rival club. The only way that happened in 1982 was if a comic wore a Comedy Store T-shirt on the Improv stage.

Most acts chose the fraternal order of comedians over club loyalty, but sometimes a little hostility surfaced from the dark undercurrent. One night, as I was rushing to make a time slot at the Store, a couple of comics blocked my entrance to the rear doorway. One of them, Carl Wolfson, said, "What are you doing here? You're an Improv comic." His friends grumbled in agreement. Anger always had a strange way of boosting my energy while calming the preshow jitters, so I welcomed the confrontation. "Hey asshole, I'm an everywhere comic. And if you don't move you'll be an on-your-ass comic." I heard a cackle and turned to see a smiling Sam Kinison. LA wasn't going to be any different than New York or Washington, D.C. Some comics you embraced and some you straight-armed.

# 33. "DON'T GIVE A DAMN FOR
JUST THE IN-BETWEENS"

I
t's a shame that young comics never got to see Jay Leno in the clubs during the 1980s. Judging Jay's stand-up solely by his monologues as the host of *The Tonight Show* was similar to viewing Michael Jordan's basketball skills only by his Nike commercials.

After driving into LA in 1982, the first thing I did was go to the Melrose Improv where I watched Leno dismantle the room. He wasn't completely foreign to me, having watched a couple of his late-'70s TV appearances. But what Leno did that night in that club was a revelation to me. He was stand-up's big secret.

Just like in New York, if I wasn't on the road, I was in the LA clubs. Night after night I saw Leno destroy the Melrose Improv, always following a murderer's row of the hottest young comics in the country doing their best to smoke the room. Inevitably, Leno did the impossible by raising the level of laughter in the room.

His style was the equivalent of a three-chord rock song – straightforward, powerful, and hypnotic. Planting himself behind the mic, Jay was fairly economical with his gestures, making the mime he did do all that more effective. His booming voice put the force of a wrecking ball into a punchline. Nobody spoke of a jokes-per-minute ratio in those days, but Jay surely had the highest of our generation. Jay's routines, like his classic "late night shopping at the Sunset Ralph's" or "small town carnival" were marvels of tight, efficient writing. He was the master of the tag, stacking and balancing them like a plate juggler. When Jay got the crowd rolling he used the mic as if it were a judge's gavel, calling for disorder. Each punchline was punctuated by pounding the heavy base of the stand onto the stage, signaling a fresh explosion of laughter. Jay worked a tight drumbeat. The audience convulsed with laughter, rocking back and forth in unison. Guys banged their fists on the tabletops. Comics in the back of the room laughed, even if we already knew the routines.

Jay owned the Improv, being a favorite with the crowds and Budd Friedman. He had the power to run the red light any time but always stuck to his time in deference to the comics who followed. He was honorable, original and everyone admired him.

As impressive as Jay's onstage behavior was his offstage demeanor. A comic moving to LA in the early '80s found a one-man welcoming committee in Jay Leno. He helped find housing and transportation. One day, Jay was outside as I parked my 1962 Chevy in front of his house. "Shydner, your car sounds a little rough. Let me check the timing." Two minutes later Jay was under the hood giving the car a tune-up.

A hair-raising ride through the hairpin turns of Mulholland Drive in Leno's jet-fuel-powered Mustang Shelby was a rite of passage, maybe a test of courage. No way was I going to say, "Hey, you wanna slow down, Jay?"

He even helped with gigs, driving many of us to Hermosa Beach to audition for his friend Mike Lacy, the much-loved owner of the Comedy and Magic Club.

When Jay was in town, his house was a late-night gathering spot for comics. No booze, or drugs, but lots of grilled burgers and M&M's, and lots of spritzing. Comics competing for laughs from other comics can be brutal with each other. Jay provided safe scratching posts for the comics by showing horrible movies like *Plan 9 From Outer Space*.

The road called Jay more and more. Comedy clubs were spreading like McDonald's franchises and Jay was the Marines of stand-up, always the first to hit a new club.

There were no wild road stories because Jay didn't drink or do drugs. Not, did them and quit. Never did. He was what my kids called "straight-edge," out there on the natch.

What I heard Jay did to wind down on the road shocked me more than any tale of drunken debauchery. After his shows, Jay held informal workshops for local comics, at no charge. He was passionate about stand-up comedy. If Jay wasn't performing, he loved discussing it. Maybe Jay fed off the enthusiasm of the new recruits, or the dialogue inspired new material for his act. Regardless of the reason, the King of Clubs, still trying to make it himself, constantly took the time to help younger comics, for fun and for free.

There's an old joke: Two comics see each other for the first time in months. The first comic says, "I killed in Boston." The second comic is silent. The first comic says, "I tore them up in Cleveland." The second comic stares ahead. The first comic says, "Oh, but I bombed in Denver." The second comic says, "Yeah, I heard about that." Good reviews traveled slowly on the comedy grapevine, if at all. Yet, in those early days on the road, all I heard from other comics was of Jay Leno taking a room apart.

The first thing I asked when playing a new club was the house record for onstage time. The first night I started running the audience to break it. It was a silly, inconsequential record, existing only in the minds of a few comics and club owners. If nothing else it was a little extra incentive to stretch and write new material. Usually the mark to hit was two hours. After Leno finished a lap on the circuit, the story became the same in every city. Jay was consistently doing three-hour shows. Even more impressive, Jay wasn't setting these time records by holding the audiences hostage. He was doing it with multiple standing ovations. Jay Leno was the Bruce Springsteen of comedy.

In baseball, scouts looked for a five-tool player who could run, throw, catch, hit for power, and hit for average. Jay was a five-tool comic. He had great material, a commanding stage presence, a unique comedic point of view, and the ability to start quick and stay long.

So it was no surprise that when David Letterman started his late-night talk show in 1982 he quickly made Jay his most-frequent guest. Jay was to Dave what Don Rickles was to Johnny Carson a decade earlier, a killer act who could tweak the host. The secret was out.

Jay was the first breakout comic in the early '80s. As with all widely popular comics, Jay matched the times perfectly. His philosophical approach to stand-up echoed the country's go-go business approach — do the jokes, collect the cash, and get to the next show. His clean, non-controversial material delivered in a take-no-prisoners delivery suited a busy, time-challenged public. His style of stand-up was the template for the first half of the Comedy Boom. What Jay Leno accomplished just in the clubs in that period was enough for inclusion in any stand-up hall of fame.

## 34. "GREAT EXPECTATIONS, EVERYBODY'S WATCHING YOU"

In 1979, my younger brother, Robbie, made a surprise visit to the New York Improv on his way from his New England Coast Guard Base to our South Jersey hometown. Since I was the MC that night, I only had time to give him a beer, and a place to stand in the back of the packed room. As the show continued, a couple of the comics even got laughs by referencing the big guy in the Coast Guard uniform "guarding" the kitchen. Robbie laughed right along with them. He told me later that other comics bought him beers. It was a kick to see my brother enjoying himself at my place of business. And to be honest, I was still feeling new to the New York scene. The comics' treatment of Robbie made me feel a little more accepted.

Things got memorable when I introduced the hottest comedy star in the country, Robin Williams. The crowd burst into wild applause. Unlike most performers, Robin didn't march to the mic. His performance began on the way to the stage. He was shouting, gesturing wildly and stopping to interact with audience members. Usually there was a clear demarcation when the performer took the stage, the applause stopping and then, hopefully, the laughter beginning. That night, Robin began getting laughs while the applause was still strong and turned the volume up on those laughs while the applause faded. The only person in the room not laughing was me because I was completely confused. For my part I stood onstage like an idiot, not knowing what to do. As the MC, I always waited for the new comic to take the stage before leaving. Finally I realized the stage was wherever Robin stood and moved along to my perch near the spotlight. My brother was laughing and giving me a big thumbs-up, surely because of Robin's appearance. It was another nice moment for me, in that my brother got to see me, if not share the stage, at least introduce Robin Williams. Success by proximity. At that point, every little moment like that was needed to tamp my ever-burning fires of self-doubt.

After Robin left the stage, he stood by me as the next comic staggered through the wasteland that an hour earlier was a hot crowd. In retrospect, Robin didn't seem to know where to go next. It was almost as if he was as stunned as the audience by the whirlwind that just destroyed the room. He made a couple of comments, more to himself than me. I didn't know what to say, so I went for the chemical bonding and offered him some cocaine. It wasn't really a risky move. Robin made more than a couple jokes about the "Peruvian marching powder." His frenzied performing style was almost a tribute to the drug.

We started that '80s dance where you pass the coke back and forth until waiting for the other guy to return from the bathroom became so unbearable you both ended up in a stall. For some reason we felt safe from a police bust in the bathroom, like we had smoking pot at a '70s rock concert.

The Improv bar was always percolating with comics waiting to go, and customers waiting to get a seat to watch them. With Robin now playing at the bar, the place was way more fun than the showroom. My brother and I were in the circle. I had the drugs. My uniformed brother had comedy fodder, especially his cap. Robin did 10 minutes with it.

Robin attracted a lot of women. The other comics were doing okay, picking off his scraps like feeder fish following a big shark. My brother sat alone. The uniform was not a chick magnet in 1979, at least not in New York City. Then I noticed a young woman talking to Robbie. After a while, she left. I caught Robin whispering to another woman, who then moved to my brother. Robin and I made eye contact and he sort of laughed, busted. He was a better big brother than me that night.

Later, as my brother drove us to my East Village apartment, he joked that he spoke to more women than I did that night. Coked and drunk, I stupidly told him that Robin told them to talk to him. My brother didn't react to that until a while later. As we both lay on futons in my little studio, staring at the ceiling and grinding our teeth, he blurted, "Shit, Ritchie. Why didn't he tell them to have sex with me?" Oh, the humanity.

I didn't see Robin again until I moved to Los Angeles in 1982. He was still attacking the stage with the same ferocity I saw three years earlier. Performing was by far the best way to grow as a comic. Watching other comics doing it was a distant second but was far better than bullshitting in the bar. They usually taught me something, what to do, or not to do. The only thing I learned from watching Robin was I couldn't do what he did.

Robin was the greatest performer of my generation. It was more than just the skill set of mimicry, mime and quickness of thought and speech. He had that X factor, that innate vulnerability that drew an audience to him. There were always those comics who wanted that laugh a little more. The audiences seemed to recognize that need and gave it to them.

If he wasn't performing as a stand-up, Robin was improvising with whoever had the courage to play with him, usually Rick Overton or Billy Crystal. One night, Robin and Billy were dueling on the Improv stage. Robin moved upstage to deliver a line. Knowing how proximity to an audience affected laughter, Billy also stepped forward to deliver his next. Robin kept moving forward, Billy with him, until Robin stood on the lip of the stage. Billy moved next to Robin to deliver his next line. Robin then jumped into the audience and started working the crowd. Billy good-naturedly threw his hands up, smiled and moved back to the piano and sipped his water. There was nothing for him to do but wait for Robin to return. Finally, Robin realized that in his laugh lust he had abandoned his partner and sheepishly returned to the stage for more play with Billy.

When Jimmy Miller first visited LA around '83, we saw Robin do an hour at the Improv. Jimmy was blown away that Robin could do an hour like that, just improvise it, off the top of his head. I laughed to myself. The next night we watched Robin improvise pretty much the same hour. The jokes weren't in the same order or even done the same way, but it was all recognizable. Lenny Bruce once responded to someone marveling at his ability to totally wing it by saying something to the effect, "If I can come up with five truly fresh minutes out of an hour up there ... That's a lot." Since the Revolution of Lenny and Mort, the art of comedy had been to make the act seem off-the-cuff and conversational. Nobody ever did it as well as Robin. Everything he said or did seemed created on the spot, completely of that moment. It was ironic that the most notable joke thief of his time had the one trick nobody could steal.

That Robin sometimes lifted jokes was common knowledge in the stand-up community. To me it was a combination of his insatiable desire for the laugh and his improvisational style. Anybody who ever dealt with a heckler, or did any kind of crowd work, knew how easy it was to nip a line or two. The success of a line depended on a speedy delivery. Delay is death. The ego grabbed the first joke the memory offered and sent it to the mouth, no matter how that joke initially got into the mind. Robin's whole act was performed in this state.

It's not as if he didn't have remorse for snatching other comics' jokes. He regularly paid comics four figures for jokes when the going rate was a hundred dollars.

Around 1988, a lot of preachers were scaring the flock with talk of the antichrist. I did a joke on *The Tonight Show*, "Everybody's looking for the antichrist. Well, it's not me. I checked my scalp. I got two sixes and a five." A few days later, Robin did the joke on *Saturday Night Live*. Somebody must have said something to him because the next week Robin approached me at the Improv, saying, "I understand I owe you for the antichrist joke." I told him to forget it. It really didn't bother me. Maybe because I had done it on TV first, or that he acknowledged it was mine. Maybe because of his style the thievery didn't seem so premeditated. It was more a crime of passion. He picked up the line, used it and when called on it, paid it. Maybe it didn't bother me as much as other thieves because he was so gifted a performer and such a nice guy.

We weren't friends. I only hung out with him that one time in New York, but people I knew spoke highly of his generosity and loyalty. It always struck me in seeing photos of Robin with other people, especially comics, how they bent into him and the way he returned their affection. I had a lot of respect for him.

Many times a stand-up gets a sitcom, becomes a television star and stop going to the mic. Not Robin. He never lost his lust for the laugh whether he had hit movies, an Academy Award, or bigger hit movies. He was always in the clubs, working it out, genuinely going for laughs. One of the traps of stardom is the temptation to trade laughter for approval applause. Preaching to the choir is a lot easier than making the effort necessary to create something funny. Robin had a defined sense of justice, but I never saw him sacrificing the laugh to make a point.

Robin first hit it big in 1978 with the hit ABC show *Mork and Mindy,* the 1978 HBO special *Off the Wall*, and a Grammy-winning album, *Reality... What a Concept*, in 1979. His stand-up really thrived in the '80s hothouse. *An Evening with Robin Williams* (1982) and his stunning *Live at the Met* (1986) showed Robin still growing as an artist.

In my opinion, he never gets the credit for his influence on the art form. In the 1970s, Robin Williams recognized the audience's shorter attention span and faster comprehension. Technology often shapes comedy. Robin was the first remote-control comedian. His style dovetailed with the rise in America's use of the television appendage. His act was the stand-up version of someone clicking through the channels — a commercial, a cooking show, the news, a movie scene. Robin cut out the segues that most comedians used to connect one unrelated bit to another. He minimized the setup, sometimes eliminating it completely, using a recognizable character or pop reference as the all-in-one setup/punchline. He shortened the bits, making their running order a high-speed lottery drawing and the audience followed joyfully.

The one moment that said more to me about Robin than anything happened around 1989 in front of the Melrose Improv. I was pulling away from the curb in my 1962 Chevy convertible. Robin ran out the club's front door, past a gaggle of loitering comics and dove onto the hood of my car, begging me not to leave him, like some jilted lover. A big star risked physical injuries just to make a bunch of comics laugh, and we all did. He was a funny man.

# 35. "THIS AIN'T NO DISCO, THIS AIN'T NO FOOLING AROUND"

At the beginning of 1979 there were three of the new-style comedy clubs featuring only paid stand-ups, all in Southern California: The Comedy Store in the Pacific Beach area of San Diego (1976), the Laff Stop in Newport Beach (1977) and the Comedy and Magic Club in Hermosa Beach (1978).

These three comedy clubs exposed a hunger for a new version of the post war dinner-and-show nightclubs. In the late 1960s, young adults shunned their parents' supper clubs into extinction. Those maturing boomers now needed a drinks-and-a-show date experience to replace rock concerts.

The non-paying LA and New York showcase clubs were teeming with young, hungry comics. Half a dozen other cities had smaller comedy scenes, also with comics on the prowl for work. As the 1970s drew to an end there were far more comedians than jobs, but within two years comedy clubs opened all across North America and suddenly there were far more jobs available than there were good comedians. The 1980s was a gold rush for stand-up. The old heckle got a new twist, "Do quit your day job."

For example, when Richie Minervini opened the East Side Comedy Club in November 1979, the first show featured the best of the local comics, including Jackie Martling and Bob Nelson, plus New York City's Paul Reiser, Eddie Murphy, and Jerry Seinfeld. Everyone got $10 except Seinfeld, who had done TV by then. All that comedy for a $5 cover.

```
                        RITCH SHYDNER
                       COMEDIAN/ACTOR
                         SAG/AFTRA

Height:    6'1"
Weight:    175 lbs.
Hair:      Blonde
Eyes:      Blue

ACTING:    (currently) Jeff Corey/ Al Ruscio
           (    "    ) Michael Shurtleff

                       Joan Darling
                       Warren Robertson Theatre Workshop (N.Y.)

TELEVISION: "Good Morning New York" WABC-TV - resident
                   stand-up comic 11/81 - 2/82

                "Evening at the Improv"
                     1982 -  Shelly Berman
                     1983 -  Ruth Buzzi

COMMERCIALS: "Maxwell House"
                     February 1982
                     July 1982

CLUB APPEARANCES:

                Catch a Rising Star   N.Y.
                Improvisation N.Y. and L.A.
                Comedy Store   L.A.
                The Comic Strip   N.Y.
              . Dangerfield's
                Comedy & Magic Club, Hermosa Beach, Ca.

OPENING ACT FOR:

                Chicago
                Mose Allison
                Tower of Power
                Spyro Gyra
                Busboys
                Haircut 100

SPECIAL SKILLS:

                Improvisation, Bowling, Wrestling, Swimming,
                  Baseball, Football, Water Skiing,
                  Motorcycling, Bicycling, Marksmanship.
```

Resume on the back of 8x10 headshot, 1982

By the end of 1980, there were maybe a dozen professional comedy clubs nationally. They were small rooms, but paid cash and included airfare and hotel.

Five years later there were probably 150 comedy clubs paying comics more, but housing them in comedy condos, thus saving the club money and costing the comics years of their lives.

The peak year was probably 1990, with maybe 500 clubs nationally, and enough touring comics to service them all. By now the comedy condos were on the CDC watch list.

Then the bubble burst, and by 1995 there were fewer than 100 comedy clubs nationally. Those club owners who dropped the mechanical bulls and the disco balls for comedy during the boom then went into the martini bar and karaoke businesses.

In 1982, a touring headliner generally made between $1,000 and $5,000 per week, most settling in the $2,500 range. The middle act was paid around $400, and the MC, $150. By 1990 the headliner could get up to $20,000 a week. The middle act was getting $600-$800 and the MC $300. You met a lot of openers and middles driving two-year-old Hondas with 300,000 miles.

There was plenty of work in the new comedy clubs for younger comics, but generally not the older generation.

In 1980, I followed 70-something Leonard Barr — Uncle Leonard on *The Dean Martin Show* — into Montreal. I heard he had to be helped onto the stage, but did great with the audience. What always stuck with me was the former vaudevillian's promotional picture offering "comedy, pantomime and rubber leg dancing."

One weekend in 1981, the East Side Comedy Club headlined London Lee, a '60s comedian. It was a stunning example of how fast comedic tastes can change. London Lee had a comedy record in 1967. He wasn't 14 years past his prime, but his style and material were so outdated, he had no chance of connecting with a younger crowd. The first show Friday night, four young comedians literally ran him off the stage. London bombed so badly that he virtually ran up the white flag, calling us back to the stage to do encores for his last 20 minutes. He actually said, "Aren't these kids great?" The next night he showed up with much longer hair, explaining, "I had the wrong hair. I didn't know it was a young crowd." The fresh wig didn't save him from making long lines at the bathrooms again.

All these touring comedians and packed comedy clubs were bound to inspire a franchise, and several arose. It was surprising one of these chains didn't put in a drive-through window in their clubs, for customers hungry for a laugh but without the time to take in a full show.

In 1982, Jeff Schneider and Gerald Kubach opened the first Funny Bone, in Pittsburgh. The "Bones" owners looked for locations in secondary markets, and in short order they were in St. Louis, Virginia Beach, Richmond, Hartford, Columbus, Dayton, Cincinnati, Omaha, Denver, Toledo, Huntington, and Des Moines.

The granddaddy of all the modern comedy clubs, Budd Friedman's Improvisation, didn't start franchising until Mark Anderson opened the first one in San Diego (1984-1994). The rest followed in mostly major markets: Dallas (1985), Irvine (California in 1987), Addison (1988),

Tempe (1988), San Francisco (1990-1993), Washington D.C. (1992), and Brea (1993-1995).

Mitzi Shore never got into franchises, stopping with one out-of-town Comedy Store in La Jolla (San Diego), although she once had her banner inside the Las Vegas Dunes.

Plenty of American acts went north of the border and profited from playing one of Canadian Mark Breslin's many Yuk-Yuk's clubs.

Childhood friends Brad Greenberg and Ken Phillips started their Comedy Zone empire with just a single night of comedy at a club in Raleigh, N.C., in 1984. By the end of the decade, there were Comedy Zones in 75 cities and towns, mostly in the Deep South, but as far North as Burlington, Vt., and even on Paradise Island in the Bahamas.

*"Most of these comedy clubs are run by people who ran the go-kart tracks in the trampoline centers." — David Letterman.*

Music booker Tom Sobel in 1981 started a one-nighter at the Jefferson Davis Inn, in Lexington Ky. Soon, Sobel booked a "Comedy Caravan," where comedians could do 13 one-nighters in a row, and pray they could recognize themselves in the mirror afterward.

In the Great Northwest, David Tribble, another music booker, went to the Seattle Underground to watch comics and unwind from his job before booking his first comedy tour in 1986. "The Spud Run" went between Pocatello and Boise, Idaho, to Ontario, Ore., pop 7,000.

Television definitely helped ignite the explosion. The first Midwest clubs, like Mark Ridley's Comedy Castle, got a lot of comics featured on Norm Cosby's *The Comedy Shop* (1978-81), which ran on the local UHF channel competing with the three news channels at 11 p.m. It gave hundreds of unknown young comedians their first TV experience. Another syndicated TV show featuring Los Angeles stand-ups, *Make Me Laugh* (1979-80) was a huge hit. The Comedy Castle in Detroit could count on a sold-out weekend when booking one of the regulars, including Garry Shandling, Mike Binder, Vic Dunlop, Denny Johnston, Bruce Baum, and Gary Mule Deer.

The basic cable channel Arts and Entertainment (A&E) began *An Evening at the Improv* in 1982 (it produced new episodes until 1996). The shows were an abbreviated version of a comedy club experience, without the cigarette smoke and two-drink minimum. Critical for the television audience was the laughter from a live audience. Most important for the television industry was the extremely low cost. In Hollywood, nothing succeeds like cheap success.

So many stand-up strip shows followed, including *Comedy Tonight* (1985-1986), *Comic Strip Live* (1989-1994), *Caroline's Comedy Hour* (1989-1996), Showtime's *Comedy Club Network* (1987-94), Fox's *Com-*

*edy Express*, MTV's *Half-Hour Comedy Hour* and even a prime-time network show, *The Sunday Comics* on Fox (1991-92). *Star Search*, hosted by Ed McMahon (1983-1995), anointed stand-up champions in the two-minute and under category. *Solid Gold*, *Nite Flight*, and even, briefly, *American Bandstand* featured stand-ups. At the end of the '80s, when the TV shows in LA and New York finally ran out of competent comedians, Showtime's *Comedy on the Road* came along to drag the lake for bodies. If you ever used any of those credits in your intro, you might be an '80s comedian.

The top showcase and most sought-after TV credit for most stand-up comics in the early 1980s was *The Tonight Show Starring Johnny Carson*. One appearance didn't make a career as it did for comics such as Joan Rivers in the early '60s, but it still signified a certain level of showbiz acceptance. Steven Wright was the exception who proved the rule.

The King of Late Night enjoyed Steven's first performance on Friday, Aug. 6, 1982 so much he invited him to appear again the following Thursday, a rarity on *The Tonight Show*. His back-to-back appearances helped put his fledgling career into high gear. He was instantly a draw in the clubs and in theaters, and soon found himself performing his surreal one-liners on *Saturday Night Live*, and *Late Night with David Letterman*, and numerous return trips to *The Tonight Show*. Wright's 1985 debut album, *I Have A Pony*, earned him a Grammy nomination. A fellow comedian once remarked that Wright was a great writer, but a bland performer. A closer examination revealed a remarkable slyness in Wright's performing style. The far-off look, monotone delivery and aimless wandering about the stage all perfectly served the disconnected, trap-door nature of Wright's material.

The fledgling pay cable channel Home Box Office began the long-form stand-up special with Robert Klein in 1975. By the early '80s, HBO and Showtime became the dominant purveyors of stand-up by presenting comedians in their most unadulterated form, delivering long sets with uncensored language. The most influential stand-up showcase in the second half of the 1980s was Rodney Dangerfield's *Young Comedians* specials for HBO. It featured R-rated comics, pulling an end-run on the Carson "Work Clean to Succeed" model. The show gave huge career boosts to Sam Kinison, Andrew "Dice" Clay, and Robert Schimmel.

Comedy is a reflective art form, a fun house mirror of the times. Ronald Reagan was ascendant in 1980, promising a new dawn in America, as in, get up and get to work. No more blowing your brains out at a rock festival and blowing off your job for the next three days. The yuppie work ethic demanded a quick break for a couple of laughs and then back to the grind. This favored comics who packed as many laughs as possible into tight, clean, and safe acts. The two poised to take the most advantage of this climate were Jay Leno and Jerry Seinfeld. They shaped stand-up comedy in the first term of Reagan more than any other young comics. Seinfeld did not take on big, risky subjects like religion or politics, but dissected every topic that interested him with the precision of a surgeon. Seinfeld was a wordsmith as skilled as anyone since Jack Benny in comedic timing and joke construction.

Just behind Leno and Seinfeld was Garry Shandling, who debuted on *The Tonight Show* in 1981 and only two years later was a guest host for the show. He had the best bad-date jokes of his generation: "I just broke up with my girlfriend because she moved in with another guy. I said, 'That's where I draw the line,' and I dumped her, sort of."

In addition to the legion of white male monologists (most wearing the standard sport coat with the sleeves pushed up on bare arms, or a suit vest over a T-shirt with blue jeans and tennis shoes) there were characters.

Yakov Smirnoff was a Russian comedian who provided comic contrast to President Reagan's harangues on the evil empire. Laughing at Yakov's relentless put-downs of his homeland gave Americans a feeling of superiority and helped soothe those Cold War jitters.

Emo Phillips had a sickly look (a pageboy haircut, ill-fitting second-hand clothing and paper belt) and a mind to match. "I don't know about you folks. I have a lot of love for old women going through garbage cans. They saved my life so many times as a baby."

Howie Mandel was a class clown, life-of-the-party type. Steve Martin inspired quite a few comics to become one-man vaudeville shows. Mandel, and crowd killers like Bruce "Baby Man" Baum and Bill Kirchenbauer, used anything — props, funny faces, little kid voices, old gags, and audience spritzing — to get that mighty laugh.

Eddie Murphy started as a stand-up at the age of 15. By the time he was 19, Murphy was offered a contract with *Saturday Night Live*. In his second season, both the show and the stand-up stage were his. He was a crowd-pleaser, not a groundbreaker like Richard Pryor. His HBO special *Raw* was one of the best stand-up performances of the decade. Other black comedians making a name for themselves at this time were Arsenio Hall, George Wallace, Sinbad, Damon Wayans, and Robert Townsend.

There were terrific stand-ups working almost exclusively in the topical/political vein like Barry Crimmins, Jimmy Tingle, Will Durst, Randy Credico and, of course, Bill Maher.

Somewhere in the late '80s, Sam Kinison's rage started a wildfire in comedy. Society had gotten meaner, and some comics mined that dark vein. Comedians rarely get away with anything the audience doesn't want.

Guys who developed a sense of humor to avoid getting their asses kicked were now barking like professional wrestlers after a steroid injection. Someone pointed out that "Tony," Gilbert Gottfried's thick-headed character from Brooklyn, foreshadowed a lot of this, but we laughed at Gilbert's Tony for the knucklehead he was.

Some comics began shifting their aim from the top shelf to the lower. The search for fresh targets led to mockery of the most vulnerable groups. Suddenly there were jokes about the homeless by comics desperate not to become the same. Dennis Miller tapped into the humor of the uppity white man; just a white man trying to make it in a white man's world. Dennis got *SNL*'s "Weekend Update" job in 1985 and took the sarcastic attitude of his influence, Richard Belzer, to a level of unfettered snarkiness that inspired comics from David Spade to Daniel Tosh.

This shift in the audience demographic might have been part of the reason why some of the younger, more forward-thinking comics left the corporate comedy clubs around this time to create the alternative scene. The '70s showcase clubs were the baby boomers' prep schools. Generation X needed new rooms to freely develop their voice. The relocation of training camps was a time honored tradition in comedy — in the late 1950s, comics like Mort Sahl and Lenny Bruce avoided the nightclubs in favor of coffee houses to develop a new style of comedy.

Women broke through as well. In the '70s, Elayne Boosler and superstar Lily Tomlin finally bumped the total number of name female stand-ups into double digits. The '80s saw the number of women push toward triple digits, with as much variety and funny as their male counterparts.

One of my favorites was Judy Tenuta, who sold herself as the Goddess of Comedy. She took a page from the Phyllis Diller playbook by hiding her good looks in order to beat the audience with sexually aggressive material. Tenuta showed how comedy lived in the contrasts — she wore a chiffon prom dress, played the accordion, and talked like a dominatrix.

Sandra Bernhard was more performance artist than comic; one critic blasted her as "the most successful open-miker ever." To me, her stand-up completely obliterated sexual standards and practices. She stripped sex to an angry power play. To a man seated ringside she would take a provocative pose while saying, "I'm very attracted to you ... and yet there's something about you that makes me want to hurt you. I'd really like to smash your face."

Marsha Warfield, from Chicago's tough South Side, had a killer opening line: "I'm a virgin," which helped her become the first woman to win the prestigious San Francisco International Stand-up Comedy Competition, in 1979. Liz Torres, a Puerto Rican, was the first Latina stand-up. Robin Tyler was one of the first openly lesbian comics. Other professional female comics making names for themselves on the '80s talk show and comedy club circuits were Carol Siskind, Margaret Smith, Emily Levine, Dottie Archibald, Pam Matteson, Joy Behar, Lotus Weinstock, Carol Montgomery, Carol Leifer, Diane Nichols, Monica Piper, Judy Toll, Abby Stein, Marjorie Gross, Beverly Mickens, Paula Poundstone, Cathy Ladman, Wendy Liebman, and Carrie Snow. Later in the decade, comics like Andrea Abbate and Felicia Michaels brought a new edginess to stand-up.

The biggest and best was a dumpy-looking housewife with one of the best comedic minds of her generation. Roseanne Barr took the call of *Network*'s Howard Beale ("I'm as mad as hell, and I'm not going to take this anymore") home to her husband and kids. She was the anti-Nancy Reagan, and any man within earshot had two choices: laugh or run. "When my husband comes home from work, if the kids are still alive, then I've done my job."

A couple of older comics jumped on the '80s wave for big career resurgences. Jackie Mason was more popular than ever with his 1988 Broadway hit, *The World According to Me*. In 1981, George Carlin released *A Place For My Stuff*, his best album since *Class Clown*, and, incredibly, produced three more before the decade ended: *Carlin on Campus* (1984), *Playin' With Your Head* (1986) and *What Am I Doing in New Jersey?* (1988).

Because VHS tapes gave the visual performance as well as the audio, comedy records were not as prevalent as they had been in earlier eras. Laughing Hyena Records was one of the only independent comedy labels in the '80s. As Laff and Dooto did in the 1950s, Laughing Hyena targeted a select audience, this time truck drivers. The legendary road dog John Fox was the first comic they released.

Everything was primed for the '80s rise of the comedy clubs and nationally touring stand-ups. Everyone in America drove the same cars to eat at the same fast-food restaurants before shopping at the same mall stores. The taste of the citizenry was being standardized nationwide for optimal consumption of advertised products. Regional differences usually didn't matter much; a Pop Tarts joke in Oklahoma got the same response in Oregon. But it wasn't totally homogenized. Certain references and jokes worked better in one part of the country than another. Jokes about the doughnuts at Krispy Kreme might kill in Atlanta but get stares in Boston.

Mainly it was boomer comics performing for boomer audiences. Comics could score easily with just the mention of a shared memory — a few bars of the *Twilight Zone* or *Dueling Banjos* got laughs. Jack Nicholson became the go-to impression, the Ed Sullivan of the cable generation. There were bits about growing up, so that young couples on the cusp of parenthood could laugh at the absurd child--rearing methods of their parents before finding their own ways to mess up their kids.

In the beginning, the clubs marketed the comics. All the stand-up had to do was show up in order to face a full house. As the number of comedians entering the business grew exponentially and the novelty of a stand-up show wore off, the comics needed to do more than provide an 8x10 or make a hungover appearance on a morning radio show to draw a crowd. Comics hired publicists and started collecting addresses of club patrons for mailing lists. In order to stand out from the stand-up herd, comics began using easily remembered names, like Sinbad, Spanky and Russ T Nailz. Some comics got 1-800 numbers to make it easy for the bookers to contact them.

The new vaudeville created its own personality, the Three-Act Show Format. Like the term "comedy condo," both the East and West Coast comedy camps claimed to have invented the three-act show. Clearly the big city formula, which consisted of a strong personality like a Lenny Clarke in Boston or Richard Belzer in New York City doing as much time as he or she wanted and then handing it off to one top comedian after another, would not work on the road because you could not afford to fly in 20 comics. It appeared that, independent of each other, club owners across the country set a general show length at about 90 minutes (maybe because most movie comedies were that length) and then hired the appropriate number of comics to fill that time.

According to the great Argus Hamilton, Mitzi Shore started out the Pacific Beach Comedy Store with four acts because she thought San Diegan Larry Himmel would introduce the show with a local flavor. Her initial impulse, and Mike Calley's at the Laff Stop, was to just load up each show with what would later be considered three headliners, with the prop or music-bells-and-whistles act going last, or from cleanest to dirtiest.

When Jerry Stanley started his Jersey one-nighters, he hired three comics, asking each to do 30 minutes. Even though the pay was equal, an unofficial hierarchy quickly developed. Either the comics or Jerry decided it, but the weakest act opened and the strongest act closed. The Law of the Jungle prevailed in comedy. The comedy clubs opened and the order became formalized with corresponding time and pay differences. The three-act show — the local MC (15 minutes), the regional middle (25 minutes) and a national headliner (minimum 45 minutes) — quickly became the standard.

Nobody claimed responsibility for the creation of the check spot, which was actually a throwback to the dinner club shows of the '50s. The New York and LA showcase comics of the '70s never dealt with it, as those shows went on from 9 until last call, and the sporadic leaving of customers was easily managed. In the early days of the comedy clubs, the owners put no time limit on the comics, hoping to sell as much booze as possible. But too many walk-outs when the comic unexpectedly hopped offstage led to the creation of a set time for the check drop. Headliners dealing with the dreaded dead zone, when the audience got hit with their checks, learned to tread water with crowd work before going into their big closer.

There were all sorts of theories for the '90s crash — too many comics, not enough customers, club owners got greedy, the comics wanted too much money, the comedy was too dirty, it was too clean, etc. But it just came to down to physics: what goes up must come down.

There were early signs for anyone paying attention.

In 1984 I played the Comedy Corner, a new club inside a huge bar called Papagaio's in downtown Milwaukee. It was a great room with a large, elevated stage and a state-of-the-art sound system with a wireless mic. Milwaukee's best and brightest showed up every night, packing the 350-seat room, large by comedy club standards at that time. The laughs, the booze, and the party favors flowed all week. I told Bill Hicks about this comedy/party paradise and convinced him to be my middle six months later. On the ride from the airport, Bill and I noticed that we were passing downtown Milwaukee. Our driver told us that the club had moved. We finally pulled in to the Silvernail Plaza, a little strip mall in the suburb of Waukesha. The club was between a Payless Shoe Store and a hair salon. Hicks started singing the John Lennon song *#9 Dream*: "Was it all a dream?

# 36. "SATURDAY NIGHT I LIKE TO RAISE A LITTLE HARM"

The Comedy Boom was well underway in early 1982. Clubs were sprouting like mushrooms. Pittsburgh now had two. The owners of the Pittsburgh Comedy Club on W Liberty Avenue opened a second room, Tickles, in the Holiday House in suburban Monroeville. One week, legendary road dog Ollie Joe Prater headlined the downtown club while I played the suburban room. He was an LA comic, whom I only knew by reputation.

Ollie Joe, the former Gilbert Hartzog, was 5 feet 5 inches, 300 pounds, and costumed as a cowboy with a beard, boots, big buckle, and cowboy hat — the fastest joke-tellin', beer-guzzlin', drug-snortin' comic there was. He was a prototypical club act who not only got the big laughs but caused audiences to drink more alcohol than anyone on the circuit. He drank through his entire set, encouraging the crowd to match him swig for swig and shot for shot.

Back then, a sold-out show was pretty much a given. The comic made a hungover morning radio appearance, the club thumbtacked an 8x10 picture of this week's monkey to the front door, and that was marketing and publicity. What really bought an owner's love was selling drinks. Ollie Joe's deal required a club to provide X amount of Quaaludes and cocaine before his first show. The clubs had no problem providing whatever kept the monkey hopping about the cage.

He also had a reputation as a bit of a joke thief. There was a saying about him, "If Ollie Joe comes up to you in the club and offers to buy you a drink, it means he just did one of your jokes ... if he offers to share a joint, it means he just did one of your routines ... and if he offers you a

# WANTED

# OLLIE JOE PRATER

### ALIAS: The Renegade White Man

## OLLIE JOE IS WANTED IN 27 STATES FOR PUTTING AUDIENCES IN HYSTERICS

**REWARD** — IF YOU SEE THIS MAN YOU WILL RECEIVE A NITE OF FUN & LAFFS.

You can catch Ollie Joe at:

the
Comedy Club

2800 20th Street South • Homewood, Alabama 35209

Gilbert Hartzog, aka Ollie Joe Prater

line of coke, it means you just played Cleveland."

On Saturday night, I finished my second show and went to the Pittsburgh club to watch Ollie Joe's third show, and party with the club owners.

When I entered the room, Ollie Joe was killing, but obviously wasted. He swayed to the rhythm of the laughter, with both hands gripping the microphone in an effort to keep the audience from tilting. His nose started to bleed. Thinking it was simply nasal run-off from the coke, Ollie Joe wiped his nose with the sleeve of his white shirt, until it was streaked with blood. Many in the audience were probably seeing live comedy for the first time, but even those first-timers knew that blood wasn't a normal part of the show. A few grossed-out ringsiders voiced their displeasure. Finally spotting the blood on his sleeve and realizing his nose was bleeding, Ollie Joe shot back, "What, you guys don't party?!"

His nose stopped bleeding and to celebrate he suggested everyone drink a shot with him. This was the tipping point, literally. The alcohol and Quaaludes finally overpowered the cocaine. The little fat man drank the shot and fell straight back onto the stage, still clutching the mic and mumbling jokes. The audience now faced the soles of his boots while Ollie Joe worked the ceiling.

Bruno ran to me and said, "We got to get Ollie Joe. You finish the show."

I pried the mike from Ollie Joe's hands and three guys dragged his carcass from the stage. The audience, sufficiently primed by Ollie Joe, was pretty loose and went right with me. It was a circus act; the tightrope walker fell off the wire. Quick — bring out the dancing bear to distract them while we scrape up the mess.

An hour later I watched as three guys struggled to stuff a still comatose Ollie Joe into Bruno's Camaro for a funeral ride to the Viking Motel.

I formally met Ollie Joe about a year later in the Comedy Store parking lot. He easily recounted every detail of that Lost Night in Pittsburgh, including bits from my act. No matter what his condition, Ollie Joe never forgot a good time or a usable joke.

I went right from Pittsburgh to the Cleveland Comedy Club. Their monkey cage was the legendary Swingos Celebrity Hotel, for 20 years a safe house for every visiting pop, rock, and soul star. The staff was deaf, blind, and invisible. The room numbers were gigantic, covering practically the entire door, just perfect for the bleary-eyed entertainer desperately searching for shelter.

Early one morning, I returned from a long night in celebration of fooling the audience one more time. The tour bus for the English New Wave band A Flock of Seagulls was parked in front of the entrance, which was a big glass door. The band staggered through the lobby, still dressed for the stage and probably suffering from their bout with Cleveland's then-seedy lakefront bar zone known as the Flats. The lead singer with the big, teased blond hair was wearing sunglasses and walked face-first into the glass door, knocking him flat on his back. He just lay there on the floor, like a turtle on its back, and finally said, with a British accent, "I've 'ad it wid dis fuckin' shit. Fuckin' 'ad it."

*Rolling Stone* magazine called stand-up comedy the rock 'n' roll of the '80s. For one moment there, as I stepped over the fallen seagull, I felt the power of those words.

The road was long hours of time-killing, only briefly interrupted by work. There were bound to be some accidents. Anything you could walk away from was just a good story.

## 37. "EASE OUT SOFT AND SLOW"

In 1982, I was performing at the Comedy Workshop in Houston when they sent me to a one-nighter in Beaumont. By now, the fallout from the comedy explosion had spread across the entire country. A gravel road circuit of low-rent comedy had formed parallel to the nicely paved highway of the big-city clubs.

First show, I wasn't onstage for five minutes when a guy sitting dead center of the room barked, "Do some nigger jokes!"

It was so shocking that someone might yell that that I just stared at him. He probably thought my hesitancy was due to not hearing him, so he slowly and clearly said, "Do nigger jokes."

I was caught in Lenny Bruce's routine about Shelley Berman and the Chicago mobsters who couldn't believe the comic would speak to them disrespectfully. I physically heard what he said, but it was so outrageous that my brain could not process it. It's not as if I had never heard the word, but to hear it yelled in a public place — at my comedy show — that angered me. I hated the word.

My dad cured me of using it when I was about 10. We were fishing on the Delaware River when I used it. My dad knocked me into the river. When I pulled myself back into the boat he said, "There are only two kinds of people — good and bad."

What was happening that moment in Beaumont was the most extreme version of a scene that occurred a few times in my comedy career ... people assuming because of my blond hair and blue eyes that I might like a bigoted joke. Usually it was someone approaching me after the show. "Here's a good one for you, two niggers ..." I stopped them, even if they managed to clean it up for modern sensibilities, "A black guy, a Jew, and a Mexican ..." "Stop. It's a racist joke." Sometimes, even that admonition was not enough, and I had to explain why. "If it wasn't, then the joke would just be about three guys." Some just weren't up for the lesson and shot back, "But then it wouldn't be funny." That's when I excused myself to go to the bathroom, in the hope that a pee and a little cocaine might erase that exchange.

Maybe all this was playing through my head, but I wasn't talking, not good for a monologist. For his part, the heckler was sick of asking politely to hear some good, old-fashioned racist humor.

Again he yelled, "I said, do some nigger jokes."

My joke-center tried to help me out of a very uncomfortable situation by making this one up on the spot: "I believe people should make fun of their own kind. Let the Jews make fun of the Jews, and the blacks make fun of the blacks. That's why I make fun of assholes."

It got laughs from the crowd ... and me. It was always a real kick when the joke-center surprised the rest of your mind like that. I was happy, but not for long.

"Don't you got some nigger jokes!?" Now he was accusing me of coming to the club unprepared, insulting my professionalism. I went after him. It wasn't hard to run him down; he was short, with an oversized cowboy hat, easily tagged for the audience as "Yosemite Sam." Within three lines, everybody, including his date, was laughing at him. I pounded on him until he left. There were few better stage experiences than chasing a nasty heckler out of the room with mocking laughter. The audience was mine, all mine.

I finished the show and headed for the bar. The club owner intercepted me and hustled me into the kitchen. "Whatever you want I can bring you here."

I wanted to drink in the bar. That's where my worshippers were gathering.

The owner explained that Yosemite Sam was presently out front, waving a gun. "I can't afford for you to get shot here. One more violation and I lose my liquor license."

The last thing I remember was drinking from a bottle of tequila. I awoke in the bartender's trailer, 20 miles out of town. I couldn't get to the airport because the bartender's ex-husband stole her pickup and "cabs don't come out here." She finally called her ex-boyfriend, "... If you ever want another shot at me, you better come get this sumbitch out of here."

I have ridden in a car trunk and been handcuffed in the back of a police car. No ride was as long and stressful as riding with this beaten, angry dog. In between sips of his beer and drags on his cigarette, he glared at me. I didn't know whether I was going to the airport or the landfill.

I didn't stop drinking for another three years, but swore, when it came to comedy, to stick to the main road. Not every town deserved to laugh.

## 38. "THE DEVIL'S ON THE LOOSE"

In late 1983, I ran into something that made me long for the Beaumont experience. Breaking my promise not to do small-town one-nighters — my drinking lifestyle was not conducive to keeping promises, even to myself — I did Tuesday night in a bar somewhere in Kentucky. Most likely it was sold to me as an easy couple hundred bucks between two comedy club weeks.

When I stepped into that Kentucky bar I felt thrown back to those cash-and-dash Jersey gigs of '79 ... A Long Day's Journey Into Slight.

Part of my preshow ritual was to listen to music on my Walkman. It served two purposes: to jack up my energy, and to discourage people from talking to me, thus allowing me to focus on the task at hand. It also gave me an entrance; I'd dance on stage, place the headphones on the mic, and lip-synch a few seconds from whatever was playing me on stage. This night the batteries died before the show began. I don't remember anything about the MC, but the feature act made an impression.

He was dirty out of the gate, opening with the Newlywed Game joke, a favorite stoke joke at that time. On an episode of the 1970s game show, host Bob Eubanks asked the couples, "Where is the weirdest place you and your wife have ever made whoopee?" One of the husbands replied, "That would be in the butt, Bob." It aired one time, but the comic, like every other comic who did the bit, swore to the audience that he had seen the show. The guy worked dirtier and dirtier, nothing original or insightful, just nasty old jokes I hadn't heard since the locker room in high school. Even more disturbing was that the audience ate it up. Just when I determined that at least it couldn't get worse, it did: he began doing racist material, again old jokes peppered with the words "coon" and "nigger," which he probably learned on his daddy's knee at Klan picnics. And he was killing with these. I saw one or two people leave, but I wasn't sure if they were disgusted or merely reminded they'd forgotten to light the cross.

I was furious, not just with the comic, but with the audience. I had experienced the difficulty of trying to make an audience laugh when they didn't particularly like me, but for the first time I experienced the other side of that equation — making an audience laugh when I truly didn't like them. And after experiencing both, I'd much prefer the former. I probably should have just jumped in the car and sped out of town. I have no idea why I stayed. Maybe it was a sense of duty, that "show must go on" mentality that I was incurably infected with. Maybe I held an idiotic belief that I could power-wash them with my comedy. Probably I just wanted the money.

When the MC introduced me I was still angry. There's not much good I ever got done when angry, and comedy certainly wasn't one of them. Over the years I had been angry at a few opening acts, but it always passed as soon as the offender was out of the way. This night the anger extended to the audience, and nobody was going anywhere. I hit the stage, and the longer I looked at them, the less I felt like being there. In no time, I was flatlining. I never had the skills or material to get the laughs without putting my ass into the act. I punished them, and me, with a glum reading of my act. I didn't purposely tank it — there wasn't a plan or purpose in any of it — but the effect was the same. At some point I probably could have switched gears and started hacking my way through a thicket of dick jokes, but I didn't. Instead, I worked totally clean. I probably left them with a good case of comedy blue balls.

The bar manager handed me the cash and said something to the effect of, "We heard you were funny," not finishing his thought: "So what was that?" I left with as much dignity as any comic can ever have, but feeling sick and in need of a shower. The middle act probably went back to his job at the Lexington Sewage Treatment plant thinking he had nabbed the thinning scalp of an LA headliner.

From then on, I wore my Walkman while the other comics were onstage not just to focus, but to keep the audience fresh. Sure, I risked tripping in a field of subject matter already plowed over by the opening act, but that was minimal compared with the risk of thinking the audience was a bunch of idiots, or worse, bigots. I carried plenty of back-up batteries.

In the 1960s, a white reporter once asked Moms Mabley why she worked so blue. Moms gave a one-line civil rights history lesson: "It's you and others in your position who keep me working where I have to use that kind of material." Moms was referring to the fact that black comedians were not allowed to play white rooms before Dick Gregory broke through at the Chicago Playboy Club in 1961.

You can't elevate the audience. Like water, laughter seeks the level of the audience. Comedy is a reflective art form. It doesn't educate or change people's minds, but rather exposes their belief systems. No matter how reasoned the material is, if they don't share that value, they won't laugh. This wasn't my first drink from a poisoned well. Beaumont, Texas, was never far from my mind. Short-money gigs normally lived down to their pay. Since my goal at that time was *The Tonight Show*, from there out I avoided the B and C rooms.

A few years later, I tried to pass along my experience to a friend. He came late to comedy, having been sidetracked by acting and alcoholism. There wasn't much difference between the two, so he split the difference and sold drugs to actors.

When he decided to try slinging jokes, it was 1986 and he was nearly 30. As with anyone else, it would take a few shows to transform his off-stage funny into onstage laughter. I wasn't worried. He was as funny as anyone I'd ever met. So I convinced Mark Anderson to hire him as the MC when I worked the Improvs. My friend did the job and was progressing nicely. The problem was he was a little older, and felt himself funnier, than the middle acts he was introducing. Impatient, he found an arena where he could headline quickly, the B and C rooms.

A comic who wants to succeed in those kinds of venues has to play to the level of the room. All you can do is set the mower low and brush the grass from your legs when you're done.

I advised my friend to stay the course at the Improvs, be patient and work his way to headliner in the A rooms, but he opted to grind it out on the back road.

After headlining a few too many of them he returned to LA, his once-promising act covered with road stink. It wasn't just his material that suffered, but his entire performing style. He'd begun mugging a lot, because dumb audiences need a big flashing sign to know it's time to laugh. He was as funny as ever offstage, but working those dives stunted his professional growth and warped his stand-up. My friend never recovered, and eventually left LA. The hammer shapes the hand.

James J. Thornton was a sophisticated vaudeville comic, walking out holding a newspaper, as Mort Sahl did. One night, Thornton was playing in Wilkes-Barre, Pa., when a young comic on the bill, who was wowing the audience at every show, approached him. "Mr. Thornton, you see what a riot I am here. Why can't I get a date in New York?" Thornton fixed him with a stare and said, "Because you are a hit in Wilkes-Barre!" Same as it ever was. Same as it ever was.

# 39. "THURSDAY TO SATURDAY, MONEY'S GONE ALREADY"

In the early 1980s, the cash flowed into comedy clubs and the club owners did just about anything to keep the comics happy. It was common for comedians to draw against their pay during the week, often to purchase drugs. It was almost a tax-deductible business expense, like gym equipment for a professional football player.

For some comics, enraged and inflamed nerve endings are the equivalent to an athlete's finely tuned muscles.

One Sunday night in 1983, I was in the office of the Atlanta Punchline as the co-owner, Ron DiNunzio, counted out my week's pay. His partner, Dave Montesanto, fielded a call and quickly put it on speakerphone.

John Fox, the ultimate wet road dog, was calling from the Punchline's franchise in Columbia, S.C.

Dave asked how the week went.

John said, "Great. Dave, I need an advance."

Dave shot Ron a puzzled look and then shouted into the speakerphone, "What are you talking about? Didn't you get your pay tonight?!"

John was almost insulted by the question. "Didn't I just say I had a great week? Now are you going to send me some fucking money so I can get home, or not?"

The Legend had spent about $2,500 on cocaine that week.

I hated to work a club immediately after Johnny Coke-seed. The waitresses always had such high expectations, and desperate need to

John Fox

avoid a painful withdrawal.

A few weeks before John Fox died, I called him in hospice to say goodbye and ask if there was anything I could do. John was ready for his last request for me. He immediately croaked out in a weakened but still familiar, gravely voice, "Shydner, you gotta set 'em all straight about that mayonnaise shit."

That was a reference to the classic '80s road tale that the first thing John Fox did upon entering a comedy condo was to go to the refrigerator and jerk off into any available condiments. I laughed at the thought of the old story, and told John that it was part of his legend, like the morning at the Atlanta Punchline comedy house when he exited his bedroom half-dressed and paraded a famous CNN anchor past a couple of breakfasting comics. The version I heard had John closing the front door behind her and sauntering back the headliner's bedroom. Before closing the door he gave the stunned comics a wink, a smile and said, "Yeah. That's right."

"Goddamn it, Shydner. I was in a comedy condo with some young comic and the dumb shit was eating all the stuff in the refrigerator. I told him, 'What're you doing? You don't know how long that shit's been in there and what anybody put in it. Hell, the first thing I do when I come into a condo is jerk off in the mayonnaise jar.' Goddamn, Shydner. It was a joke. I was just trying to teach him something and the dumb fuck told everyone like it was true. Hell, I was getting so much ass back then why would I waste it in a jar."

Funny to the last.

# 40. "ALL THE BOYS THERE, AT THE BAR, BEGAN TO SING ALONG"

In 1983, my first ex-wife, Carol Leifer, and I worked the week of New Year's Eve at the Punchline in Columbia, S.C. The opening act, Ronnie Bullard, brought his new bride, a waitress from a club in North Carolina.

There was a bar, Pug's, directly below the Punchline, where everyone did their post-show partying. One night, the bar owner complained of being short-staffed, so the young opener volunteered his wife to help. She worked there the rest of the week, every night, while the opener sat at the bar drinking for free.

After the New Year's Eve show, Carol and I returned to the comedy condo to find the opener's bride tossing her suitcase off the second-floor balcony.

The opener arrived just as she got behind the wheel of their big '70s Oldsmobile Land Yacht. He tried to calm her, but she cursed him and floored the accelerator. A car fishtailing in a gravel parking lot was always one of my favorite sights. It got better. She ran the side of the car along a stone wall, sending up a strip of chrome and a shower of sparks. The car bounced hard upon exiting the steep driveway, sending a hubcap spinning down the street.

Ronnie watched the car disappear into the night. He then turned to us and with a smile said, "So, where's the party?"

I just knew Ronnie was going to keep doing comedy, but not with that wife.

## 41. "TO THE COMFORT OF THE STRANGERS, SLIPPING OUT BEFORE THEY SAY SO LONG"

*How many comics does it take to screw in a lightbulb?*
*Three. One to screw it in and two to say,*
*"How long is he going to be up there?"*

The worst part of the night was waiting to go onstage once the show began. Some of the stress was simply performance anxiety, the fear of failure. The jokes might not work this time, the laughter might not show.

I heard a story about Sammy Davis Jr. In his Las Vegas dressing room before a show Sammy was pacing, chain-smoking and muttering to himself. Someone remarked, "I can't believe Sammy Davis gets the butterflies." Sammy shot back, "Because I care, baby. I care." I liked that story, knowing that Sammy Davis Jr. got nervous. I also liked it because I cared. Maybe too much, but to me there could be no limit to how badly a comic wanted to kill.

The Sammy Davis story helped rationalize the existence of the pre-show jitters. It didn't help when they hit. Nothing did. I know others calmed the nerves with a little alcohol, or weed, or sex, or working the room like a politician. The best approach for me was to isolate and pace to keep the surging adrenaline from blowing the butterflies into an attacking flock of seagulls.

No matter how many times I performed stand-up, there was always the fear I would take the mic and not be able to find the funny. And by that I mean literally not able to find my act. The mind always went

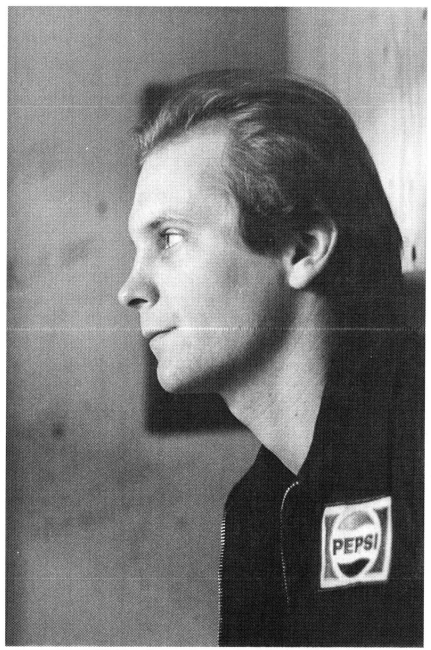

Waiting for another comic to finish, 1980

completely blank just before I stepped on the stage. I could not think of one joke. Nothing came until I faced the crowd and their welcoming applause stopped. Then for some reason I knew what to say. That was one more reason why I wore the Walkman, to distract my mind from obsessively looking for an act it could never find. With all that panic it was hard to relax and enjoy even the most wonderfully creative opening act.

The comics who bombed generally didn't present much of a problem. They usually at least hinted at the possibility of funny. It usually didn't take much to pull an audience, eager to be rescued, out of the crater.

The toughest acts to endure were the middle acts that killed. The physical act of laughing required energy and eventually even the most lubricated and stimulated audience tired. Every audience had a lifespan, had so many laughs in it. Maybe it was irrational but I had this fear the other acts might suck all the laughter from the crowd.

Carol Leifer and I worked together at the Atlanta Punchline one week in 1984. One night I was pacing in front of the bar as Carol rocked the room, ignoring the red light. To be fair, it was not a good fit for Carol. She was a headliner trapped in a middle act's time slot.

Each time she scored another big laugh, I grumbled. "Close with it. Close with it."

The MC, Jeff Foxworthy, tried to calm me.

"Hey, man. We gave her the light. Take it easy."

I shot back. "You take it easy! That's my wife!!"

We managed to stay married for one more year.

In the New York showcase clubs in the late '70s the first act of the night, the MC, was an important position, usually handled by the club's best comics. But on the road, the MC was the lowest paid, and usually the least experienced of the three acts in the show.

As a headliner, I only hoped for three things from the openers: don't piss off the audience, work clean, and stick to your time, and of those three the first is the only felony offense.

I understood that the only way for an opener to reach the next level was to make an impression on the club owner. The best way to do that was to make it difficult for the headliner to follow them. You could normally detect the level of resentment the middle act had for their position by their exit line ... if they failed to mention the headliner by name and instead just spat out an "Enjoy the rest of the show."

It didn't bother me if they wanted to run the headliner off the stage as long as they played by the rules. Since I worked mostly clean, I preferred someone who worked similarly. In the early '80s, an opener getting too dirty too fast usually unsettled an audience. At least give the couple on a first date a half-drink head start before you whip out your first dick joke. But I could drive through any sewage mains the opener ruptured.

My only real concern was time. If the comic ran the light and ate into my time, they heard about it, even if it was in bed later.

By the early '90s, it was a free-for-all. The landscape was littered with Shade Tree Comics, weekend warriors who had no intention of quitting their day jobs. They were hobbyists, looking at a few moments onstage as a good excuse to drink and drug. Glorified amateurs who probably realized they had a better shot at getting laid by hopping onstage than by elbowing for space along the bar with their fellow local losers. Raised on open mics, bringer shows, and Comedy Night at the Thunderdome, they were the unaware taught by the ignorant. They never learned a sense of responsibility to the whole show, just a jackal's instinct to snatch what they could and not worry about the mess they made.

By the late 1980s, I was a veteran comedy club headliner but on several occasions opened for bigger names, such as Jerry Seinfeld, at the Charlotte Comedy Zone, and for Robert Klein, at the Atlanta Punchline. I worked clean and stayed under my time. Coming down from headliner time was a nasty detox for me. Nonetheless, I did my best to help the audience to enjoy the rest of the show ... yet still miss me a little.

# 42. "FUNKY LITTLE BOAT RACE"

In 1984, Sam Kinison and I were hired to perform a midweek show at UCLA for $250 each. I always thought that the pay should be in direct proportion to the gig's distance from my front door, so this wasn't a bad night's work.

The young opening act/agent was driving us from the Comedy Store to the Westwood campus when Sam suggested I close the show. I laughed.

Sam was the reigning comic's comic, not a star at this time, not even close. For a long time, he was locked into closing the Comedy Store show, usually performing at 1 in the morning to three or four tourists too drunk to get out of their seats, and comics in the back of the room. However, Sam was starting to attract a cult following of Sunset Strip hipsters, strippers and metal rockers. Anyone who saw him recognized his power as a performer. As cocky as I was, I wanted no part of following the howling beast.

Stand-ups are a very competitive species. When two or more headliners were booked for the show, the order became problematic. The usual struggle was for the bragging rights of closing the show, so I was suspicious of Sam wanting to middle. About a year prior to this I worked with another headliner in Claremont, who asked to middle because he really needed to get back to LA. The current game and talent show host proceeded to do more than an hour, leaving me to push a limp crowd up the hill. When I came offstage, he was still in the bar.

Sam promised me that the "kids" were going to hate him. I loved Sam, but knew he was a bit of a con artist. I suspected there was an angle I wasn't seeing and balked. He then made this offer: If I was unable to follow him, his pay that night was mine. So I agreed to close the show.

The small cafeteria was only half full, but the young opener pulled them together nicely.

Sam was right. Those students hated him from the start. Here was the Dark Prince of Comedy pulling black clouds onto the horizons of their sunny futures. Sam laughed at their groans and silence, and never took his foot off the pedal, railing against women, charitable organizations, and organized religion. He was a professional, doing his 25 minutes before introducing me in the sweetest, most sincere way possible.

I easily followed Sam. Not that it mattered to either one of us afterward. This was before cellphone cameras and YouTube. The live performance was the most perishable thing on the planet, nothing but a vaporous memory when the applause ended. Shtick and move. You're only as good as your next at-bat. *Out here in the fields ...*

The show was over; it was time to make a scene. Most of our pay didn't make it out of Westwood. I always loved partying with Sam, up till dawn, looking through the Bible for loopholes.

In the summer of 1985, Rodney Dangerfield's HBO *Young Comedians Special* shot Sam out of a cannon. A few months later, Sam walked up to me at the Comedy Store. "I'm going back to UCLA, for $15,000."

That night Sam entered and exited the stage to a standing ovation from a packed auditorium of UCLA students, some of whom surely stared at Sam six months earlier.

Same Sam. Different results. Insanity.

There is joke timing, and there is career timing.

# 43. "FIGHT YOUR SECRET WAR"

*"You don't know what is enough until you've had more than enough."* — *Billie Holiday*

As much as I fell in love with stand-up that first time in 1977, I had already committed to alcohol and drugs in 1965. When I took that first swig of DuPont's ethyl alcohol mixed with lemonade at age 12 magical things happened — I suddenly found the confidence, a sense of purpose, and feeling of connection with people that I had never before experienced.

The laughter I heard and felt performing stand-up comedy did those same things for me. It quickly became apparent that they were competing highs, and that I couldn't perform under the influence. As a monologist, it was important that the audience understand my words easily and clearly. It didn't take but two or three beers to turn my mushy South Jersey accent into an impenetrable swamp. Of course, once I got the mic in my hand and gained the confidence that laughter brought, my natural instinct to try to increase any high took over and I often started drinking onstage.

I did manage to ban alcohol and drugs from my preshow preparation. My plan was to keep them separate, to perform straight and use the alcohol to bridge the offstage valleys. Of course it's hard to build a bridge or even find it when you're wasted. That plan had the sort of success you might expect from a steadily progressing alcoholic.

The stage was the place for all sorts of experimentation, creative and chemical.

In 1979, I was scheduled to open for Robert Hunter, lyricist for the Grateful Dead, at the Cellar Door. I decided to first go camping on Assa-

174

From beer (1979) …

… to bloated (1985)

teague Island with Alice, my girlfriend at the time, some friends, and a few tabs of acid. I was still tripping when I hit the stage, and spent much of my set repeating a fairly nonsensical setup with different punchlines, "God in his infinite wisdom, and man in his infinite stupidity have joined forces to bring you ... the leisure suit. God in his infinite wisdom and man in his infinite stupidity have joined forces to bring you, Spagettios ..." I wasn't getting any laughs with my trippy improvisations, from what was essentially a Grateful Dead audience. Not that I noticed either of those facts. Apparently I kept this up until Alice knocked the needle across my broken premise by throwing a roast beef sandwich at me from her seat in the audience. The sandwich hit me in the head. Pulling slices of the meat off my face and eating them were just enough laughs to get me booked with Hunter a couple more times.

On a Friday afternoon in 1980 I started snorting cocaine with John Cochran, the owner of Giggles Comedy Club in Columbus, Ohio. By the time I hit the stage in front of a full house, the coke had turned my mouth into a waterfall of words. I went through 10 minutes of material in my first two minutes. The whole audience stared at me, slack-jawed. There was not a space for them to laugh, even if they could understand what I was saying. The bar was in the showroom so I proposed a toast to the Buckeyes, ran to the bar and downed a couple of double shots in an effort to slow the word flow. A few more shots were sent to the stage and in no time I needed cocaine to tighten my diction. My solution was to call for a bathroom break. Yelling jokes the whole way, I ran to the bathroom, where John Cochran packed my nose. More shots meant more bathroom breaks. Most of my act that night was performed going to and from the bathroom.

Not long after the great Bob Marley died in 1981, I had a chance to open for one of his former Wailers, Peter Tosh, in Washington, D.C. My friend Rich Hall had opened for them somewhere the previous weekend. Rich told me to stay away from backstage. Before the show he got a contact high and could barely do his act. I just figured that Rich did not have the tolerance level my years of drug usage gave me.

That night I was pacing around backstage and a dreadlocked guy called me over to his group. He handed me what looked like a burning baseball bat. I took one hit off this giant spliff. My marijuana experience to this point had been low-grade shake weed — stuff pulled out of a ditch in Mexico, sprayed with Raid and sent north. Colombia Gold, Panama Red and Jamaican Ganja were just references in rock songs. I exhaled this smoke and time stopped. The next thing I knew, I heard my name being introduced as if I were underwater.

A friend who was in the audience told me later that I was laughing hysterically when I walked onstage and didn't stop until I left. He doesn't remember me doing any jokes. Luckily the audience was just as high as I was and laughed at whatever they thought I was laughing at.

It was around this time that a drug experience gave me a reminder of the power of laughter. One night on a cross-town ride from the Improv to Catch, my friend Mike Cain and I met a cab driver who dealt in high-grade hallucinogens. The fact that psychedelics became a topic of discussion in a 15-minute cab ride had to be due to Mike, who could find trouble in a monastery. The cabbie, who we called Nos, because of his resemblance to Nosferatu, became our go-to guy for all things kaleidoscopic for the next couple of years. He supplied the mushrooms I gave to Bill Maher and Ron Zimmerman for their first trip. Things were going well until their minds expanded beyond the capabilities of my small East Village studio. I tried to warn them that we were in no condition for the public consumption but the vote was two two-headed lizards to one. We headed for a St. Marks Place bar. I thought we might be okay, just keeping to ourselves and playing pinball, but this machine turned out to be the funniest game ever. We laughed nonstop. What I expected might happen, based on an experience with Paul Kozak and a couple of other comics in Pittsburgh a few months prior, happened. Our loud laughter quickly dominated the bar. A couple of local toughs approached our table and asked specifically, "What was so funny?" People always want in on the joke, especially if they think it may be them. It was hard for me to tell them nothing while Ron and Bill looked at the tough guys and doubled over in laughter. I had to tell them the truth. We were doing mushrooms and everything was funny. Understandably they wanted some, and weren't happy to learn we didn't bring enough for the whole class. I had to quickly wrangle my two howling friends past tables of humans quickly morphing into angry demons. Our recurring joke for the rest of the trip was a parody of an old '60s song, "Don't bogart that laugh, my friend ..."

I already knew drugs didn't work for me onstage. It took a little longer to realize they no longer worked for me offstage, either.

But they served a purpose, at least initially. Alcohol provided liquid courage and a social lubricant. It helped those early road experiences. It enabled me to walk in the door of any club in the country for the first time and fit into whatever scene I faced. When I finished a show, I chased that stage high — partying until the inevitable crash and burn. I rationalized much of my drinking and drugging as necessary for the operation of my research and development of jokes.

Pot was probably the most creative drug for writing new jokes, sending my thinking into unexplored places in my brain, until all that was left were the dark corners where anxiety and paranoia waited in ambush.

In 1976, my first experience with cocaine led me to the immediate conclusion that it had to be a part of my life from that day forward. Finding the balance between the alcohol and blackout-preventing amphetamines was always difficult, but my twisted mind deemed it easier to regulate the upper intake by snorting cocaine. Banks helped the addiction by making late-night purchases possible with the advent of the ATM. I decided to deal coke, like an overeater becoming a fry cook.

I bought an 8-ball of cocaine — one-eighth of an ounce, three and a half grams — for $225. The plan was to sell three grams for $300 — a $75 profit, a free half-gram to celebrate. I snorted the half and immediately came up with a new business plan. If I snorted another full gram and sold the remaining two, it meant a gram and a half of Peru's best only cost me $25 — a savings of $125. Again, I was halfway through my new plan when the obvious occurred to me: Sharing the last 2 grams with the beautiful medical intern next door might get me laid. She wasn't home. I decided to keep snorting the cocaine in order to stay awake for when she did return. Sometime around dawn, I heard her door open and close but thought it might be a DEA ploy to get me into the hallway. Later that day after three heart attack scares and hours of compulsive masturbating to daytime television, I ended my career as a drug dealer. At that time my denial was such that I didn't see it as a problem with drugs, just a failure as a businessman.

I don't remember ever being able to write on cocaine, just talk. Every cocaine conversation followed the same pattern, night after night — a couple of hours were spent chronicling every event of your life, then world politics before winding down with God and death before lockjaw set in just as the last line disappeared up a burning nose and the eyes began the frantic search for more. The chirping birds signaled the start of the death march about the living room, the muffled screams of a brain on fire. I couldn't get my mind off my mind.

Cocaine was the least creative drug, not that I would ever admit it. The focus necessary to examine and analyze was impossible. Cocaine made my mind an out-of-control merry-go-round with ideas flashing past, but impossible to snatch, or even determine whether the thought was worth reconsidering. It did serve to jack the performance, sticking a live wire into the monkey's brain and sparking the incessant chatter that might eventually toss out a sequence of words that might pass for a joke.

Alcohol and drugs promised truth, boldness, and freedom but eventually delivered deception, rationalization, and confinement. In 1982 I was working Tickles in Pittsburgh over the Thanksgiving holiday. Jimmy and Dennis Miller invited me to their family's feast. It was difficult for them to roust the vampire for the late-afternoon meal. They took turns pounding on my door before I finally let them into the vault. I had aluminum foil taped over the windows. The room had the rank smell of cigarette smoke and stale beer. It not only smelled like a bar in the daytime, it looked like the clean-up crew never showed. I smoked while I dressed. The Miller brothers pointed out all the full ashtrays, empty beer bottles and cocaine snow seals but no evidence that any food was ever there. They also commented on my sickly appearance. Dennis said something to the effect that I looked worse than the room. I told them I was ahead of them on this, had done the research, and found the solution. I'm sure they were stunned when I pulled the half-dozen vitamin bottles from my bag.

The chemical intake was definitely affecting my career. Around '83 or '84 I was auditioned for a role in a proposed film adaptation of *The Hitchhiker's Guide to the Galaxy*. I felt the script didn't do justice to the humor in the book. As a service to everyone involved I stayed up all night — drinking, snorting and rewriting my audition scene. I'm sure I reeked when I entered the producer's offices the next morning and announced the script sent me wasn't very funny but had taken care of that problem. I always wondered if I got cut off with one of those classic, "Thank you." They immediately hustled me out of the office before the writer could stab me with his Mountblanc. My agent fired me by answering machine — the 80s version of ending a relationship by text.

By early 1985, the alcohol and drugs were affecting my stand-up comedy. No combination of substances produced any new material worth repeating. My performances became angry exhibitions marked mostly by the amount of perspiration they created. My most precious possession, a sense of humor, was MIA.

To paraphrase *Cool Hand Luke*, "I started out real fast and strong ... but I got to admit it's beginning to get to me."

I quit all mind-altering substances on May 11, 1985. Like any relationship that only brings drama and chaos, I had to let it go. The road finally became just stand-up and me. It was different, but not much of a problem — I knew how to avoid all the traps because they all contained old, dried pieces of my flesh. One thing remained the same ... the stage high was the purest and best I ever scored.

# 44. "REVEL IN YOUR ABANDON"

Not long after moving to LA, I became a regular "B" guest on *The Merv Griffin Show*. If an A level guest ran long, I was bumped. Merv's talent booker, Les Sinclair, a very gentlemanly Australian, was great at quickly rebooking a bumped comic. Sometimes, though, a rebooking was almost a guaranteed rebump — like when I was called in as insurance in the event a morbidly obese Orson Welles was not able to chat for a full hour.

In 1983, I started a string that, in just a few weeks, reached eight bumps in a row, a record at that time, according to Les. The security guards waved my '62 Chevy Malibu convertible into the parking lot. Everyone backstage knew my name.

It didn't take long for my sense of entitlement to kick in. I began to believe that my new job was to be bumped on *Merv Griffin*. I'd awaken around noon, lounge around the house until 4, get dressed, drive the 2 miles from my West Hollywood rental house to Merv's Hollywood studios, get bumped, drive home and get a check for about $600. I finally had steady employment, just like dad. And just like my dad, I was entitled to a cocktail, or two, or six, after a long workday. *The Merv Griffin Show* had a full bar backstage, serviced by a bowtie-wearing bartender who lit your cigarettes. This was old-school show business. Each night, as soon as Les made my bump official, I signaled the bartender for my regular, a shot of Jack Daniel's and a Heineken. Then I'd slide a tip toward the bartender who would tap the bill on the bar and wink at me before pocketing the money. Old school was fun.

On the ninth day at my new job as Merv's Bump Comic, I entered the Green Room and my alcoholic brain announced a new plan. "Why

Merv Griffin congratulates me for finally making it to the stage, 1983

wait for a drink? You're going to get bumped anyway." So I ordered a
shot and a beer. Those were good so I ordered two more. In no time the
alcohol had driven me past "fuck dinner" and well on my way to "who's
that chick," when Les entered and announced I was on next. I knew I was
a little too drunk to perform but as an ex-Boy Scout I was prepared for
any emergency. I slipped into the bathroom and took a few hits from my
little cocaine dispenser known as a "bullet." In no time, I was in the
proper frame of mind to do a talk show, confident and talkative, even if I
wasn't real sure of what I was going to say. I knew the set I had prepared
to perform was somewhere in my head but my mind was moving too fast
to find it. Naturally I thought another shot of Jack Daniel's could correct
my over-correction, but Les said there was no time for that.

My set was a frightening experience. I did whatever jokes came into
my mind, mostly the freshest, which meant the ones I did the night before at the Improv, narrowly avoiding doing a dick joke. The biggest hit
from the alcohol and coke was to my physical ability to perform. My
normal poor diction wasn't going to get me invited to any speech competitions, but with alcohol and drugs added, it became difficult to know if I
was speaking English. Onstage that afternoon, I had a terrible combination of a machine gun brain and numb tongue. The words were coming

out fast and slurred. I was animated and unintelligible. It's one thing to work half-lit in front of a nightclub crowd also fluent in Drunkenese, but this was a stone-cold sober *Merv Griffin* audience, filled with hard-of-hearing elderly folks looking for a couple of light laughs before they hit the Denny's early-bird special. The audience mostly smiled. They knew something funny was happening, but weren't sure what.

I drove away from the studio scared to death. I took my usual approach, pouring on more liquor and drugs to disguise my fear as a lust for life.

My managers took one look at the tape and promptly announced they finally understood why I wasn't getting further in comedy: No one could understand what I was saying. They were as clueless as I was and sent me to a speech therapist. That poor guy gave up after six sessions, baffled that he couldn't correct my 90-proof speech defect.

# 45. "NOTHING TO DO, NO WAY TO GO HOME"

My first trip to Alaska was in 1984 to play an Anchorage strip joint, PJ's, booked by my friend David Strassman. The club's bouncer and DJ, Lanier, a big black guy in a cowboy hat, greeted me at the airport curb in his old pick-up truck.

We exchanged names and Lanier pulled a joint out from behind his ear. "Wanna smoke?"

The only rule I had back then was to stay straight until after the show. Once the chemical intake began, anything other than more intake became a secondary consideration and the show became an iffy proposition. I knew I was an alcoholic long before I knew I was an alcoholic.

I politely declined the joint.

He pulled a beer from under his seat. "Beer?"

Again, I declined.

He pulled a pint bottle from the glove box. "Whiskey?"

I turned him down again.

He pulled a vial of coke from his shirt pocket. "Blow?"

I said, "No thanks."

"Motherfucker, you're in Alaska now, you better start doing something." He wasn't angry, just frustrated with my ignorance.

Lanier dropped me at the comedy condo.

The first thing I saw upon entering the apartment was a young, naked woman seated at the kitchen table. She looked at me, snorted a line of cocaine and yelled, "Vic!"

I knew she was yelling for Vic Dunlop, the other comic on the two-act bill. Vic had a reputation as a killer comic and an even better guy.

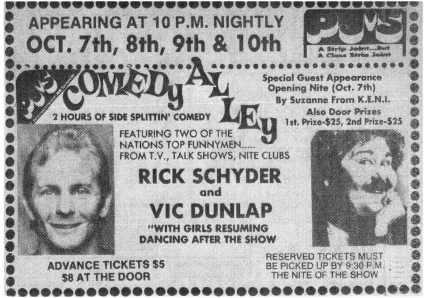

A long week one night in Alaska, 1983

The late, great Johnny Torres told a story about the first time he met Vic in 1982. Johnny was at the Austin airport to greet Vic for his week at the Comedy Workshop. Instantly, Johnny realized Vic's face was familiar for other than his TV appearances. Johnny was sure he saw Vic providing comic relief in a porno, dressed as a Nazi, and brandishing a riding crop while heckling the couples performing sex. When asked if it was him in the porno, Vic smiled, winked, and said, "Yeah, Johnny. I do it all."

Behind me a bedroom door opened and a big, naked man of a comic slammed into the door frame, struggling just to stay on his feet. His voice was as shot as his legs, but he was very happy to see me. "Thank God you're here."

Vic then stumbled backward, and collapsed on the bed.

The man knew how to make a first impression. I had assumed he would close the show since he had much bigger credits than me, such as The Richard Pryor Show and Make Me Laugh. Now I was thinking my gun was getting another notch.

On the drive to the club, Vic, who landed two days earlier to MC hot-oil wrestling contests, tried to explain Alaska. He was a veteran road dog, but had never experienced anything like Alaska. "The license plates read "The Last Frontier" for a fucking reason. It's the Wild West up here, man."

Backstage, all the strippers greeted Vic with familiarity and warmth, or as much warmth as an Alaskan stripper can muster. Like everyone else in Alaska, most of these women were running from arrest warrants in the Lower 48, so any questions about their personal life were answered with the question, "You got any blow?"

About 15 minutes before showtime, the last stripper left the stage and Lanier made an announcement. "We're going to have a comedy show now, so anyone who wants to stay for the show can pay another fifteen bucks. If not, get out, and in two hours the girls are back."

The place was soon packed. Comedy club crowds were mostly composed of couples. This one had a large percentage of single men, probably because in Alaska the ratio of single men to single women was roughly the same as elk to elephants. This probably explained why so many guns were checked in the coatroom. If you had a woman, you wanted to keep her, at any and all costs.

Vic and I loitered backstage with the off-duty strippers, who offered a greater variety of drugs than a DEA training seminar. I again abstained.

Vick pulled me over for a preshow huddle. He showed me a substantial pile of cocaine on a mirror, sitting on a two-by-four in the back of the stage wall. "Here's the deal. I'll go out and intro you and you'll come out and you'll do some jokes, however long you can last, and then bring me back and you can come do a line and then when I need a break I'll bring you back out."

I didn't understand what he was talking about, especially with that, "However long you could last." This guy obviously didn't know he was talking to Marathon Man. "Look. I'll do my 45 and then you do yours."

He tried to explain. "That ain't going to work up here. It's … "

I was frustrated and cut him off. "Let's just do the show, man."

"Okay. But remember." Vic pointed to the cocaine. "This is here when you need it."

Vic walked onto the stage to a lot of whooping and hollering. He quickly had them laughing and gave me a fine introduction.

Taking the microphone, I turned to the audience and came face-to-face with a waitress holding out a large shot of whiskey. I tried to ignore her and start my first joke but a deep, strong male voice boomed, "Drink!"

I tried waving her off, saying something like, "In a minute." The whole room was instantly chanting "Drink! Drink! Drink!" Being especially prone to peer pressure, I drank the shot. The audience roared with approval.

As soon as their applause stopped and before I could even begin a joke, a second shot was handed to me. More applause and then a third shot appeared. I was three shots and three applause breaks into the show before even coming close to my first joke. Fortunately, I spotted Vic waving from backstage. Boy was I glad to see him.

I reintroduced Vic, staggered offstage and dove into the cocaine to level off my free-falling drunk.

Vic managed a few jokes between mandated shots and brought me back onstage.

That's how it went. I did my little joke dance until the forced shots made me bring on Vic, who did the same until he needed relief. When we weren't doing individual stand-up, we improvised and did old jokes together. Somehow we managed to finish the show, but we were wired like nuclear power lines.

PJ's was crawling with crazed oil workers, fresh from eight weeks of isolation on the pipeline. They had big wads of cash, sandwich bags of coke and boot guns. I knew this because they were always pulling one of the three out to make sure it was still in their possession. A Giant Texan grabbed me and said, "You're funny. Let's go." It didn't matter whether it was a group of Vietnam vets in Virginia Beach, or New York City mobsters, tough guys loved having a pet funnyman. The tough guy gets laughter. The comic gets drunk, drugged, and a story to tell.

We walked from the club into the Alaskan winter for a night of bar-hopping. Every other house was an after-hours joint with gambling and prostitution. For a long time, I watched the Giant Texan play blackjack and did my best to earn the free drugs by making fun of everybody but him. I guess the Giant Texan thought a blowjob might change his luck because he said those exact words. The gamblers were five deep waiting to play so he gave me cash and coke and placed me in his seat before disappearing into a back room.

A few minutes later, the Giant Texan returned to see how I was do-ing. The dealer offered his opinion about my blackjack playing. "He ain't betting shit."

The Giant Texan grabbed the back of my neck, and my head sudden-ly felt like a balloon ready to burst. "I'm going to get fucked now, and you better bet some goddamn money, and hold my seat."

I was addicted to everything but gambling. For whatever reason, the pain of losing was always so much greater than any joy from winning. I did learn this that night — alcohol and drugs mixed with the fear of a broken neck made me a silly gambler. I bet on every hand, and won. Twelve? Stand pat. I won. Eighteen? Hit me. I won.

The Giant Texan returned, saw his new pile of chips and tossed me from the stool like a soiled seat cushion. "This is a lucky chair."

When we finally left Satan's most northern franchise, it was still dark outside. Not being familiar with the lack of daylight in the Alaskan winter, I was relieved to be heading home before the dreaded dawn. We passed Lanier in PJ's parking lot. I asked him what time it was and he said, "Seven o'clock." I was happy to be able to have 12 hours to rest before the show. Lanier probably observed my condition and a general lack of awareness, so he set me straight. "Seven o'clock at night. The show's in an hour."

That's how it was for three days.

"Welcome back, my friends, to the show that never ends."

Sunday night, Lanier led me on a leash into the airport. The only security in those days was a metal detector calibrated to detect nothing less than an artillery shell. He walked me onto the airplane, buckled me into my seat, slipped a large vial of cocaine into my hand and said, "This should get you home, brother."

The flight attendant gave me a double Jack Daniel's before the plane was finished loading. Later, she noticed that I was making a lot trips to the bathroom between chain-smoking and whiskey refills. She asked if she could join the party. It was a redeye so no one really noticed her joining me in the bathroom. We tried to have sex, but my dick was just a mushroom cap surrounded by pubic hair. Her only shot would have been to punch me in the stomach and grab my dick when it popped out.

A few days later, when I was finally able to work a telephone again, I called Strassman. "Get me back to Alaska."

I became a huge Vic Dunlop fan that weekend. He was a funny man, a generous performer to share the stage with, and had the stamina of a rhinoceros. I saw Vic from time to time before he died from complications of diabetes in 2011 at age 62, and we always laughed about PJ's. Cheers, Vic. We'll always have Anchorage.

# 46. "I'M THE INNOCENT BYSTANDER"

One night in 1984, two customers greeted me as I left the stage of the Punchline in Columbia, S.C. They asked if I wanted to do some blow, so naturally I overlooked the fact that both were covered in tattoos at a time when body ink was more of a declaration of war than a fashion statement. The three of us soon took residence in a men's room stall.

One of my new best friends pulled out a large Buck knife, dug into a plastic sandwich bag half-filled with coke and stuck it under my nose. The high-grade cocaine immediately numbed my face to the pain from a knife point imbedded in my upper lip. After a few more snort-stabbings, my new best friends said they had some funny prison stories to tell me. They suggested relocation to their place, adding hookers to continue our bonding.

We left the bathroom and headed for the door. The club owner, a prominent local defense attorney by day, grabbed me by the arm and said, "Your wife is on the phone."

I told him to tell her I was off on assignment and expect a call from me in two or three days. The owner insisted I take the call and strong-armed me into the office. He informed me that these guys were suspected of killing a drug dealer the day before, only three days after being released from state prison. Although everyone admired their ambition and drive to get back to the civilian life as quickly as possible, the authorities had the parolees under 24-hour surveillance.

I let the bag of cocaine leave without me.

The morning paper featured an article about the arrest of two suspected drug dealers and killers. At about 3 a.m., local and state police, along with members of the DEA, stormed a house. Inside they found large quantities of drugs, a suspected murder weapon and four women in their early 20s.

Every day for the next week I stared in the mirror at multiple puncture wounds in my upper lip, a reminder that some stories just weren't worth it.

# 47. "IF DREAMS WERE THUNDER AND LIGHTNING WAS DESIRE"

In 1962, when Johnny Carson made his debut as host of *The Tonight Show*, there were three channels on the TV. The other two played old movies. In no time, Carson was the King of Late Night, and for the next 30 years, the most powerful man in the world of stand-up comedy. Cable TV started to bite into the broadcast pie in the late '70s and early '80s, but nobody touched Johnny's slice.

A young stand-up comedian of this era heard the overnight success stories while learning joke structure. *The Tonight Show* Starring Johnny Carson was the launching pad for Joan Rivers in the '60s and Robert Klein in the '70s, Steven Wright in the '80s. Do not stop. Pass Go and collect a career.

At the very least, an appearance on *The Tonight Show* was a marker of show business success that even a comic's worried family recognized.

My first Tonight Show was on Aug. 30, 1984. As a stand-up, this date was more important than my birthday. This birth I did. This birth I sweated. This birth I remembered every moment.

The comic's midwife was Tonight Show talent coordinator Jim McCauley. He decided when the new Jester was ready and what jokes to present to the King. His power was immense in the stand-up world. Whenever Jim McCauley entered the Improvisation or the Comedy Store showrooms, doubt disappeared, hope materialized, and the push for the stage resembled the Oklahoma Land Rush.

After several successful minor-league stints on The Merv Griffin Show and Evening at the Improv, Jim declared me ready for the majors

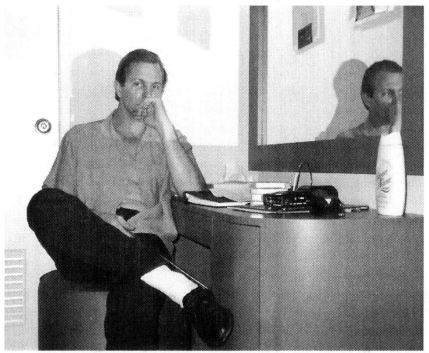

Entertaining a self-destructive thought, 1985

in the summer of '84. He cherry-picked jokes from my act. I then fashioned segues to stitch up the unrelated pieces and practiced those five minutes night after night, word for word, until it became part of my DNA. I even managed to stop drinking and drugging two weeks before my scheduled date. However, the preshow stress caused painful shingles blisters to break out on my right hip and thigh two days before my due date. They could have broken out on my face and I would have performed in a Phantom of the Opera mask.

The day of the shot, my message machine filled with well-wishes. My acting coach, knowing my tendency to speed-talk my way to incoherency said, "Speak slowly. If you're worried you're speaking too slow, then slow down some more."

Jerry Seinfeld said, "You already hit the home run. Just don't trip rounding the bases."

When the applause began after my final joke that night, I did as instructed and looked to Johnny for my next move. He had three basic signals for a new comic. The first was a wave to come do panel, a sign of total love and acceptance. The second was an outstretched hand with the forefinger and thumb forming a circle, meaning a passing grade, nothing special, but you lived to fight another day. That's what I got. At least Johnny wasn't tapping his pencil on the desk, while smiling and nodding to the music. That was the third option, the equivalent of a trap door opening beneath the comic. Few ever returned after getting the pencil tap.

A very happy Jim McCauley greeted me behind the curtain. Jim lived and breathed with the comics he brought to *The Tonight Show*. His job was on the line as much as yours.

As the show ended, McCauley positioned me along the path Johnny took every night from the set to his office. For my efforts, I got the standard reward for most first-time comics, a handshake, a photo-op, and a second appearance. I was relieved, happy and soon on my way to drunk.

My second *Tonight Show* shot was scheduled for February 1985.

This time I decided I wanted more say about the material. Spending a lot of time with booze, coke and Kinison gave me a blurred, but intense vision of a need to be edgy.

My idea was to end it with two jokes about suicide, which were scoring well in the dark, boozy clubs. Jim knew the difference between nightclub-funny and TV funny.

A couple of relationship jokes were Jim's choices for my closing. I agreed, but soon became obsessed with new jokes about Barney Clark, the world's first artificial-heart recipient, and the life-saving technique of defibrillation.

The Barney Clark joke was a reaction to a doctor's assertion that, "Mr. Clark would lead a pretty normal life." I complained that it would at least hinder his bowling game, and ended the bit by mimicking Clark trying to pick up a spare while dragging the 200-pound heart-pump. I then pointed out that the defibrillator caused the patient's body to jump off the bed. Some sadistic doctor was sure to turn up the juice in an effort to set a record height. This bit ended with doctors using two sets of paddles to volley a patient back and forth in a game of tennis.

To me there was nothing wrong with this material. I was getting laughs by complaining and pointing things out. That's what stand-ups do.

Almost every night I practiced with a different closer. The drinking and drugging was by now a daily chore, a tedious job. It was a huge effort to abstain the night before the show. It was not so much as a sober night as the start of detoxification. I placed a post-show gram in the pocket of my show suit, an addict's security blanket.

The night of the show, I begged Jim to let me do the heart material, arguing it was a perfect fit with the rest of the set's jokes of broken bones, doctor advertising, and brain storage capabilities. McCauley was reluctant, doubting if it suited Johnny's taste.

I was a crazed comic begging for his artistic soul, which at that moment meant being the first on TV with a Barney Clark joke. The Devil was bargain shopping.

Jim finally relented.

The set went fine; the laughter coming at all the right places. I closed and looked for my signal. Johnny was tapping his pencil, smiling and nodding to the music.

As soon as I stepped behind the curtain, Jim hustled me straight to my dressing room. He gave me a beer, but offered no pretense as to my situation. There was a problem with my set. Although all the blame clearly rested with me, Jim was the one apologizing. "I should have known Johnny would hate that heart stuff. He smokes three packs a day and worries about having a heart attack. He's really mad."

I drank my beer quickly and looked around for another. Jim shook my hand and left. There wasn't anything that needed to be said. We both knew my second *Tonight Show* was surely my last. There were a lot of ways to self-destruct in show business. My choice of alcohol and drugs was so hack.

I left the NBC Studios with that old, familiar unease of angering Dad and drove straight to the dealer's house.

# 48. "CAUSE THERE'S SOMETHING IN A SUNDAY THAT MAKES A BODY FEEL ALONE"

Sam Kinison was the most influential stand-up to emerge from the 1980s comedy boom. The evolution of stand-up is fairly fluid but some comics are rings in the tree. Every so often, a comic indelibly alters some aspect of the art form, whether it's the style of performing, subject matter, comedic language, or even joke structure. In 1917, Frank Fay changed the game when he wore a sharp suit and worked the crowd with a sharper wit. Mort Sahl sparked a revolution in 1955 simply by talking in a conversational tone about things that mattered to him. There are many other trailblazers who reset the compass heading, but this story is about one comic in one particular time period. Sam Kinison, in August 1985, not only made anger a commodity but also cut a new path to the mountaintop.

Like many an innovator, Sam spent a lot of time alone in the shop. When I arrived in LA early in 1982, Sam was a late-night act at the Comedy Store, relegated to entertaining the show's remnants, three or four tourists nailed to their chairs by drunken inertia. Of course the back row was filled with comedians. Sam developed the perfect opening. The former preacher sauntered onstage and in a calm, reassuring tone, addressing the stragglers as if it were the start of a Sunday morning service, said, "You have seen quite a show here tonight at the world-famous Comedy Store ... a lot of funny people. Some of those names you're going to want to remember. Well, I'm a little different. (cranking up the intensity) You're going to wish to God you never saw my face, because this is the face of hell! I'm in hell!!" Sam then leaned forward, putting his face as close as possible to his victims before unleashing his bone rattling, bi-level scream, "Ahhh! Agggghhhhhh!" The comedy prophet awakened the dead to listen to his dark take on love, parents, and religion. While the comics in the back of the room howled, the reanimated visitors usually stumbled for the exit. Traditionally, the ninth and last act in a vaudeville show was chosen specifically to clear the room. Sam was a latter-day "chaser."

We were always friendly, sharing a Pentecostal upbringing, a chip on our shoulders, and a fondness for all things mood-altering. Like me, Sam was a bit of a pirate. One night at a party at my house, we passed the hat for contributions to the drug fund. When Sam and I got in my car for the short trip to the dealer's, he asked me, "How much we got there?" I counted about $700. Sam smiled, "Looks like we got enough for some coke and a couple of blowjobs."

When Sam walked away from the pulpit he left the Christianity but brought along the charisma. He attracted followers more than any comic I've ever seen, and not by accident. No comic had a greater messiah complex. Sam once "crucified" himself to protest a comedy club banning by covering himself with ketchup and mounting a cross in a parking lot across the street.

He was always on the lookout for new disciples, to provide quick cash (don't call it a loan) or hold his drugs (felony possession). The man had an entourage before he had money and fame. One dawn, as we were about to part ways, Sam teased me, "You could be an Outlaw." It wasn't a sincere invitation to join his inner circle as much as just a drug-fueled show of affection. I loved hanging with Sam occasionally but saw him clearly, and let him know it. "You ride with Colonel Sam at your own risk. If you fall off your horse, the Colonel says, 'Grab his horse and leave him.'" Sam let loose his little laugh that was an odd combination of enticement and warning. Comedy lives in the contradictions, and Sam was a crackling blue arc of electricity between the poles of good and evil.

The summer of the 1984 Los Angeles Olympics, Sam and I decided to skip out on the traffic jams and clubs filled with non-English speaking tourists. I suggested New York and Sam jumped at it. This was his first stand-up expedition into New York City. Of course, New York audiences loved Sam's cynicism and anger. It wasn't just the city. We did a Jersey one-nighter where Sam was practically carried off the stage. It boosted his confidence. One night he showed up at Catch with Steven Stills. Sam was starting to lift off.

It continued back in LA. I remember going on the road for a month, and by the time I returned, Sam had turned that last, wasted slot at the Comedy Store into his own concert. He was no longer just a comic's comic. The typical overnight sensation who was years in the making now packed the original room, which buzzed with anticipation for the arrival of the Antichrist of Comedy. The comics preceding Sam died, bouncing their jokes off a bed of cocaine crosstalk. Sam did not disappoint. He walked onstage like the rock stars he was performing for, and owned the room from start to finish.

With his breakout performance on Rodney Dangerfield's *Young Comedians Special* on HBO in 1985, Kinison led stand-up comedy through an angrier, darker phase during President Reagan's second term. Decades are often divisible. The button-down early '60s became the hippie late '60s. In the early '80s, Leno and Seinfeld represented the bright flash of the comedy explosion. Sam was the heated wind and darkness that followed. By 1985, many people began realizing that Reagan's trickle-down economics meant a steady stream of piss on their heads. Sam exposed that mood. His horned impression of "The Beast" mocked and celebrated the excess and indulgence unleashed during the Reagan era.

Kinison was pedal to the metal from the moment he hit the stage. He did nothing in moderation. Sam was the first guy I ever saw drop the mic when he finished, either in disgust or as an end-zone celebration dance.

His primal scream, honed from years of actual preaching, was Sam's hook, but his fury was his gift. He ripped off the smiling mask of comedy to expose a grimacing prankster. Kinison made anger a commodity in stand-up, influencing those who were to come after him (Lewis Black) and more remarkably, those who came before him (George Carlin). Sam Kinison led a charge of angrier, edgier comics from Bobcat Goldthwait to Roseanne Barr. Virtually overnight many comedians got Kinisized; guys sprinkled expletives over their nostalgia bits about breakfast cereals.

As with athletes, you can only fairly evaluate a comedian by a comparison with their contemporaries. Some current comedians fail to find Lenny Bruce funny. I totally disagree but I understand that sentiment. Comedy is not a good time traveler. At least consider Lenny Bruce from a historical perspective and contrast what he was doing with what the rest of the comedians did in the late 1950s and early '60s. While most everyone else was still doing cookie-cutter jokes about women drivers and mothers-in-law, Lenny was attacking religious institutions and social dogma. Nobody was talking about sex and religion. Lenny was the equivalent of archaeologists digging up a Stone Age village and finding a Maytag washing machine. To truly understand Sam's impact, you have to put him in the context of the comedy scene at that time. Nearly everyone was doing nice, clean comedy, trying to get on *The Tonight Show*.

As for his material, Kinison had the goods to back up the onstage intensity. His classic "African Aid" routine was a chainsaw at a pajama party. While every other comic did jokes about the star-studded recording session for the song *We are the World*, Sam went for the source, uncovering the public's frustration with the world's endless problems, and our pathetic attempts to solve them.

Sam went to places no one else went, even with his heckler lines. "I only wish I had a list of your sacred dead, so I could wipe my fucking ass with it!" He didn't bother with clever put-downs, he just threw the offender into the lake of fire, and the rest of the sinners sought redemption with laughter.

Shock humor seeks a constantly moving target; each bit of outrageousness shifts the line. There is no rest for the wickedly funny, because once you've decanted the unthinkable, you need to find the next taboo to expose and mock. Sam faced that truth with his necrophilia routine. It was the most outrageous bit of the era and he worried with good reason that he might never equal it. The edge is a hard line to hold.

The problem with being a trailblazer is it's never your path to own for long. Sam allowed himself to be distracted by comics whom he felt stole from him. Andrew Dice Clay surely was influenced greatly, but not Bobcat Goldthwait, who was an original, the first punk comedian. Even though Bobcat also yelled his punchlines, his was more a tortured cry of adolescent pain and confusion. These showbiz dust-ups are ultimately just another form of entertainment, schoolyard shoving matches this time attracting a crowd of reporters. And as with all showbiz feuds, like that between Fred Allen and Jack Benny in the 1930s, the result was more publicity for all parties. Sam, Dice and Bobcat all got tremendous amounts of air time on the most popular morning radio show in America, *The Howard Stern Show*.

Sam also showed a new path to the mountaintop. Every stand-up comedian has a following of some size hidden in the general population; the question is how to get on their radar screen. Since the late 1940s that answer has largely been network television. Before Sam's breakout on the *Rodney Dangerfield Young Comedians Special*, cable giants HBO and Showtime largely featured established acts like Robert Klein, Robin Williams, and George Carlin. Sam changed that. He was the first comic to use cable TV as a springboard to stardom, and in doing so took the pressure off working clean for quite a few comedians, including the earthy Robert Schimmel.

Sam was one of the first comics from our generation of stand-ups to become famous, surely the first that I knew fairly well and shared time with in the trenches. He taught me a few lessons about stardom. Not that I ever needed to use them.

When he first started, Sam flashed a lot of anger onstage, but it was obviously a defense mechanism. Onstage, Sam played the underdog, the chubby little guy who had been pushed around for too long and was now fighting back. It was funny.

He was sort of a generational answer to Rodney Dangerfield, but Sam wanted revenge, not respect. His material on women clearly showed frustration, but also that necessary vulnerability. I saw a shift when he became famous. Sam became more of a bully onstage and off. I know some of it was the booze and coke, but I think some of it was an adjustment to fame.

Some erratic behavior when a performer first hits that rarified air of stardom is predictable and understandable. I imagine the view from up there must be dizzying at first. My theory was that for those who thought fame and fortune would fix them — fill that empty hole in their gut and make all the wrongs in their life right — the realization that it didn't do any of those things must be more than a bit disconcerting. If fame couldn't fix it, what could?

Sam got a little mean. I confronted him one night and his response was basically, "You don't understand. It's all fucked. Nothing is going right." He was playing big venues to adoring crowds for big money and nothing was going right.

Ambition is necessary to make it, but it can be a corrosive stimulant. Somehow you need to learn to be happy wherever you are because the ambition is never quieted, never soothed. There is nothing but discontent when comparing yourself with others. In the beginning the comic says to himself, "If I could just become a regular at the Improv, everything would be okay." He becomes a regular and then it's, "If I could just get a great weekend spot. If could just get a *Tonight Show* shot. If I could just get role on a sitcom. Just get my own sitcom. Just get a movie. If I can just get offered scripts. Why can't I get to see the scripts before (insert hottest movie star here)?"

When I got sober in 1985, obviously I was no longer hanging with the Dark Prince of Comedy. Sometimes I would make a brief appearance at Sam's weekly Sunday night Comedy Store show. Sam knew I was sober and playfully called me his "double agent from God." One night my friend Mike MacDonald and I were sipping our Cokes and enjoying the scene when we noticed a very agitated Mitchell Walters circling our table. He was not directly engaging us, just eyeballing us. We mentioned it to Sam, who dismissed it as coke paranoia — Mitchell worried that we now worked for the DEA. Sam then walked to Mitchell, locked his arm around Mitchell's neck and dragged him to our table. While Mitchell struggled to escape, Sam pointed to Mike and me: "See, Mitchell? They have no power here. We rule the night." We all laughed until Sam finally released Mitchell, who took off, probably heading straight for a bathroom stall.

Before he died, Sam was trying to get sober. His biggest fear was that he had peaked artistically. Specifically, that he had painted himself into a comedic corner with a bit like the necrophilia mortician, and might never be able to top it. I told him the same thing I told Bill Hicks. There's no denying that alcohol and drugs can bring bursts of creativity — Bill even did material about some of the great art produced under the influence. But after he got sober, Bill took his comedy to another level and I felt that sobriety would bring new energy, new vision, and new material to Sam too.

Sam Kinison died in April of 1992 driving to a gig in Laughlin, Nev. A drunk driver hit his car, ironic because Sam had a famous routine justifying drunk driving.

Like Kurt Cobain and Jimi Hendrix, it was impossible to say whether Sam had another great comedy album in him. One thing is certain; he sure shook it up while he was here. Some are meant to be rockets, screaming and exploding in the night sky.

## 49. "MAN, YOU'VE BEEN A NAUGHTY BOY, YOU LET YOUR FACE GROW LONG"

Some comics liked to work the audience before they hit the stage. They kibitzed with the people standing in the line outside, and hopped from table to table once the room filled. Maybe these comics figured it's never too early to get a little audience goodwill or establish their funny. Generally, because of either shyness or superstition, I kept a distance, saving that first impression for those first steps under the lights. There were also periods when I probably hoped to hide my personal problems until they might be obscured in a joke fog.

In 1984, after my *Tonight Show* debacle, I traveled to Lubbock, Texas, to open a new comedy club, the Laughing Stock of Texas.

My first night went well, which at the time meant that the audience laughed, and then I met a local drug dealer. I partied at his house until the club owner tracked me down the next day to do a 4 p.m. interview with a local television station. He drove me straight to the club, where I did the interview in my stage outfit from the previous night, clothes now made 4 pounds heavier with smoke and sweat.

I sat on the edge of the stage for the interview. As soon as the reporter and camera crew left, I fell back onto the stage and passed out.

Sometime later, a waitress prodded me awake. "Sir, you have to get up now."

This week the Alamo was in Austin, 1985

I sat up and stared into the faces of a packed house.

Maybe the look on my face indicated that I still didn't fully grasp the situation because the waitress continued, "Sir, we have to start the show."

I stumbled through the crowd.

Some of the audience had to be surprised when the drunk shooed off the stage returned a short time later to perform on it. My personal problems were front and center for the crowd, and the club staff.

The manager reacted quickly when I wasn't in the club for the start of Saturday's show. Fortunately I was staying in the motel next door. The opener was sent to check on me. Allegedly, I opened the door naked with beer in hand, inviting the young comic to wait in the room while I dressed. On the bed was the mirror from the wall, covered with lines of cocaine. Under the bed's covers was the club waitress, who had called in sick. Again, reportedly, it took a long time for me to dress since every article of clothing put on deserved a celebratory line of cocaine, cigarette and beer. The show was what you might expect from a tired, bloated, drugged-out comic. I would have been the perfect opener for Elvis' last days.

After Lubbock was finished with me, the next stop of my Dragging the Lake Tour was Huntsville, for a show at the annual Texas Prison Rodeo. My opener was a tall, young black comic with orange hair, parachute pants and a long feather earring, Sinbad.

From there we drove the rental car to a couple more one-nighters on our way to the Austin Comedy Workshop. Sinbad was enthusiastic about his new career in comedy and extremely gregarious, making friends wherever we went. He started talking about five minutes before he got up in the morning and didn't stop until five minutes after he fell asleep. My hangovers were lasting until show time. I barely had enough words for the stage.

It didn't take long to see Sinbad had a real gift for stand-up. His outsized personality made jokes superfluous. The saying, "The jokes are just something to say while you're being funny" was never more apt. Sinbad loved being onstage and the people loved him being there. He had a smile, a swagger and a laugh that was contagious.

For the first time, I struggled to follow a middle act. Sinbad kept to his allotted time, did his own material, worked squeaky clean and killed it in 25 every night.

I spent a lot of stage time talking about drinking and drugging, but as if it was a prison sentence not a party. My notebook was filled with whiny complaints and unfinished thoughts. "Booze is a Grizzly Bear. Cocaine is a cobra. Pot is a python." Half-finished jokes were delivered half-heartedly to the audience.

I was shot mentally, and physically. I ran all night with the party crowd while Sinbad saved his party for the crowd. I tried to rev the engine and hit the stage running but my crankcase was filled with sludge.

Up to this point I was pretty good at compartmentalizing my offstage and onstage lives. But walls were crumbling. My personal life was a dark star, sucking the laughs from my act.

After the last show of the week, everyone went to a bar. I sat there bloated with drink and blow, unable to take my eyes off Sinbad. He joked and laughed and drank only Coca-Cola.

Sinbad was still having a good time, reveling in the joy of making people laugh, wherever he was. My feeling of loss was enormous. I was tanking stand-up comedy; the one thing that put me in the moment, eased all my doubts and made me feel connected to people.

No doubt, alcohol and drugs had blown off the door of my cell and released me from a lot of childhood fears and inhibitions. I don't think I could have danced without them. Then one day they turned on me and I awoke on Donkey Island. My liberators had become my captors. The alcohol and drugs robbed me of my most valuable possession, a sense of humor. Suddenly the reason for that difference between Sinbad and I became obvious. It was not skin color, or age, but the fact that Sinbad was stone-cold sober.

Other people, most notably Brett Butler, said things to me about my drinking and drugging along the way but I never listened to any of it. For whatever reason, and no intention to do so, Sinbad was the one to pull back the curtain on the Wizard ruining my life. It was just lifting my foot to take that step in a new direction, but ultimately the most important one I ever took.

# 50. "LIVING JUST A LITTLE, LAUGHING JUST A LITTLE"

I
n 1979, Robin Williams popped into the New York Improv to do a guest set. He was the hottest stand-up in the country and the crowd gave him his due, welcoming him with a standing ovation. To say he killed did not come close to describing what he did to that audience. Every word, every gesture, every facial expression convulsed the audience. If he stepped back and put his hand on the piano, they laughed. This went on for about an hour. When he finally left the stage to another standing ovation, the MC/me had to face the debris, now more a chattering town-hall meeting than comedy audience. I paid some dues for a while before bringing up the next act so he could pay some too. When I returned to my MC perch, Robin was still there. His eyes scanned the crowd, with a look of consternation on his face. He said to no one in particular, "I don't know what's funny anymore." At that point he must have been experiencing that night after night, a dream to be the funniest turned into a nightmare — if they laugh at everything, then nothing is funny. This would have been a great *Twilight Zone* episode. I didn't say that, or anything. I was just getting the feel of getting on a roll.

I never would have the pleasure of feeling the pain of killing too hard.

Comedian Scott Record told me a story of when he was opening for Rodney Dangerfield at the Carlton Celebrity Theater in Bloomington Minnesota in 1982. They stayed at a large suite in a health club, with a big living room and two bedrooms. At 3 a.m. one morning, Scott was watching

TV in the living room when Rodney came out of his bedroom, holding a stack of papers containing submitted jokes. Tears ran down Rodney's face as he flipped through the pages. Finally, Rodney looked at Scott and said, "I don't know, man. I tell you. I just don't know what's funny anymore." Finally Rodney threw down the papers and went to bed.

Richard Pryor, at the peak of his powers in the late 1970s, once told an interviewer about aborting a Hawaiian vacation after only one day. One of the greatest stand-ups of all time scampered back to LA because he feared if he wasn't onstage every night he would "lose it."

Losing the funny is a comic's biggest nightmare. Self-doubt is both the drive and curse of all artists. Getting the levels right requires daily calibration.

The gift of comedy is a nebulous thing. Perhaps most infuriatingly, in order to keep it, you must give it away to strangers who then tell you whether you still have it.

Everyone in the business has seen the wrecks on the side of the road, formerly funny people who could no longer turn the trick. The first question is always, "How did it happen?"

Success seems to destroy the funny as easily as failure. Comics operate on a delicate blend of self-centeredness, hunger, and humility. A big, fat bank account and a thousand pats on the back can wipe away a need to please while leaving the ego intact.

Age may be the No. 1 destroyer of the funny. Comedy requires buoyancy. The effective stand-up floats above the frustration and anger, which is at the core of every joke. Age brings responsibility. Marriage, kids and mortgages carry weight. The burdens of life can drag a comic into a boiling cauldron of resentment, turning a light and funny fuming into a bitter and grave rant.

An 1871 review in a Brooklyn newspaper claimed Mark Twain was not as funny as he had been the first time he came through town. The reporter offered possible reasons for Twain's slippage: "He isn't a bit funny now he's married ... He's got a baby and that takes all the humor out of him."

In May 1985, I found another way to lose the funny when I completely quit drinking and doing drugs. For the first time since age 12, I was without my sidekicks, and missed them badly. Rehabs were not so much a part of the recovery process then, so instead of spending that first messy month in a safe cocoon, I physically and emotionally detoxed from 20 years of chemical abuse on the Improv stage.

One of the reasons to quit drinking was losing the ability to laugh. I heard other people laughing but no longer got the joke myself. It seemed the party was over.

Since the start of my career I had worked every day to have new material for my show. If not a complete joke, the daytime effort always produced at least a premise that made me excited to grab the mic. Sometimes the ideas came while I was dozing or driving or even fucking, but they always appeared. All of a sudden, they stopped. For days and days, nothing came into my head that seemed even remotely funny or worth talking about.

There was no refuge in my old act. Without a new joke, all of the material that had worked so well a month ago was incomprehensible, completely unfunny. I no longer knew how to assemble the old bits into a set, as if the instructions were suddenly in a foreign language.

Every night I walked onto the Improv stage only to flounder for a few minutes before apologizing and abruptly exiting. Sometimes I angrily tossed the microphone and stomped off without saying much of anything.

One night, I was working hard to transform the Improv into a tragedy club and in the audience sat a man who later became one of my best friends. Tony Vicich, a former drug-addicted drug dealer making the transition to a laugh-addicted joke dealer, managed to find something funny and let loose with a loud laugh. I snapped at him, "What are you laughing at?!"

Thank goodness Budd Friedman kept giving me spots.

I was sleeping too little and smoking too much but I never quit going to the Improv.

Luckily, I was running one day and a new joke came into my head, all in one piece.

I couldn't wait to get to the Improv that night. In the past an untested bit was slotted into the middle of a set, to be cushioned on either side by laughter. That night I opened with this new joke.

"I don't care how much you love each other. How much you need each other. There are going to be those moments in any particular day where one minute you're thinking to yourself, 'I want to spend the rest of my life with you.' And your next thought could be, 'How can I fake my death?' "

The audience laughed and gave me back my funny.

# 51. "HOCKED ALL MY YESTERDAYS, DON'T TRY AND CHANGE MY TUNE"

**B**y early 1986, about nine months after I totally quit drinking and drugging, the laughs were louder, the rolls longer, the applause more sustained. A couple of comics, not surprisingly former party teammates, actually told me that I wasn't as funny after stepping off the downbound train. Maybe recognizing that alcohol and drugs nearly took me down would have forced them to look at their own behavior. Maybe, with the same fear-based cynicism that made it entertaining to watch another comic bomb, they had enjoyed watching me skid off the road. Their opinions didn't matter to me. I told them I was no longer willing to die for their sins.

One night, Jim McCauley approached me after a set at the Melrose Improv. He was impressed with my new attitude and material and told me another *Tonight Show* appearance was possible. He called his friend Les Sinclair at *The Merv Griffin Show* to arrange a rehab assignment there. Another shot at *The Tonight Show* was not the reason I got sober, but I saw this as a nice little flower along the path I was trudging.

The night of my *Merv Griffin* appearance/*Tonight Show* audition, Les said something strange as we walked to the stage. "I know I didn't mention this, but ... our audience ... well, almost all of them are from a Jewish retirement home."

"Don't worry, Les." I was a little confused as to why that was relev-

Tonight Show redemption, 1986

ant to my safe little set of jokes about driving, children and fashion.

With that Les led me behind the curtain where I watched Merv finishing his chat with the actress Dyan Cannon.

"All right, Dyan, you got, you got a movie here you want to talk about?"

"Merv. I felt so strongly about this movie that I cut my hair." She barely restrained her big actress tears. "It's called *Jenny's War* ... the story of a woman trying to rescue her son from a German prisoner-of-war camp."

They then played a clip of a Nazi officer roughly interrogating the second-most recognizable Los Angeles Lakers fan.

The clip ended. Merv said, "All right, that's great. Terrific work, Dyan. We'll be right back."

The commercial break proved to be the exact amount of time necessary for the audience to remember all the loved ones lost to the Holocaust.

Merv introduced me to the shell-shocked audience.

A tall, blond-haired, blue-eyed man with the last name of Shydner entered to the minimum amount of applause to be considered a smattering. I might as well have goose-stepped onto the stage.

I wanted to tell the audience my family fought for the Allies, that I was a big supporter of Israel, and married to a Jewish woman. Instead, I launched into my first joke. It got nothing, not one laugh. Through the silence I thought heard a few people sobbing.

Into my fevered brain came a cooling thought — someone once told me said that if a joke didn't work on television, just smile at the camera for a moment so they could later fill that space with canned laughter.

For that failed joke, and every one that followed, I grinned and paused after the punchline before launching the next into the abyss. I was never much for smiling when the laughter flowed. Mustering a fake smile when joke after joke was sent to the slaughterhouse felt painful and blasphemous.

Naturally, the gaps between jokes became a bit shorter with each fresh blast of silence. I felt like a man performing in a glass coffin. The weight of the dead jokes sank me deeper and deeper. It had become quickstage. I kept banging the jokes and smiling to the end. Then I thanked them, waved and left to the sound of Merv's lonely applause. It had been a frightening five-minute metamorphosis. I walked onto the stage 6 feet and 1 inch of comedic confidence, only to return a baffled cockroach.

Les tried to steady me. "I didn't want to tell you beforehand about the movie because I was worried you'd lose your confidence. Don't worry. We'll sweeten it in post."

Les was a good guy in an impossible situation that night. It was his responsibility to get the comic to the stage on time. There was no way for him to bulletproof a confidence solely dependent on laughter.

I drove back to my tiny West Hollywood apartment totally convinced that there was no future for me on television, certainly not on *The Tonight Show*. Some of my new friends said I had shown up and done my job, and that the results were out of my control, always. The most important thing they added was that I not drink or drug over it. I didn't sleep well for a couple of nights, but I hung with my new friends and stayed sober.

A few days later Jim McCauley approached me at the Melrose Improv to tell me he heard about my *Merv Griffin* appearance. Before I could excuse myself to quit the business, he continued. "What a mess ... but you didn't bail or blame the audience. You handled it like a total pro. I want to give you another shot with Johnny." It was a great lesson. What I had thought was the end of the line was actually a new beginning. I went from a guy who had always seen the glass as half empty, cracked and leaking to a guy who did his best to ignore the glass.

In 1986, my third *Tonight Show* went so well that I did 11 more until Johnny retired in 1992. One of those shots made it onto the DVD of *The Tonight Show*'s Greatest Stand-up appearances. That *Merv* was the best bombing I ever had.

I finally watched a tape of the *Merv* appearance. The canned laughter was indeed added after each and every failed joke. The problem was when the camera cut away to the audience. In direct contradiction to the sound of the happy laughter was the sight of a studio full of stressed and stunned old people. In that way the *Merv* bombing actually ended up being very funny.

I never did fully thank Jim McCauley for what he did for me, and a lot of other comics, in his 25 years at *The Tonight Show*. Rest in peace, Jim.

# 52. "I'M GONNA RIDE THE SERPENT"

The day after my third appearance, my comeback shot, on *The Tonight Show*, Phyllis Diller shocked me with a phone call. She told me that she saw the show and had to talk to such a funny man. At first I didn't believe it was her. I asked her how she got my number. She did her patented laugh and told me to call her Phyllis. That phone call was just a goof for her, but it was a lot of validation for me. I grew up watching this lady on television. My dad loved her. Whenever she was on, my dad would have one of us turn up the volume on the TV and then laugh like crazy. I knew what was funny before I ever got the joke, and Phyllis Diller was funny.

Over the years she sent funny cards, had me over to her house and usually called after a TV appearance. The phone conversations were the best. "I give great phone, honey." And advice. She gave great advice.

That first phone call, she told me, "That man-woman thing is yours, honey. That got the biggest laughs tonight, so do more of that. Whatever they like the most — always do more of that." It was basically the same thing Rodney told me. If two of the all-time greats tell you something, bank it. One of Phyllis' favorite themes was eating shit. "You have to eat shit in this business. You have to learn to like eating shit." She would call and get right to it. "You eat any shit today?" She loved swapping showbiz horror stories, especially hell gigs.

I know it wasn't just me. I have heard countless stories of Phyllis calling comics out of the blue, being nice to comics on every level of the showbiz hierarchy. As friendly as we got, it was always on my mind that I was talking to a showbiz legend.

We shared an interest in the history of stand-up comedy. She encouraged me to write a book, even sending me a note after one long discussion. It's hard to fathom today, how important Phyllis Diller, or Ms. Diller as she insisted on being called by everyone but friends, was to that story.

When she took the stage in 1955, at age 37, with a chronically unemployed husband and five children, Ms. Diller wasn't looking to be a trailblazer, just a breadwinner. Taking the stage as a solo act during World War II, Jean Carroll was undoubtedly the first female stand-up, but Phyllis Diller was the first star female stand-up, the first to make the whole country laugh.

When Ms. Diller took the stage at San Francisco's Purple Onion in 1955, there were only a few scattered women barely scratching a living on the outskirts of Stand-upville. Post-war America saw a return to traditional gender roles. Rosie the Riveter was replaced by Betty Crocker. Women in the 1950s had little authority outside of the home. In the rawest terms, making someone laugh is powerful, their laughter an act of submission. Even today some men aren't willing to give in, finding women unfunny. For a woman in the 1950s to take the stage and control the sense of humor for a packed nightclub was just too radical to be considered possible, but Phyllis shattered that glass ceiling with laughter. By 1965, she was as big as any of the boys and inspiring younger women to do it.

She created a devastatingly effective stage look. By hiding her good figure beneath clownish outfits Ms. Diller neutralized both the baser male instincts and any competition with other women. It was absolutely key for that era, if audiences were to hear her at all.

What they heard were one-liners delivered in the machine gun, barely-let-them-up-for-air style of her hero and mentor, Bob Hope. She developed a distinctive, braying laugh to punctuate the punchline or goose the audience to laugh.

Ms. Diller's true subversive side can be found in her jokes. Women in the 1950s were expected to raise perfect children on nutritious meals in spotless homes. Phyllis Diller turned "My wife can't cook" jokes into "I don't clean, either" jokes like, "Housework can't kill you, but why take the chance?" Men were the strong, unchallenged breadwinners. Ms. Diller chopped them all down to size with a barrage of jokes about her lazy, unromantic, beer-guzzling husband, "Fang." It is rather ironic that at the same time Mort Sahl and Lenny Bruce were conspicuously changing the discourse in stand-up comedy, Phyllis Diller was leading a one-woman charge up the other side of the hill. As a stand-up comic, this alone is enough for me to love and respect her. Then she made it personal. Thank you, Ms. Diller.

# 53. "JUST THIS SIDE OF DERANGED"

Anyone with a microphone in front of a group of people would attract admirers of some sort. I'm sure even carnival barkers had groupies. The kind of quick action comics attracted didn't compare to musician-camp followers in numbers, temperament or quality. Comic-camp followers tended to fall into two categories. In the first were women who thought themselves funny too, but sought professional validation before facing an audience's judgment. Then there were the delusional or naïve, guilty victims who thought the comic might distract them from a dreary, senseless life, just as he had done for a whole crowd.

Making people laugh like they hadn't in years was bound to lead to sexual encounters with audience members, but some comics felt the need to chum the waters. I hated it when comics would pitch for women during their act. Stage-trolling, even writing specific bits as bait, seemed underhanded, went against the stand-up's prime directive ... not that we weren't all in it to get love, in some form. Some guys were subtle: "I'm single, but really looking to settle down and start a family ..." Some were not so subtle: "Ladies, it's my last night in town ..." Some were blatant: "A lot of people don't know it, but there are problems with having a big dick ..."

I once worked with an opener whose whole act was an effort to get laid. Hacky jokes, cutesy posturing and pathetic pandering: "Austin has the most beautiful women in the world and they're all here tonight."

215

First marriage, Carol Leifer, 1981-1985

"Women are smarter than men …am I right, ladies?" After every show he'd stand by the door, nodding and smiling blankly at the exiting crowd, coming alive when a potential victim passed: "I hope you enjoyed my show. It was a pleasure performing for you." After the audience left, he'd try to recruit someone to go fishing elsewhere: "How about we go down to Sixth Street and check out the women there?" One night I snapped, "You just gave it your best shot, pal. If you can't snag a woman after being onstage, you're done. Now you're just Clark Kent again."

After being onstage it didn't make any sense to return to standing at the bar with the other losers whose best move was a lonely look. And if a woman did approach me after a show, I made absolutely certain she was more than interested before I showed my hand. It would just be too painfully ironic to have your sexual move be dismissed with a line that would normally be welcomed as a compliment: "You're so funny."

To me, road sex served the same function as alcohol and drugs — a Band-Aid over a gaping wound of insecurity. I used any treatment available, but none of it kept me soothed for long. Besides, thinking you were cool because you snagged a woman by being the star of the show was about the same as thinking the drug dealer was your friend. Rodney Dangerfield once said as much one night at Catch A Rising Star's bar. "All these girls who come up to me ... Do you think if I wasn't 'Rodney Dangerfield' they'd come up to" (pointing to himself) "THIS guy?"

Without that stage and the opportunity it provided to be introduced as a funny, charming guy, some comics were a tough sale. Around 1984, at Atlanta's Limelight one night, I was standing at the bar with Ron DiNunzio and Dave Montesanto, the owners of the Punchline. We were preparing to move the party to an after-hours club when a road comic approached us. We were surprised by his sudden appearance, but not shocked. At the time, the Punchline's big rental house was a crash pad for comics in between gigs. Nobody was thrilled to see this guy. He was a bit of a hustler, always looking to con somebody out of something. On his best days, he wasn't the most attractive guy, but on this night he was particularly unappealing, sporting greasy hair and unkempt clothes. True to form, the first thing he said after "I knew I'd find you guys here," was "Hey, Ronnie. You got a bump?" Ronnie slipped the guy a little bag of coke. As soon as the comic left for the bathroom, Ronnie declared his intent to ditch the guy. He turned to a prostitute who was hanging out at the bar. "When this guy gets back, take him off our hands." He then slipped her a couple of $100 bills. The comic returned and joined Ron, Dave, and me when we left for the after-hours bar. Later, when the guy was once again off treating himself to more of Ronnie's coke, I asked Ronnie why he was still with us. Ronnie said when the comic came back from the bathroom at the Limelight, the hooker took one look at him, slipped the money back to Ronnie and left.

It was hard enough just being funny up there without also having to deal with the jealousy of some of the guys in the audience. You'd glance down at a ringside couple. She was laughing, but the guy glared at you, as if to say, "I never make her laugh like this. Back off, pal." He'd pull her a little closer to him, as if after the next joke you were going to leap off the stage onto her. My strategy to drop these guys' shoulders was to do a few jokes about my girlfriend, or later, my wife.

A road comic generally worked for one hour a night and thus had 23 hours a day to kill. The typical time traps were alcohol, drugs, gambling, and women. More sensible comics might play golf, sightsee, write a script ... and then chase women. Obviously, the especially degenerate comics didn't have to do as much chasing, since a generous supply of alcohol and drugs usually attracted the right kind of wrong woman.

Some comics who were married or in long-term relationships rationalized the road as a guilt-free zone; that what happened out there didn't count as cheating, that it was just a part of surviving. And by "some comics," I mean me. Not proud of it, but that's who I was.

Nobody was tied to the whipping post. Everybody was using everybody, the women only with more subtlety. And I'm not referring to the out-and-out professionals like hookers and strippers. The connection between comics and strippers is ancient. It makes sense since the two professions are related: strippers bare themselves physically, comics bare themselves emotionally. A stripper and a comic hooking up are just two drowning rats climbing onto the same piece of driftwood.

The comics enjoyed being able to hit and run, living a secret life left on the road. Of course, that worked both ways ... sometimes the woman liked the fact that when the comic left town, her secrets went with him.

In 1983, after a show at Joker's Comedy Club in Tulsa, Okla., I was approached by a very prim-looking woman, an associate pastor at a local Baptist church, who ostensibly wanted to talk to me about my religious jokes. It took us all night in my hotel room to finally come to an understanding about God and the Devil.

I played that club about four more times over the next two years, and each time she got us a hotel room under the name of Mr. and Mrs. Louis Cypher. Not surprisingly, she called me her Devil Boy. It was thrilling to me that she essentially financed her sins with church funds. There were a couple of other quirky aspects to being her secret, out-of-town temp lover. She neither drank nor smoked but loved that I did plenty of both. And she had quite an appetite; everything was in play except vaginal sex, as she was determined to walk down the aisle a virgin. About two years after we met, she got up from the bed, dressed and announced that this was our last time as she was getting married in a week. My conscience bothered me a bit, but then it occurred to me that at least she would be walking down the aisle a virgin ... and I had actually helped her accomplish her goal.

The best road sex story I ever heard was from a former comic from San Diego. The morning after performing at a Christmas Eve one-nighter, the comic came out of a blackout on the floor, lying next to a fully lighted Christmas tree and surrounded by wrapped presents. He was instantly aware of a pain in his chest. Despite his severe hangover, it didn't take but a few seconds to find the source of his discomfort: An unfamiliar man was straddling the comic's naked body, pounding on his chest with a revolver. The man pointed the gun at the comic and said, "You have one minute to get out of my house." Not knowing the man with the gun, the comic erred on the side of caution and assumed the fellow was a man of his word. He grabbed his clothes and stumbled out the front door. The man stood in the doorway, gun still in hand, glaring as the comic dressed on the front lawn. The comic happened to spot a woman in a nightgown watching him from a second-story window. She smiled and waved at him. Now, there were all sorts of possibilities here. I imagined the woman brought the comic home as payback for crimes her husband had committed, purposely leaving a naked stranger under the tree with the other Christmas presents. The comic quit drinking not long after that.

Considering all the random and anonymous road couplings that happened in the '80s, it was pure luck that no comic was shot for accidentally, or purposely, messing with another man's woman. I once heard that

God looks after fools and drunks. Fortunately, I had both covered.

Before changing the chapter titles theme, this was to be called, "Road Hard And Put Away Wet." The title I settled on doesn't cover it all either, but it tested funny. Funny stays.

Not every comic love affair was a hit-and-run. A long-term relationship with a civilian was possible, but there were obvious problem areas, like the day worker versus night comic schedule clash. The most common cause of break-up was the fundamental inability of the civilian to understand the singleness of purpose that stand-up required. Every attempt at cross-pollination yielded the same empty field. The guy would come to the club with his beautiful new girlfriend, introduce her to everyone and plop her down in the back of the room. She howled at him like she had two nights earlier at Freddy's in Bernardsville. The second night, she laughed a little less, and the third a bit less as she realized his off-the-cuff brilliance was an act. By the sixth night her ain't-the-circus-grand smile had dropped into a what-is-that-smell grimace, not just because she knew the jokes and their exact running order. No, by now she realized every date began and ended in a comedy club. Eventually she would pop the question: "When are you going to quit this and get a real job?" She would reconsider her boss' advances, and the comic would work on his new "my girlfriend just dumped me" bit until the next cute ringsider laughed just a little longer than everyone else.

The New York comedy scene I first encountered in 1979 offered two romantic options: a female comic or a comedy club waitress. It wasn't long before I became involved with a comic, Carol Leifer. We were two competitive, ambitious people who understood that our relationship always was a distant second to stand-up comedy. Our biggest fights were over stage time, billing and material. In 1981, we got married. The first thing we said after "I do" was, "That would go better in my act."

After Carol and I moved to LA in early 1982, our agent sent us to meet with a manager, Irvin Arthur, who specialized in comedians. He urged us to become a team, to become the next Nichols and May. We told Irvin that we were separate acts, but he sold us with talk of "great things," and "television."

The next week Carol and I played Tickles' Comedy Club in Warren, Ohio. The fact that Warren, Ohio, had a comedy club in 1982 proved that the mushroom cloud was still rising. The first night we shortened our solo acts so we could perform together at the end. We did about 15 minutes together, mostly simple improv games. Afterward, we fought over who got the most laughs. The next Nichols and May didn't even become the new Bickersons.

Every day we competed for premises, jokes and laughs. Every success one of us enjoyed the other experienced as a failure. We finally called it quits in 1985. Our marriage was one of the first casualties of my new sobriety. One of my jokes was, "I quit doing alcohol, cocaine and my wife the same day. Coincidence?'

Carol was in New York writing for *Saturday Night Live,* and I was chasing an ever-changing dream in Los Angeles. There wasn't much left to fight for, in any area. There was a brief squabble over the custody of Beatles albums, as if they weren't making any more of them.

About two years after the divorce, I dated a woman who had a steady job in television as an assistant director. Things were going fine until one night she announced that she wanted to do stand-up. My palms started to perspire, my back locked up and I became very tired. I stopped seeing her two days later. She did a few sets as a stand-up before quitting to concentrate on her career in production. We are still friends today, but I would never date her for fear she might do stand-up again.

## 54. "HEARTACHES ARE HEROES WHEN THEIR POCKETS ARE FULL"

I n 1989, I was newly married and performing in St. Louis. After the first night's show, a well-dressed black man approached and offered his hand. "I'm Rahn Ramey. I heard all about you. We're going to do some partying this week. I got some cocaine and ..."

I cut him off. "I don't drink or drug anymore."

Rahn didn't lose one gram of cool. "That's okay. I got a line on some bitches here."

"I'm married."

Rahn kept his smile and said, "Well, it looks like we won't be seeing much of each other this week."

I said, "I guess not."

With the same enthusiasm he began the conversation, Rahn said, "It was nice meeting you. Enjoy your stay in St. Louis."

He shook my hand and I never saw him again that week. That was too bad. He seemed like a cool guy with a quick, sharp wit.

Later I realized Rahn was working off old reports of me. It had been four years since my last drink or drug. It would take some time to build a new reputation but I was determined to do just that, one day, and one missed night out, at a time.

# 55. "CAREFUL WHAT YOU SAY, YOU'LL GIVE YOURSELF AWAY"

In the early '80s, the resident philosopher at New York's Improvisation on 44th and 9th was Bob Altman, aka "Uncle Dirty " He rose through the Village rooms in the '60s with George Carlin and Richard Pryor, became an opening act for Led Zeppelin, and recorded a gold comedy record in 1970, *Primer*. Dirty was in his 40s, with a longer view of the road, but was still banging it out with the young maniacs swarming the New York showcase clubs.

One night, a comic was complaining about his lack of agency representation. Dirty said, "Hey, kid. When they can make money off you, they'll be there." Everyone went silent.

Another night, a few comics were discussing the strategy of when to move to LA. Dirty said, "Don't go to LA until they say there'll be a car for you at the airport." Quiet time again.

Then there was the night Dirty and I sat in the back of the Improv, watching the show. He began assessing the acts. "This guy's got great material and the audience likes him ... Stand-up. This guy's got great material, but the audience doesn't like him ... Writer. This guy's got no material and the audience doesn't like him ... Agent."

There was no way I had the courage to ask Dirty to categorize me. At that time I was only concerned with the where and when of stand-up, and not much with the how and why. I was basically a showbiz amoeba reacting to light, heat and applause.

223

Performing and writing, 1983

I knew there were two sides to stand-up — writing and performing — and those two creatures were not always equal partners.

The writer goes onstage to have a mind-set validated. If the audience doesn't laugh at the thoughts expressed in his or her jokes, then the comic feels stupid or, worse, crazy.

The performer takes the mic to get a pat on the head. If the audience doesn't laugh at the jokes, then this type of comic will make funny faces, sing, dance ... whatever it takes to make the audience pony up.

At the beginning most stand-ups are better at one than the other. I had no performing skills, but had a little confidence that I had funny ideas. My first appearances were awkward, memorized regurgitations of my writings. It took time to get an effective transfer from the page to the stage, to wring a laugh out of the notebook.

Maybe this was why I was attracted to the stand-ups with great material. I grew up listening to comedy albums which favored the comics with the best jokes; a funny face or body language didn't come across. I fell in love with the comics before I ever saw them perform. All my early favorites were consummate writers, George Carlin, Lenny Bruce, Bob Newhart, Robert Klein and Richard Pryor. Years later I learned that when Bob Newhart recorded his seminal album, *The Button Down Mind of Bob Newhart*, it was his first time on stage — not doing the material for the first time, but doing stand-up for the first time. Of course he had the instincts and became a great performer, but still ... that was some kick-ass material.

Of course, stand-up comedy was always performance dependent — no monkey, no show. The audiences tended to favor the performer but comics honored the writer. The title of Comic's Comic always rested with the stand-up whose material was bold, different, and just out of reach of the mere mortal.

When I first got to New York City in 1979, Gilbert Gottfried was the reigning Comic's Comic. Gilbert was a marvelous mimic and impressionist but it was his daring assaults on forbidden subjects that caused the other comics to bow at his feet. There is a danger in that sort of reverence. Once, after watching Gilbert a few too many times, I took my notebooks down to the East River and burned them.

I always believed that most comics identified more as a writer or performer. Not that it ever mattered to the audience. They just assumed whatever came out of the comic's mouth originated in his mind. Since the late '50s revolution of Mort Sahl and Lenny Bruce, the audience put a premium on the comic's point of view. They wanted to believe that what the comic said was personal and distinctive, that the material and the comic were the same, existing as one. Before them, during the age of the Top Banana, the big personality of a Milton Berle or Bob Hope drove the act. The jokes were interchangeable, one-size-fits-all, and their origin not important. The fact that Will Rogers or Fred Allen wrote nearly all their material didn't score any more points with the crowd. Milton Berle crowed about his stealing, publicly owning the title, the Thief of Badgags. Comics like Jack Benny and Bob Hope bragged about their large writing staffs.

A certain suspicion exists between writer and performer types, a distrust based in mystery. Performer types wonder how the Writers are able to create killer material. The Writer types marvel at some Performer types seem to conjure laughs out of thin air.

Sometimes the Performer type's remarkable (and enviable) connection with the audience goes beyond a big smile or any sort of identifiable likability. My friend Bob Nickman calls the comic who soars way above his material a "Charismatician."

I once heard some comics trying to explain the remarkable success of a comic who was a big smiling Performer type. Someone said, "Well, he's a nice guy." The great satirist Barry Crimmins said, "He has to be a nice guy. He has no act."

The joke thief was more likely to be the Performer type who needed to hear those laughs by any means necessary. The Performer didn't care whether it was old, stolen or purchased, as long as it got a laugh. That's why the joke thief baffled and infuriated the Writer. Why would anyone want credit for a thought that wasn't his own? What's the point of getting up there unless it was to test your observations, to share your opinions and live and die by your thoughts?

Even after doing stand-up for years I always identified as a Writer, believing that my stage work was at best a mediocre delivery system for my jokes.

My growth as a performer was slow and painful. From the outset, it took the audience a while to warm up to me. I lived with being a slow starter as if it were an unalterable condition, like my blue eyes. My strategy was to wear down the audience's resistance, and with enough time I'd eventually get to them.

In 1980, the New York Big Laff Off showed a major flaw in my approach. With 100 comics in the competition, the set times were less than half the normal showcase minimum of 15 minutes.

In these competitions, the luck of the draw — your placement in the long string of comics — was crucial. I drew some choice slots in the early rounds and became one of the 10 semifinalists.

I had a problem getting started in my semifinal set. By the time I got rolling, the red light flashed. The finalists were Rick Overton, Carol Leifer, Eddie Murphy, Mark Schiff and Steve Mittleman. They were the funniest, and time has proven them all to be great stand-ups.

Naturally I didn't like feeling left behind, especially by my girlfriend, but there was a real lesson in that defeat. I marveled at Steve Mittleman's fast start, noticing that his opening jokes were very self-deprecating. Being open and vulnerable established his humanity and a created a fast connection with the audience. It was a revelation.

An overweight or minority comic established their vulnerability and outsider status, building blocks of stand-up audience rapport, as soon as they walked onstage. I was a straight white male and needed to show an audience why I was a comedian. I developed jokes about my shortcomings, such as my balding head, or inability to do math. These things might be elemental and instinctual for most comics but for a guy who had such a fear of looking weak, even when I was clowning, it was a slow, hard turn. But I did come about, because back then my hunger for those laughs always overcame any fear.

Nothing thrilled me like that new joke smell. Unless it was an audition, I felt it was a waste of stage time not to try at least one new bit. In the late '80s, I had a new joke about a new-fangled car option, the power door locks. The gist was they enabled the fearful driver to lock the doors quickly. It was maybe the second time I did the joke when Jerry Seinfeld approached me as I left the Improv stage and said, "I've been trying to figure out an angle on the door locks, but you nailed it." It gave me great satisfaction to beat one of the best writers of my generation to a fresh concept.

The first time I bought a joke was around 1988. A *Tonight Show* set included three jokes on religion. The first was my favorite: "Pat Robertson said he's running for president because God told him to run. When God tells me to vote for him, I will. If I'm walking down the street and I hear a burning bush go, 'Vote for Pat,' you got it." Then there was a joke about preachers playing rock albums backwards, looking for satanic messages. I said, "Why bother? Just look at the album cover. AC/DC's *Highway to Hell* seems pretty upfront to me." The third was the search for the Antichrist, which was a big deal at the time. My punchline was, "I did my part and checked my scalp. I had two sixes and five. That close."

A friend and fellow comic at the LA Improv, John Pate, had a joke on the Devil that I loved. "The Devil had to be the dumbest person ever. He's sitting in heaven, thinking, 'Let's see … God's all powerful. He's everywhere. Yeah, I think I can take him." Pate watched me practicing my *Tonight Show* set and offered to sell the joke.

John accompanied me to *The Tonight Show*, probably to make sure I didn't botch his joke. Everything went fine. Afterward, talent coordinator Jim McCauley entered my dressing room with a bit of nice information from the post-show meeting. "Johnny raved about you the whole time and how strong your act was. He absolutely loved that one joke."

My heart froze with the fear that he was about to name John Pate's

"Devil" joke.

McCauley continued. "That one about Pat Robertson."

That was a big moment. For one joke on one night, I envisioned myself a comic's comic.

# 56. "DANCED MYSELF RIGHT OUT THE WOMB"

"Humor must not professedly teach, and it must not professedly preach, but it must do both if it would live forever. By forever, I mean thirty years." — *Mark Twain*

**B**ill Hicks and I met at the Houston Comedy Workshop in 1982. Before his death in 1994, we worked together a few times, hung out a bunch, and talked on the phone a ton. In no way was I as close to Bill as some others, especially his much-loved Texas Outlaw Comics, but we were friends. Our first road gig together was the Austin Comedy Workshop. There was nothing memorable about his material at that time. I certainly didn't tag him as the next Lenny Bruce, but then nobody pinned the young Leonard Schneider as a future comedy icon either. At 20, Lenny was conning his way out of the Navy on a homosexuality charge while Bill was a very funny and creative middle act.

What was obvious was Bill's passion for comedy and music. Bill was about 10 years younger than me, but his knowledge of '60s stand-ups and rock groups was remarkable. There was an old soul behind that baby face.

Austin was a wonderful city, a bizarre blend of cowboys, hippies, politicians, and students. The music scene rivaled Nashville. After my first show, a University of Texas  horticulture professor handed me a bag

*Between Shows* — A 2015 drawing by Peggy Reid, based
on an unfinished 1982 Bill Savage painting

of psilocybin mushrooms, and kept me supplied for the next three years.

I could drink, to paraphrase ZZ Top, with anyone just this side of insane. Getting drunk was pretty much a slow climb up a rain-slicked hill. There was usually time in the process to adjust to the odd personality. On the other brain lobe, tripping was a North Korean rocket launch. The ascent was sudden, the direction unpredictable, and connections easily missed. A tight mind on acid might come at you like one of those crab-like creatures popping from an egg in the movie *Alien*.

The Workshop sometimes housed the comics in the Villa Capri Motel, famous for themed rooms. They first checked me into the Darrell Royal room, featuring pictures of the legendary UT football coach, a burnt-orange color scheme and two long horns above the bed. That was not a good atmosphere for hard drugs. I quickly moved to the Red Skelton room, which was outfitted with his clown paintings. Mushrooms worked in that space.

During this period, tripping was part of my R&D department, a dubious aid in the search for new material. At the very least, with the right crew it was a lot of laughs, with a few spiritual moments along the way. The mission fit Bill's agenda perfectly. Creating a funny moment and figuring how to translate it to the stage was more important than anything to him. All night, a young woman tried to pull Bill out of the room, but the laughs were flying and he stayed. Before he left at the dawn's early light, Bill pointed out the universe in a clown painting. I had a new lab partner.

We got along so well that when I got the call to hit two new clubs in Oklahoma City and Tulsa, Bill came as the middle. That's how it was in those days. Comedy rooms were opening so fast that a two-week tour easily became a five- or six-week run.

After the high tide of Austin, Oklahoma City was a tidal pool. The main problem was the barely furnished condo, located in an isolated apartment complex about a half hour out of town. Every night Bill and I asked the staff if anything was happening and every one of them claimed to be heading home for bible study. Nobody wanted to be stuck driving the comedians into the wilderness after a long night. The shows ended and we were driven straight to Fort Apache, as we called it. It was all we could do to convince the bus boy to stop at a U-Totem for cigarettes, luncheon meats and beer. Another week in Oklahoma City, and we would have been trapping our food and wearing animal skins.

It was Bill, me, and an old black-and-white television set. The late-night TV preachers drew our ire. We cracked jokes about them and railed against religion all night long.

By the time Bill and I got to Tulsa, our bags were full of bile. The first night, we fell in with Bill Savage, an ex-pro ball player and local purveyor of fine potions and tonics. Savage was a funny man with some sharp opinions on organized religion. To top it off, he was painting a piece, titled *Between Shows*, of a dejected clown, with his head down, smoking a cigarette, and sitting on a small crate outside a circus tent. Clown paintings, religious jokes and drugs ... Hicks and I were home. We spent every moment not on stage that week at Savage's house. Each night the whiskey and cocaine put a fine edge on our anger, and the next night Bill and I punished the audience for our sins.

We were both doing religious material, but with a huge difference. Hicks burned down the temple and challenged the very existence of God. My jokes mocked the institutions.

Bill was a progressive, disappointed by mankind in general — crack the shell of any cynic and you find the withered body of an idealist.

In Tulsa, Hicks went after Jesus and Elvis Presley, who also had many sightings after being laid in the grave. Bill's approach was diametrically opposed to the flattering impression of the King done by Andy Kaufman — different generation, different comedic approach. Hicks lampooned the wasted talent and degenerate hillbilly that was the Fat Elvis. Knocking down the twin icons of Elvis and Jesus was more than some Southerners could take. By the time Bill finished, half the audience was gone. Nobody laughed as loud as me and Savage in the back of the room. It would have been even funnier if I didn't have to then perform for a dispirited half-house.

Surely Bill saw the exodus, but was in a zone and didn't realize the ramifications until he left the stage. He walked up to me with a stunned and sheepish look and said, "Sorry, man. I don't know what happened." I believed him. It was probably the first time Bill Hicks walked an audience, but certainly wasn't the last. That night Hicks began the long, fit-ful, and arduous process of whittling an audience to find a following.

Most comics were grocers, stocking the shelves with whatever the audience was buying. Rare were those comics willing to see the customers leave for other stores. My only purpose, my only license to be on-stage, was to make people laugh. If they didn't get the joke, I found one they did. Bill Hicks wanted that laughter badly, but had an equally strong need to make a point. The message was part of his gift and burden. It's what kept him in the desert for so many years. It was how he attracted so many rabid fans. It's why, 20 years after his death, he is still hailed as a comedy prophet.

Hicks called me sometime in 1988, wanting to quit drugs and alcohol. I was about three years sober and grateful to hear from him. People hit bottom for all sorts of reasons, from financial bankruptcy, to health concerns, to loss of companionship. Bill feared that the constant boozing was destroying the love of his life, comedy. I related totally. We connected again.

I was one of several people he called about sobriety. All my life, I was only good for a few minutes of phone conversation. Hicks was a telephone junkie. The man loved to talk on the phone — discussing jokes, books, or the news we watched together from our different locations. Bill almost made me a phone person.

The next time I saw Hicks onstage was a revelation. His stand-up had grown exponentially. There was always a purpose and intelligence with Bill, but now he had clarity and focus. Hicks still had the range to satisfy a second-show Friday night audience, or as he put it, "Pull the cord and parachute safely to Dick Joke Island." However, it was obvious that Bill was beating a path out of the comedy clubs. His takes on smoking, the anti-drug campaign, and the religious right hinted at his new direction. A short time later I witnessed even more development. Bill added anti-abortion activists, entitled children, gays in the military, and American consumerism to his hit list. Bill Hicks was becoming a social satirist in the grandest tradition of Mark Twain, Dick Gregory, and George Carlin.

One day, Hicks called with a problem. He believed that Denis Leary had ripped off his act, wholesale. The Boston comic was doing a commercial version of Hicks' act, cleverly snatching the leather jacket, pro-smoking and rock 'n' roll bits while leaving behind the more inflammatory religious material. Overnight, Leary became a parentally approved faux rebel for the kids. It was understandably upsetting for Bill to watch someone else succeed with his ideas. The remarkable part was how quickly Bill dropped any bitterness. Bill realized that he was already past that material. His solution was to write new material and keep moving to higher ground. That he did to the day he died.

In 1993, Bill called complaining about stomach pains. We had spoken of this a few times. I again told him to stop eating so much of that deep-fried road food and see a doctor. The next call was from a West Palm Beach hospital. The next was to inform me the doctor spotted a shadow on his X-rays. The last to say he had pancreatic cancer. My then-wife, Kay, pointed out that Bill and I joked and laughed through every bit of bad news. It was the only way we knew how to deal with it.

Over the next couple of months, Bill never mentioned death, but was always planning for the future. He called one day to ask if it was okay to do mushrooms. There was no need to add "one last time." Since Day 1 of my sobriety I had one unbreakable rule, "don't drink or drug no matter what." This was the exception. I told Bill to go for it. A couple of days later he called to tell me of a glorious spiritual experience with a couple of his closest friends. That was the last time we spoke. The next thing I knew he was at his parents' house in Arkansas and not taking calls.

We never acknowledged he was dying, so we never said goodbye. I regret not telling him how I felt about him. I think he knew but I won't make that mistake with my friends again. Thanks for another lesson, Bill.

# 57. "I DON'T MIND OTHER GUYS DANCING WITH MY GIRL"

The great screenwriter William Goldman once wrote something to the effect, "Nobody in Hollywood knows anything." The tricky part is to remember that also includes me.

It's hard to tell. Vegas doesn't have a line on showbiz stardom for a reason. The race can take twenty years and the winners and losers are damn near impossible to predict. Of course some stand-ups look pretty good coming out of the gate while others never really hear the starter's gun.

I've seen first timers so awful, so far from funny that the question became not whether they would ever be back, but whatever gave them the idea they could do it in the first place. Did anyone ever laugh with them? It was beyond sad to imagine them mistaking derisive laughter aimed at them as genuine laughs.

Then some newbie would come along that made me question why I bothered spewing my little jokes.

In 1984, I was the judge for a semi-finals night of the Great Southeastern Laugh Off at the Atlanta Punchline. Someone had bothered to create a judge's scorecard whereby you could rate the contestants on a scale of one to ten in categories such as "material" (was it theirs?), "stage presence" (did they face the audience?), and "professionalism," (did they put the mic back in the stand on the first try?). Supposedly the judges then put their drinks down long enough to do some addition and division to determine the winner. I just put a check next to the first comic's name and if someone came along funnier I moved the check, so I never had to put my drink down. There were people in the competition that night I had worked with on the road, and knew to be funny. At the end of the show, the check was next to the name Jeff Foxworthy, a guy I never saw before that night.

At the bar I introduced myself and congratulated Jeff, who stunned me by telling me it was his first time on stage. He said he had been nervous, but I sure hadn't seen it. I had been doing stand-up for seven years and didn't have his ease with the crowd. You can learn to write jokes and sell them on stage but that ability to connect with an audience is the eye-hand co-ordination of stand-up ... you either have it or you don't.

I remember sitting in the back of The Comedy Store Original Room around 1984 or '85 and watching Roseanne Barr for the first time. From that moment on, I was a fan. She made me laugh hard, every time. Her comedic voice, who she was up there, was loud and clear. Even so, after her killer *Tonight Show* premier I didn't hear anyone say that in three years that woman would be the star of the number one TV show in the country. You know why no one predicted it? Because no one knows anything.

Most stand-ups lock into a style and persona in their first few stage appearances. Rare is the comic who changes and even rarer for the result of that metamorphosis to become a huge hit.

I first saw Andrew "The Dice Man" Clay at Pip's Nightclub around 1981. All that I remember of his act was his medley of spot-on impressions of Italian actors from John Travolta to Sylvester Stallone to Al Pacino. He closed by perfectly mimicking Jerry Lewis's transformation from Julius Kelp into Buddy Love in the movie *The Nutty Professor*. A nice act that would land a nice little career in Vegas opening for Frankie Valli. Here I was, thinking I knew something.

Two or three years later he surfaced at the Comedy Store in LA, with pretty much the same act. Around this time, a guy approached me at the Store, introduced himself as a manager, and asked me to lunch. I didn't have a manager, so I gladly accepted.

It was a business lunch, and wanting to make a good impression, I abstained from any alcohol. The guy announced that he was Andrew Clay's manager, and that they both "liked what you do with the men/women thing." Before I could digest the compliment, the manager slapped a dead mackerel upside my head. "We're prepared to offer you $500 for your entire act."

It could only have been funnier if he had written the figure on a piece of paper and slid it across the table to me. Not that I saw the humor then. After explaining that I was getting 10 times that for a week in the clubs, I ordered a shot of Jack, a Heineken and a steak. Someone had to pay for fooling me into thinking that someone might be interested in helping my career.

It was never clear that Dice knew the manager was making a play for my act, or if he was actually, in fact, Dice's manager.

On another night at the Melrose Improv another strange guy approached me as I came off stage, and announced himself as "the guy who's gonna take you to the top." I thought he was goofing with me, and waited for him to complete his John Lennon impression from *A Hard Day's Night*, " ... the Top of the Pops." With a way too straight face my pseudo-savior gave me a business card with instructions to call him the next day. It was a Pacific Bell business card with a barely legible, handwritten "manager" above the crossed out type-written words "sales representative."

The next time I saw Andrew Clay, around 1986, his act was very different. He was now doing his whole act as "The Dice Man," a leather-jacketed, chain-smoking Brooklyn street tough: Buddy Love transformed into a foul-mouthed Fonz. His act was living proof of Steve Mittleman's joke: "Like most Jewish men, my goal is to one day be mistaken for Italian."

Dice had some new, and very effective material: a slew of filthy nursery rhymes. I easily recognized the source of the nursery rhymes, a New York ventriloquist act, Otto & George. My first thought was Dice had to pay more than $500 for those rhymes because they fit his character like one of his biker gloves.

The next I knew, Dice was selling out multiple nights at Madison Square Garden.

Like most great actors, all Dice needed was the right script to achieve stardom. It was startling to observe the creation of the character, to see it come together. Andrew Clay went from a Vegas-style impressionist to an over the top man/child, The Dice Man — that cartoon character happened to intersect with culture, and boom ... Hello, dere!

There is no denying the importance of career timing. Around 1982, Maxwell House Coffee hired a few comics to create commercials to sell their coffee to young people who were increasingly choosing soda as their caffeine delivery system. It's a wonder that instant coffee and rusted percolators didn't sterilize our entire generation. Besides myself, the only other comics I remember taping ads were Jerry Seinfeld, Carol Leifer and Arsenio Hall. I already knew Jerry and Carol, but was meeting Arsenio for the first time. He was a very likeable guy, friendly to everyone on the set. He wore a sport jacket and tie. In my mind there was nothing memorable about his act. Somewhere in the mid-80s Arsenio started hanging with Eddie Murphy. He smeared a little of Eddie's rock star swagger onto that earnest preacher kid and turned late-night TV into a hip-hop party. Every comic I knew liked Arsenio, but no one saw that coming.

Emo Phillips, Jeff Foxworthy, Dennis Miller, Rich Jeni, Judy Tenuta, Sam Kinison, and Bill Hicks all opened for me at one time or another before later blowing me off the road. Once I got back on my feet and dusted myself off, I applauded their successes.

No one knows anything, especially who might be the next phenomenon. And no one likes not knowing anything. That's why they use the phrase "overnight sensation" to explain someone who no one saw coming. Yet everybody in the business really knows that any overnight sensation had been coming a long time. It's just that no one saw them coming. Probably because we were all so busy running our own little one person races. That's probably why nobody knew anything. And really, we were happier that way.

# 58. "WE ARE VAIN AND WE ARE BLIND"

In 1986, Robert Palmer did an industry show at the legendary Whisky a Go-Go on the Sunset Strip for his hit single *Addicted to Love*. Industry crowds were notoriously difficult to please and engage, so someone at William Morris thought it a good idea to have a comic lay on the barbed wire for Mr. Palmer. There was no pay, but the gig was sold to me as a favor to the music department and a great opportunity to be seen by some of Hollywood's "movers and shakers." I never thought I'd live long enough to hear that hoary phrase used in real-life conversation. Truthfully, I was in as soon as I heard it was a chance to perform at "the Whisky." To me this was the Doors, go-go dancers and psychedelic rock 'n' roll.

No one greeted me at the crowded club that night. After a frustrating search for someone in charge that resembled Martin Sheen in *Apocalypse Now*, I approached the sound man. He told me to stand by the stage for his signal.

A few minutes later, the sound man waved for me to go onstage. Thinking he wanted me in motion for the introduction, I walked slowly while he waved me forward. This continued until I stood behind the microphone. I stared at him. He stared right back at me. After a very long moment he thrust both hands toward me, and nodded his head vigorously which I interpreted as the international rock 'n' roll signal for, "What are you waiting for, idiot?! Go! Go!"

No introduction, no lighting change, but I dutifully launched into my first joke anyway. It got nothing. Neither did the second, third or fourth; not a laugh, a chuckle, or a groan. My amplified voice bounced back at me, off a solid wall of louder conversations.

Right in front of the stage stood Jack Nicholson, whispering into the ear of Whoopi Goldberg. Everywhere I looked there were stars, all talking to each other. It was a big showbiz cocktail party and I was the carved ice sculpture in the center of the room. The most I got was a glance while they sipped from their drinks.

I ditched my jokes in an effort to protect their future and went rogue. I created imaginary dialogue for the conversations happening all around me. Nothing. I mocked my situation. Nothing. A little bitterness bubbled up through the mulch in my head. I said something to the effect of, it was a pleasure to perform for "Hollywood's boozers and fakers." One laugh.

All the savers and the improvisation would get a single laugh here and then another one over there. Whenever there was a chuckle, I turned in that direction in a pointless game of comedic connect-the-laughs.

It had been years since my last bombing, but here I was experiencing a major ass-kicking. I entered that vortex where the chill from the lack of laughter eventually freezes time.

Then with no warning, and while I was still talking, the sound man interjected with a booming voice, "Let's have a hand for comedian Ritch Shydner." For a brief moment, everyone looked at me and then immediately returned to their conversations. The guy skipped the intro, but made sure everyone got the name of the ship they just saw sink.

I left the stage as I took it, without one bit of applause. The crowd parted for the leper. Eyes averted mine. Bodies recoiled from any possible touching. Hollywood always treated failure like a communicable disease. Any contact with a carrier might kill your career.

Before I turned onto Downer Road to begin the long drive to Depression Gorge, a young man with a brilliant smile stepped into my path.

"Hey, that took a lot of courage to do what you did up there."

Donny Osmond shook my hand and then disappeared into the crowd.

One person offered one bit of acceptance, and the lame was healed.

I ran to the Improv stage and let fresh laughter wash away the stink.

# 59. "LAW OF AVERAGE PLAINLY STATES THAT CHANCES GO AROUND"

I n the fall of 1986 I auditioned for a sitcom pilot, *Married With Children*. The role was "Luke Ventura," the single, womanizing co-worker of the show's lead.

Starring in movies and television wasn't a youthful fantasy for me. That ambition was planted when I became a stand-up comedian in 1977 and learned that acting in movies and TV were steps on the stairway to comic stardom. TV and movie roles filled seats and boosted the pay. Roles on hit sitcoms sometimes transformed club comics into theater draws. At the very least, it was a new credit to give the MC for your introduction.

So I took acting classes, in New York with Ron Orbach, and then in Los Angeles with Michael Shurtleff, Jeff Corey and others. Corey, in the first class, gave everyone pencil and paper, instructing us to list whatever we might do to make a living other than act. He then announced, "If you wrote anything down on that paper … leave. The only people who are going to make it are the ones who believe they can't do anything else but act." I heard, "Don't quit your day job." Mine was stand-up. I was the happiest guy in the class.

No matter how many classes I took, no matter how much I rehearsed, I never considered myself much of an actor. I never got lost in the moment the way I did in stand-up. I was a guy worried that he was standing awkwardly while waiting for the other actors to stop speaking

Married With Children promotional photo, 1987

their lines so he could get rid of his before he forgot them. Fortunately most sitcoms didn't require much more than that.

My nocturnal lifestyle was not always conducive for daytime acting. In 1979, I dressed in a vintage 1940s suit and fedora and stood in line with hundreds of other New Yorkers for an open call on a "Woody Allen Project." The audition consisted of stopping in front of a camera long enough to state your name and phone number. I was picked to be an extra on a train scene, but was too hungover to make the bus to New Jersey. It occurred to me every time I watched *Stardust Memories* that I would have fit right in the train of "lost souls."

In 1985, when interviewing to replace "the Coach" on the sitcom *Cheers*, I was sober. I showed up early, bright and shiny, with my lines rehearsed and a plan to succeed. After a couple of call-backs, I went "to network." This audition, in front of the producers and network executives, was typically the last hurdle. Three blond actors sat in the outer office, hoping to play the young, stupid bartender. Actually they used the word "naive" instead of stupid so as not offend us blonds. Anyway, they chose the right guy, Woody Harrelson.

After a few more near misses, I went to network for *Married With Children*, sitting with two other guys in a hallway on the Paramount lot. We all participated in the usual nervous chit-chat. One of the actors had just flown in from New York, his luggage next to him.

Suddenly the show's two creators, Michael Moye, a short black man, and Ron Leavett, a tall Jewish fellow, entered the building. The New York actor sitting across from me jumped to his feet and shouted, "Hey Michael!"

Moye, one of the men about to decide the fate of this role, then embraced my competition warmly. They joked and laughed before Michael told the guy, "The wife has your room ready. You're going to love this town."

Leavett and Moye then disappeared into the offices. The third actor looked like I felt, gut shot. I considered leaving, and then for some reason just started laughing at the whole damn affair. The assistant called me into the office at exactly the right time.

For the first time ever I walked into an audition not worried about getting the part. I was loose and full of attitude, making fun of everything and everyone, including this alleged network, Fox, which didn't yet exist. I never got so many laughs in an audition, ever, as I did on that one.

A couple of days later, my agent, Bill Gross, told me to get ready to tape my first big-time showbiz Hollywood television sitcom pilot.

The pilot was shot in December 1986 and the series began filming a month later. On the first day of rehearsal, Michael Moye pulled me aside and accused me of doing cocaine during the shooting of the pilot. He said I was "acting coked up" up and that someone found snow seals on a bathroom floor. I admitted maybe I looked whacked with all my nervous Coca-Cola intake and chain-smoking, but insisted I was clean and sober. The coke culprit was later revealed to be one of the makeup artists, but I never heard anything about that from Michael Moye. He continued to hound me, hating everything I did; table readings, rehearsals, and the way I parked my car. Fortunately, I had a lot of support from the other cast members. I can't tell you how much Ed O'Neill helped me with acting tips and pep talks.

My role was small but in every episode. I worked hard and got into a groove. On Friday, the script was delivered. I worked lines with an acting coach over the weekend, and scored the expected laughs at the table read on Monday. My confidence was growing. I was starting to have fun and get loose.

The seventh show featured my character. Al Bundy, after a terrible fight with his wife, Peg, came to stay at Luke's bachelor pad. Al flew from the temptation of the two blond flight attendants offered by Luke, later bringing home a blond wig for Peg to wear. During the taping, I waited behind the wall of my bedroom with one of the flight attendants, actress Jerry Hall. She was a beautiful woman with a cute Texas drawl, cracking me up with stories of her "cheap" husband, Mick Jagger. I thought to myself, "I can do this job."

The next Friday I didn't get a script. Bill Gross said not to worry; it was probably just a delivery problem. A few minutes later he called back with the news that I was no longer on the show. That's a firing, Hollywood-style. My name was probably already off the parking spot.

My second ex-wife, Kay, became good friends with Ron Leavitt's wife, Sharon. We attended quite a few parties at their Malibu home. Ron and I never talked about anything but sports and hamburgers. One day, Sharon, pushed Ron toward me, "Tell him, Ron."

He walked me into a bedroom and said, "Look, man. I'm sorry, but

Michael wanted that role for his friend. You wouldn't believe the scene in the office the day you auditioned. Michael fought like crazy but the network insisted on you. After that, Michael wanted to get rid of the role, and you. We were fighting so many fires I finally let him have his way."

I did other failed pilots, but never think of those shows. *Married With Children* was on Fox for 11 seasons, nearly 250 shows, and continuously in syndication. Every residual check for my seven episodes reminds me how close I came to owning a really big boat.

# 60. "I WAS CROWNED WITH A SPIKE RIGHT THROUGH MY HEAD"

In June of 1987, I played a club in Metairie, La., a suburb of New Orleans.

The first night, I was heckled as soon as I took the mic from the stand.

"Al Bundy!"

I shot back with my standard replies for a non sequitur from the audience. "White, heterosexual man. Are we playing word association?"

Not two minutes later, a different voice heckled from the same area of the room.

"Talk about Al Bundy!"

I knew they were referring to the lead character on the Fox sitcom *Married With Children*." The problem was, judging by the confused looks on the audience's faces, nobody in the crowd knew anything about Al Bundy or *Married With Children*. This was two years before the protests of that idiot Michigan housewife made *Married With Children* a hit.

I gamely tried to placate the heckler. "Yeah, Al Bundy is cool, let's move on to these little jokes I brought along …"

One table started a chant.

"Al Bundy! Al Bundy! Al Bundy!"

The rest of the room was silent.

Years before, in 1979, I saw Robin Williams take the stage at the

Married with Children credits, 1987

New York Improv at the height of *Mork & Mindy* mania. Audience members kept interrupting Williams with shouts of his character's name, "Mork," and his alien greeting, "Nanu Nanu!" I saw the same phenomenon with Steve Martin at a concert in '78 in Washington D.C. Even after Martin did his hook line, "Excuuuuuuse me," people continued shouting it throughout the show. I had just experienced the same nuisance without the fame and fortune.

When the table stopped chanting "Al Bundy," I tried to crank-start my act. "Okay … so, anyway, I had a nice drive in from the airport, on the —"

"Al Bundy!"

I snapped a little. "Al Bundy's not here, man. Remember Cheech and Chong, 'Dave's not here?' Well, that's the deal here. Al Bundy's not here. And nobody knows who you're talking about. Anyone here know Al Bundy?"

The one table cheered again. The rest of the room was silent. One of the guys at the table yelled, "He is on *Married With Children*!"

My only course was to kill this charging beast. "Nobody knows what you're talking about. Anyone here watch *Married With Children*?"

Again the room was silent except for the one table, which cheered less loudly this time.

The voice from the darkness was almost pleading now, "Don't you watch *Married With Children*?!"

"No, I don't, man. Because every night I'm in a club doing stand-up … LIKE I'M TRYING TO DO RIGHT NOW!"

The audience laughed.

"You should watch *Married With Children*, because you're on *Married With Children*."

"No. I'm right here. Do you think you're home in your living room? You're probably confused as to why your remote's not working right now." I mimed the guy pressing his remote. "I can't get this guy off my TV."

The audience laughed hard, not knowing it was a line I did for years. That was the up side of crowd work, looking quick and clever with practiced lines. The down side was worrying the continued heckling might empty my little bucket of brilliance.

The voice from the darkness now had a need to be understood by a roomful of strangers, just like I did. "You know what I'm talking about. You're on the show. He's on *Married With Children*!"

The steady cross-examination by the voice in the darkness had tripped me into a damaging confession. "No, I'm not, man. They dropped my character from the show."

The audience didn't laugh. Sympathy and laughter can't occupy the same place at the same time.

My friend in the dark wasn't finished. "You were on the show last Sunday night."

"That's because we taped the show two months ago so they can play it later. Don't ask me to explain to you how planes fly."

The audience laughed a little. Before I could segue into some airline jokes, the voice from the darkness decided the funeral wasn't complete without some dead flowers on my grave.

"Sorry. We liked your character."

"Thanks, man. Do you want to remind me of all my other failures? Did my parents send you?" I mimed my parents whispering. "Ask him how long it took him to ride a bike. Ask him if he can draw a tree."

The audience laughed, which bought a little time, but I was distracted. This was the first time I considered the *Married With Children* dismissal, and the stand-up stage was not an ideal place for personal reflection. Fortunately, my need for laughter sharpened my focus and I eventually found my groove.

After the show, the table of hecklers approached me. They were very nice and apologetic. Turned out they were employees at the local Fox affiliate, just a little overzealous about their new venture. No harm, no foul. It was just a Tuesday night in America. Live shows were the most perishable fruit on the planet, dust as soon as the applause ended.

Unfortunately, I couldn't stop thinking about the *Married With Children* situation.

A couple of minutes later I was in the office to get an advance. The manager seated at his desk, looked up from his piles of cash and cocaine and asked me, "What's bothering you?"

"Nothing, I'm just thinking."

I had that same exchange countless times during my life. People assumed something was wrong with me when all I was doing was thinking. Apparently, my thought process looked very painful.

The manager looked to his buddy, an equally obese guy. "This guy needs a bump."

He pushed his little plate of cocaine toward me. "Here."

"No, I don't do that stuff." I was a little over two years sober.

"Good. More for us." The manager did a line and passed the plate to his friend.

After doing his bump, the friend tried to pass the plate to me. "You need some of this."

I wanted to do a bunch of that, but needed to stay sober.

Watching these two grossly overweight men snort coke made me think of the No. 1 pick in the 1986 NBA draft, Len Bias, whose heart stopped after ingesting less than a gram. The problem, as usual, wasn't with what I was thinking; it was with me deciding to share it.

"Aren't you guys worried about blowing out your heart? Len Bias was a young basketball player and his heart couldn't take that stuff."

The manager did another line and said, "He was probably in too good a shape. The coke went right to his heart." I guessed he was referring to some recent scientific study regarding the ability of fatty deposits to protect the heart by filtering the lethal cocaine.

His friend was not going to be out-idioted. As he reached for the plate he actually said, "The coke probably triggered that sickle cell thing."

I had to laugh. After all, I had spent years building similar bridges of rationalization to get to my dark side. I never returned to Metairie. It only took those guys about six months to snort the entire club up their nose.

# 61. "THE SIMPLE THINGS YOU SEE ARE ALL COMPLICATED"

From the mid 1980s to early 1990s, I did about 10 appearances on *Late Night with David Letterman* on NBC, which followed *The Tonight Show Starring Johnny Carson*.

One such appearance went from not happening to never forget.

Another of the other guests was a gray-haired woman pushing a book on how to cook in the wild. She spent much of the pre-show walking around backstage holding a small white bird that looked like a dove. Everyone petted this cute little bird, including Dave.

The first guest went long and one of the show's producers informed me that I was bumped. Instead of heading to the airport early for my red-eye back LA, I watched the show in the green room and ate my flight meal of Chinese sesame noodles.

After the commercial, the wildlife chef walked onto the stage where Dave waited by a stove. She announced the first dish, wild dove, and pulled a dead dove from her sweater pocket. Before stepping onto the stage she probably twisted the dove's neck. On the studio monitors the audience saw a camera close-up of the bird's little head swinging at the end of a broken neck. Three-hundred jaws dropped. I heard their collective gasp backstage.

David looked at the bird, then into the camera and said, "We'll be right back."

The producer who moments before apologetically gave me the bump call, now rushed into the green room in a panic. She stood in front of me and yelled to no one in particular, "Is the comic still here?"

I swallowed a mouthful of noodles, and notified of my willingness to report for duty.

Finding me didn't immediately ease her pain — she had probably booked the Dove Killer.

She bore in on me. "You gotta do something!"

I thought, "Well I can't bring the bird back to life ..." To say that to her in her current state would have been cruel.

Supposedly, animal acts were always tough to follow. My experience that night on *Letterman* was just the opposite. People laughed at anything and everything to get the taste of dead dove out of their minds.

After the show, David came to my dressing room with his producer, Robert Morton. I don't remember what he said, only that we all laughed a lot.

# 62. "THEY'RE ONLY PRETTY LIES

**B**efore going onstage for the first time in 1977, without ever having read a book or taken a class, I knew how to write a joke. Years of making friends laugh, watching stand-ups on TV, and listening to comedy albums had taught me the basic joke construction of set-up and punchline — build an assumption and then a surprise misdirection.

When I prepared to do stand-up that first time, I wrote jokes without even knowing that was what I was doing. My performance of what I had written that first night was terrible. I memorized the words on the paper and then recited them stiffly and quickly. Five minutes of stand-up yielded a single, strangled "Ha!" That partial laugh was enough to elevate a bunch of words from a statement to what I later recognized as my joke: "You can always tell who's gonna win a professional wrestling match by the introductions: "In the orange tights at 187 pounds from Hackensack, N.J., Arnold Skoland. His opponent, at 417 pounds, from Parts Unknown, Haystacks Calhoun." It's the same with high school wrestling. "In the 130-pound weight class, from Oakcrest Regional High School, two-time New Jersey state champion, two-time Christmas tournament champion, undefeated senior captain Bob Ciarrochi. His opponent, from Pennsville Memorial High School ... former student council treasurer."

Mark Twain said, "... the difference between the right word and the

Tubby Boots comedy album, 1960

almost right word is the difference between lightning and a lightning bug." I instinctively knew "treasurer" was funnier, even though in real life I had been student council president.

George Carlin once said that comedy was in the specifics. He had a joke about buying contraceptives with a credit card that became much funnier when he changed it to "buying vaginal jelly with an Exxon credit card." One of my earliest routines was based on being pulled over by the police for driving under the influence of marijuana. At one point, the police officer asks the driver, "Are those your munchies?" In retrospect it was an easy rookie error that got what it deserved, a few titters. I switched the general word "munchies" for the more specific "Twinkies" and got real stoner recognition laughter.

Somewhere along the line, "Never let the facts get in the way of a good story" became part of my stand-up DNA. Not long after I moved to Washington, D.C., in 1975, I did volunteer work for NORML, the National Organization for the Reform of Marijuana Laws. There was a decided amount of self-interest in my service work, and more than a few pot jokes in my first 20 minutes. Write what you know. I had a bit about NORML. Part of it was a staff meeting where everyone smoked a little weed. The guy running the meeting, pointing to a large strategy map of the U.S., referred to Madison, Wisconsin, as one of our best chances at decriminalization. Someone said Wisconsin is famous for cheese, then someone else said the word, "pizza." and the strategy meeting dissolved into a hunt for a pizza joint. Today I'm not sure if that actually happened, or if I made it up. The only things I remember for sure are stuffing envelopes for NORML, smoking a lot of pot at that time, and the pizza bit getting a laugh.

Dick Gregory said the most important quality for a comedian to have is curiosity. I've always liked watching people. I'm sure it was a part of my survival training as a kid. It was important to be able to read adults, especially my dad. Did someone's actions match their words? Were there any verbal or nonverbal clues to predict violence? Studying human behavior was important to me. I still do it, but sadly, it has changed with age; what was once youthful curiosity is now just an old guy's cranky judgment.

The stand-ups I most admired excelled in dissecting the human condition and reassembling those observations into time tested, heckler-proof, weather-resistant jokes.

In the first few months of 1977, I was so green and alone as a stand-up that I didn't know you could repeat a successful joke. This was part of the transition from being a funny guy working friends, family, and co-workers to becoming a traveling professional comedian. The local joker needs new jokes for the same audience; the pro needs a new crowd to use the same jokes. Anyway, I temporarily shelved my one working joke, just in case that one guy at the Iguana Coffee House who thought it sort of almost funny might be in the audience at my next three stand-up experiences at the Brickskeller Inn, Jailhouse Bar, and the Gay Cabaret. Oddly, years later I did the same thing with the jokes I performed on Carson or Letterman, shelving them for days after an appearance in the event someone who saw the TV shot might be at a club.

Regardless, I knew that one joke don't make no show. I became obsessed with writing and performing new jokes. I began carrying a little pocket notebook and pen to write down any and all ideas. If I was at a party and someone said something funny I slipped into the bathroom, locked the door, sat on the toilet and wrote it down. When the notebook was filled I wrote on anything. Coming home from a night in a bar, my pockets would be filled with cash register receipts, crumpled cocktail napkins, and matchbooks covered with my drunken scrawl.

The inspiration for jokes was everywhere: conversations, real life situations, and pop culture. My second joke was a parody of a TV commercial for the new volunteer armed forces: "You're 18 years old, training on a destroyer off the coast of Virginia. You set the coordinates and fire ... the missile flies off course and destroys Philadelphia ... but, hey, you had a good time. The Navy...it's not just a job, it's an adventure."

Sometimes the idea for a joke didn't require any examination or comparison of behavior or even any imagination, it was just a matter of being alert and writing down exactly what happened. In the spring of 1979 I attended a giant No Nukes rally on the Mall in Washington, D.C. It was a throwback to the days of the '60s protests — music, speeches, tie-dye, Frisbees, and pot in the spring sunshine. It was prompted by the Three Mile Island accident, so throughout the day musical acts like Bonnie Raitt and Jackson Browne led the crowd in chants of "No nukes! No nukes! No nukes!" Finally this long-haired hippie next to me asked, "Hey, man ... when them No Nukes gonna play?" Of course, that not-so-disguised stoner joke got a big laugh the first time I took it to the stage.

The second joke inspired by that day took a lot longer to work. Most of the speeches at the rally were about the environment, and what we could do to save the planet. In college I had read Paul Ehrlich's *The Population Bomb*, a pessimistic view of the world's future, including predictions of numerous ecological disasters caused by human overpopulation. I wrote a joke as soon as I got home from the rally: "How can we save the planet when we're the problem? The streams aren't polluted because the beavers are using asbestos when they build their dams. There are too many people. If you're really a dedicated environmentalist, the best thing you can do for the planet is kill yourself."

I couldn't wait to do that joke on stage. It didn't just die from indifference, it turned the audience against me, getting groans and boos. It was my first experience with a joke I thought was sure-fire that proved to be just the opposite, a crowd irritant. I normally tried a joke a handful of times before shelving it. I favored this child and gave it a hundred chances before kicking it out.

Then, in 1991, my act was being audiotaped in San Diego for eight shows. I performed every bit I could remember and emptied every notebook I could find. I ran across this forgotten bit and tried it. After all, it contained a few things that were still dear to my heart, including rebuking mass movements and telling people to kill themselves. To my surprise, it worked. Apparently, at least some of the country had become more pessimistic that we might ever do anything to save the planet from ourselves. I experienced a different type of joke timing.

That was my only joke that time ever helped; usually it was the opposite. Most stand-up doesn't travel well. Comedy ages much faster than music. My teenagers loved the Rolling Stones, but classic George Carlin from the same era left them flat. Mark Twain said, "Often (the joke) is merely an odd trick of speech and of spelling ... and presently the fashion passes and the fame along with it.... Humor must not professedly teach, and it must not professedly preach, but it must do both if it would live forever. By forever, I mean thirty years."

In 1988 I did a goofy piece called Canyon Man, mostly mocking the first sport utility vehicle, the Jeep Cherokee, and why a city dweller needed it. Several jokes were about the newest car options, the power windows and door locks, which basically made it was easier to lock all the doors at once and keep yourself safe from the dangers presented by the outside world. Within a year or two that technology became standard in about every car; people took them for granted and the jokes lost traction. SUVs became ubiquitous and people became less likely to laugh at themselves for driving a "Fear Wagon." Canyon Man went into early retirement, while dick jokes from my early years continued to slave away in smoky rooms.

Sometimes the performer no longer fit the bit; time appropriated the material. In 1980, I worked a Jerry Stanley Jersey one-nighter with 1950s burlesque comic Tubby Boots. A classic bombing took a grotesque turn when Tubby closed by removing his shirt to reveal huge man boobs tipped with stripper tassels. He then twirled them to that classic burlesque-dancer-song-turned-shaving-cream-commercial, "The Strip-per." He didn't clear the room but he did hurt some eyes, while demonstrating that young fat may be funny, but old fat is frightening.

Like most stand-ups I was forever on an obsessive hunt for new material.

My act was always evolving, with new jokes pushing out the old jokes. Even proven race winners were set out to pasture for the new. I got bored easily. The rate of joke turnover increased in the late '80s when the enforcement and penalties for drunk driving became stricter, and club owners became more worried about fatalities and lawsuits than liquor sales. The club owners looked to shorten the show length, pretty much ending liquor service an hour into the show. The dreaded check spot appeared earlier, usually about halfway into the headliner's set. When the set was an hour instead of an hour and a half the number of jokes I used on any given night decreased and the pressure to toss out the old for the new increased.

Coming up with new material was necessary but toxic, as it required maintaining high levels of bile and contempt. I wasn't the type who could sit down and decide to write jokes about the mailbox that day. I didn't examine a subject under the microscope as much as put it in my crosshairs. I'm sure it was this way for most comedians. It was just a matter of where the comic operated on the sliding scale of frustration, from befuddlement to rage.

The style and form of a joke changed over time, but not the raw ingredients. Mark Twain again: "Everything human is pathetic. The secret source of humor itself is not joy but sorrow. There is no humor in heaven."

In 1989, I broke my leg in a motorcycle accident in front of the Comedy and Magic Club. I was lying in the street, writhing in pain, when Jay Leno exited the club. The first thing he said was, "Shydner, that's a tough way to get some new jokes." As Jay helped me into the car of club owner Mike Lacy for the ride to the hospital, Jay asked, "Hey, if you don't make it, can I have your act?" Comics ... always with the jokes. For the next month, every time a comic saw my leg in its cast they'd say, "You're gonna get a new five minutes out of that." There was always a bit of envy in their voice as if saying, "Damn, I wish I had a broken bone."

Such was the pleasure of laughter that most civilians didn't consider the pain at its source. So many times an audience member said to me after a show, "You sure to do complain about your marriage a lot up there." There would be little joy in the room if the comic stood onstage and talked about how wonderful their spouse was and how much fun it was to be married.

It's been famously said that "comedy is tragedy plus time." I slightly altered it to "comedy is tragedy, plus time and distance." Twenty-five years ago a bus went off a cliff in Pakistan, killing about 200 people. I added a cold punchline to that setup: "Whenever something like that happens, I always stop and think, 'How'd they get 200 people on a bus?'" It got a huge laugh, because the dead were not Americans. Most people, and most crowds, view the world through their eyes and experience. The farther a joke like that lands away from their life, the easier it is to find funny.

Most comics don't like to acknowledge there is work involved in stand-up so they won't feel bad about not doing it. A great deal of that work is writing jokes, specifically crafting the words on the page to fly on the stage. A crucial element is editing the joke, tweaking the timing. I heard that old joke — "What is the key to comedy?" where the teller blurts out the answer, "timing," before the listener can answer — before I knew exactly what the word meant to joke construction. The best joke gives just enough of a setup so that the punchline is delivered at exactly the moment the audience is ready to receive it. That is the snap of the whip that causes the audience to jump with laughter. If there is too much information, or the setup is too long, then the audience has time to guess where the comic is going and is there before the punchline is delivered. The laughter tends to be muted, a collective, "Yeah, I saw that coming." If there is not enough information in the setup, when the comic tosses them the punchline, then the audience is not ready for it. Their laughter is delayed and piecemeal, 200 heads nodding at different speeds, "Oh, I get it."

Figuring out the timing on a new joke is repetitive grunt work — a blacksmith hammering the blade, sticking it on the fire and hammering it again. The late great Ronnie Shakes had no patience to wait until the next night to rework a promising premise. After a joke failed to ignite, Ronnie sometimes opened his notebook onstage and offered the audience alternative punchlines to the same premise.

I always laughed when some comic would declare, "I wrote 20 new jokes today." Maybe you wrote 20 new sentences, but they're not jokes until the audience says they are. Rare was the joke that fell from my head to the page and didn't need more help to get a laugh.

The cold reality is that nine out of 10 jokes I wrote didn't work, but all 10 had to be tried onstage to find the one that did. That's a lot of rejection, the silence a painful rebuke of your cute little idea. I understand why some comics, once they finally get that 45 minutes of effective material, just stop writing.

It was rare to fully conceive and birth a joke onstage, except for a saver. When a joke fizzled, the whole audience knew it. To move on, as if nothing had happened, seemed deceitful and a breach of the basic bargain. An acknowledgment must be made, not only to admit the failure but to pay its debt. I never wrote a joke offstage to cover a misfired joke onstage. Maybe the only comic who ever did was the King of the Savers, '50s comic Jack E. Leonard, whose act was predicated on purposely bombing and digging out of the hole. My favorite saver was a twist on a stock saver. When I started, a lot of comics covered a failed joke by blaming the audience, passing their hand over their head, implying the joke was above the audience's collective heads. Most of the comics using that saver didn't have one joke in their act too clever for a first-grader, When a joke face-planted, I explained the stock hand-over-head saver and then said, "but the real deal is ..." I would hit myself on the forehead, instead of passing my hand over my head while saying, "Oh we heard you, pal. It just wasn't funny."

The comic with the best work ethic also wielded the sharpest editing pencil and, not surprisingly, was one of the most prolific and best joke writers of my generation. One of the great learning experiences afforded me when I first moved to New York City was the opportunity to sit in the back of the room and watch great comics all night long. I loved watching Jerry Seinfeld shaping a joke. A word went in, maybe two went out, and suddenly the crowd's heads snapped in unison with laughter. Sometimes it wasn't a word, but a pause, a gesture, a look. Jerry Seinfeld was one of the best since Jack Benny in using those tools to set the timing on a joke.

Jerry was the first guy I heard talking about writing for a couple hours every day. If those hours didn't yield a working joke, that daytime focus benefitted the night's performance. I found it to be true. Because I had labored on the joke and it was fresh in my mind, sometimes I would try the setup and was as surprised as the audience when the missing punchline popped out of my mouth. Maybe it was the unconscious making a last-ditch effort to save the ego from embarrassment. Whatever the reason, through rain, sunshine, and hangovers, I dragged that pen across the paper every day.

Once the construction of the joke is perfected, the comic pretty much locks in the performance of that joke. A musician bored with an old song can play with it in ways a comic can't with a joke. About 10 years ago I saw Bob Dylan in concert. Part of the fun for the audience that night was seeing how long it would take us to guess which of his classic songs he was playing. There were bulletproof jokes in my act that if I changed one or two words or altered the tempo on my delivery, the joke lost air.

For the comic, it always comes back to the new. Comics need fresh jokes nearly as much as they need stage time. If someone hears a new song and likes it, they're likely to play it 50 times in the next two weeks and want to hear it every time the singer performs it for the next 50 years. A person doesn't hear a joke and then say, "Tell me that one again." A comic tells a joke and has only a few seconds to surf on that laughter before a roomful of eyes all seem to say, "Tell me another." Like worrying about rain for a farmer, a comic's need for new material is part of the occupational neurosis. There is no resting on your laurels. Even the best, most famous comics are only as good as their next 45 minutes.

The reward for all that joke-writing was in the performance thrill of the new, or all the talk-show shots. A live show may be the most perishable fruit on the planet, but the jokes remain. Those jokes, no matter how dated and obsolete they might be now, represent my life's work. When I was younger, if someone said something funny in a conversation, my response was, "Can I use that?" Now I say, "I used to have a joke like that."

# 63. "IT'S THE SAME OLD TUNE, FIDDLE AND GUITAR"

Comics always love a post-show hang, somewhere they can get a bite to eat, swap old stories, new jokes, and affectionate insults. In New York City in the late 1970s that place was the Green Kitchen, a short walk from Catch a Rising Star. When I first moved to Los Angeles in early 1982, that place was Canter's Delicatessen on Fairfax Avenue in West Hollywood.

One night, one of our group spotted Morey Amsterdam with a few other older guys at another table. We all knew him from his supporting role in the early 1960s sitcom *The Dick Van Dyke Show*. The show, created by the legendary Carl Reiner, was more than a domestic sitcom. Van Dyke played the head writer for a fictional comedy show, giving a generation of future young comics a funny inside look at show business. Morey Amsterdam played Buddy Sorrell, a joke writer on the show, a little wiseguy, and my personal favorite.

We were all starstruck. It's strange seeing someone in real life who you only knew as a character on a black and white TV. There's a strong temptation to touch the leprechaun, especially if you're a little buzzed.

Morey was very good-natured. He managed to smile as I blathered about what a huge fan I was and how much *The Dick Van Dyke Show* meant to me. No doubt the adrenaline boosted the man-made chemicals in my brain, throwing me into hyper-drive. One of Morey's friends tried to slow me down with a joke. Covering his plate of food with his hand, he cracked, "Easy there, fella. You're kvelling all over my potato salad."

Maybe to justify our intrusion, I introduced us as comics who worked at the Improvisation, around the corner on Melrose. And maybe because I didn't think anyone as ancient as Morey (74 at the time) might understand, I began to explain the sort of comedy performed at the Improv.

Morey was polite. "Oh, sure. That's a good place for you boys to work out your jokes."

I doubled down on my stupidity. "Morey, we do things different. We don't really do joke jokes. We just talk about what we see in the world. You know, stuff about our lives."

Morey never dropped his smile. "That's good. Tell me one of these things you boys do."

I told Morey one of my jokes.

He never took his eyes off me. "That was done by Ricky Craig Jr. in 1931 ..." And then he told the joke. The language was different, but my joke was the same as Ricky Craig's.

One of us told Morey another bit.

Almost immediately he came back with, "Allen Drew did a joke kind of like that around 1947 ..." Morey did the Allen Drew joke. It wasn't "kind of like" our joke. It was, again, the same joke.

"This is fun, boys. Give me another one. You might get me with one of those LSD jokes, but most of them are just a good old, being-on-a-bender joke."

Whether we offered up a story, a one-liner or surreal take on pop culture, Morey swatted them away between bites of his sandwich. "That's Fred Allen from 1929 ... Phil Foster ... 1954."

In no time we were three slack-jawed monkeys.

"Well, whatever it is you boys are doing over there ... jokes, or bits, or shtick ... Have fun doing it."

Morey's friend gave us a parting gift. "The only new joke is an old one you haven't heard before." That was the first time I ever heard that ancient line.

The next night I told Budd of our encounter with Morey Amsterdam. He laughed and brought me to the big round table. To that point, this was the closest I had ever come to the Adult Table. Typically it was filled with celebrities. The two I remember from that night were Carl Reiner and Kenneth Mars. I told my little story and got a big laugh, undoubtedly at me.

Carl Reiner said, "Welcome to the big time."

Someone else said, "You ran into a buzz saw. Morey's an encyclopedia of jokes."

"He wrote most of them."

They quickly forgot about me and started telling Morey Amsterdam stories.

"Morey got that bastard Milton. He once sold him the same joke five times. He'd change it to a doctor, then a dentist, then a lawyer ... same joke."

In the next few days I did some research and found out that Morey Amsterdam had been a vaudeville comic when he was a teenager. At 19, he wrote for one of the greatest stand-up comics ever, Will Rogers. Morey hosted his first television show in 1948. I just thought he was a fourth lead on a sitcom.

I was embarrassed by the disrespect I had shown this man, especially considering that I had been a stand-up for only five years. Looking back, my ignorance was understandable. I was so busy trying to be funny in 1982, the last thing on my mind was how they did it in 1942. No doubt I wasn't alone in my disregard of the past in my pursuit of a place in the present. It was part of the thrill of youth to think no generation had ever loved, danced or laughed as well as we had. In order to change the world, which was our mission, the past had to be dismissed and ridiculed, if not completely torched. It's only after those attempts left us collectively face down in the mud did we wonder if anyone else had ever done this.

It wasn't even the first time I had been embarrassed by my ignorance of my chosen profession. Just a few months earlier, while staying at the Tropicana Hotel for my first taping of *An Evening at the Improv*, I stumbled into Duke's Coffee Shop for a Sunday morning coming-down afternoon breakfast. I spotted a face recognizable to me from album covers, and, without thinking, dropped down to fan mode, blurting out, "Tom Fucking Waits." Embarrassed, I didn't even linger for a reaction and sat at a table. A few minutes later, Waits stood in front of me, holding his plate of food. "Mind if I join you?"

Waits asked if I was in a band. If he stopped right there, my day was made. It was a decent guess since I wore jeans, T-shirt, old motorcycle jacket, and a wasted look. When he heard stand-up comedy was my trade he started asking questions about how I did it. I can't remember what he asked me, only that his questions were much better than my answers. It was very uncomfortable that he seemingly had put more thought into my profession than I had.

Nevertheless, it took the incident with Morey Amsterdam to prompt me to learn a little bit about the mechanics and history of stand-up.

The first thing I did was expand my comedy record collection. Visiting old record stores on the road made that easy. Someone suggested I read *The Joker Is Wild*, about the great nightclub comic Joe E. Lewis. This biography of a comic whose career peaked in the 1940s was thrilling, eye-opening, and oddly reassuring. I related to his obsessive personality and drive to get the laughs.

I collected books and albums, getting into the history of stand-up. Anything to avoid writing a new joke. Which every vaudeville comic said was the hardest thing to do. Which is why so many just used old ones. Around the turn of the 20th century, the first and only black vaudeville comedy star, Bert Williams, told a friend, "Speaking of new laughs, they are only younger than the old ones, and not quite so sincere. Did you ever hear of the origin of Joe Miller's joke book? You know, it was found in the library of Noah's Ark."

# 64. "THERE MUST BE SOME KIND OF WAY OUT OF HERE, SAID THE JOKER TO THE THIEF"

The greatest villain in the world of the stand-up comic was the joke thief, more despised than the dishonest club owner, the lying agent or the successful peer.

Jokes were the one form of currency that everyone in stand-up recognized. Jokes made a reputation, forged an identity and created a legacy. Jokes opened doors, bought cars and attracted lovers.

Even in the relatively communal comedy days of vaudeville, jokes were jealously guarded. The Vaudeville Managers Protective Association officiated over "lifted" material. Both the National Vaudeville Artists and the Variety Protected Materials Department were repositories of original scripts. But the best insurance in those days was to tip the stagehands who then guarded the material from poachers. The protection often meant vigilante actions. If the thief didn't take the warning to "lay off," then scenery would suddenly be moved loudly behind the curtain or sandbags suddenly dropped near the offending act.

If lifting material was a nuisance in vaudeville it became a capital offense after the 1950s Comedy Revolution of Mort and Lenny. As the routines became more identified with the comic's persona, the thievery felt more of a personal assault. When comics started referring to their jokes as "my babies," snatching a joke became a child abduction, a grave felony offense.

Atlanta Punchline, 1988

The problem was always determining if the comic actually stole the joke or created it independently, or if it even was the same joke.

Really about the only way I truly knew someone stole from me was if they saw me do the joke, didn't say anything, and then suddenly had the same joke. That's why if I saw a comic do a similar joke, I told them we shared the bit.

Otherwise, I gave a comic the benefit of the doubt to allow for "parallel thought." It was always possible that two comics might come up with the same idea, even a hundred years apart. In the 1870s, Mark Twain had a line, "But I never fight duels now. If a man insults me, do I challenge the man? Oh, no! I take the man (uplifting his eyes piously) by the hand, and with persuasive words lead him to a dimly lighted apartment and — kill him!" A hundred years later Steve Martin had a great joke about a girlfriend who wanted to go home. "So, I took her out to the car and — shot her."

Great minds think alike, but so do mediocre ones. The lower the hanging fruit, the more comics were likely to come up with the joke at the same time.

Sometimes it was a comic marking territory that wasn't his. In the early '60s, Shelley Berman accused Bob Newhart of stealing his use of telephone, not a specific bit about the telephone, just the phone as a device in a bit. It was as wild as if George Burns had accused Milton Berle of stealing his use of the cigar to time jokes. The telephone conversation had been a stand-up joke form since Julius Tannen did a bit about the new device in 1906, and recorded his bit on the equally new invention of the record player: "Cohen on the Telephone."

A few took it to outrageous lengths. A friend of mine once left the stage after using the classic heckler retort, "This is what happens when first cousins marry." Another comic immediately ran up to her and said, "Hey, that's my stock line."

Joke thieves created a lot of paranoia, especially among beginner comics who didn't yet trust their machine could always produce more. In 1980, auditions were held for a daytime comedy show to be hosted by David Letterman. Young Fred Stoller refused to participate for fear the producers would steal his material. The whole advantage of great material is to move a comic to greater success. To not use that material "defeats its own purpose," to quote Robert De Niro from *Raging Bull*.

Fred eventually learned, as we all did, that the only way to beat the joke thieves was to write new material. Some comics wrote 45 minutes and then built a castle and moat around their act and spent the rest of their career defending attacks, real and imagined. I preferred the gypsy model for jokes, to keep the party moving, always looking for inspiration and new pastures. When it came to joke thieves, I believed the best defense was a good offense: write new jokes. Shtick and move.

Stealing a clearly defined bit done from the stage by a certified comic was an actionable offense, but there were gray areas.

For some reason many comics viewed heckler retorts, joke savers or most any crowd-work lines as public domain. A comic in danger of drowning was more likely to grab the first line that appeared. If a comic scored with a fresh heckler put-down, you can bet that it was stock nationwide in a month. In the beginning I used stock heckler lines such as twanging a few lines of the song "Dueling Banjos" from *Deliverance*. My drive was to be as original as possible, so I worked as hard at creating heckler and saver lines as stand-alone material.

Here are a few I remember. If the heckler was a little incoherent, I said, "Anyone here speak Drunkenese?" Another drunk heckler might get, "You have one brain cell treading water in a sea of beer." If the heckler yelled something and didn't respond to my query as to what, I addressed the crowd, "Does anyone else hear that? Help me folks, I need to know if the voices are inside or outside my head. The doctor said it is an important part of my recovery to distinguish between the two." If a joke fizzled, I bounced off a stock saver at the time, "If the joke doesn't get a laugh some comics might do this — wave one hand quickly over my head — which implies the joke was over your head. But let's be honest the real deal is — *(chopping myself in the forehead with one hand)* — 'Oh, we heard you, pal. It just wasn't funny.'" I've seen comics do all those. There was a sense of pride. I learned the hard way to be satisfied with that. Claiming ownership only got skeptical looks or defensive claims of their ownership.

Different from the specific joke and far less defensible against claims of thievery is the joke concept or premise. There always has to be someone who discovers a new vein of funny, some subject now common enough for the general public to experience or at least understand. Someone in the 1950s had to be the first to do airline jokes. Someone in the

'70s had to be the first to realize Jack Nicholson was well known enough for an impression of him to score with the audience. A new concept, fresh comedic territory, was always blood in the water to comics. There were never any prohibitions against biting into a new premise.

In 1980, I was doing a lot of colleges and started to use rental cars. Next came the expected rental car jokes. I had the premise to myself for about a week. New York comics who never drove a car soon had a rental car joke or two. Nothing pushed material out of my act faster than seeing other comics modeling a knock-off version of it.

A few comics hanging out and conversing inevitably turned into spritzing contests, bound to create usable material. There were no rules here, only unspoken guidelines — the comic who provided the premise/set-up and the comic who came up with the punchline determined ownership of the joke. It might end with one of them saying, "That would work better in your act" or "This one's yours. I'll take the next." Even a comic who spritzed a wholly formed joke in conversation might get validation with a warning from one or two of the other comics. "That's funny. You have a week to take it onstage, or I am."

If a civilian said something funny, it was usually fair game. Taking something that a comedian said offstage is different than using an amateur's line. I made that mistake in New York City around 1980, using a joke that Dom Irrera said in conversation. The embarrassment from being called on that caused me to add a couple of checks to the system.

From that moment forward if a great joke came to mind, I asked other comics if it was from somebody else's act. That saved me problems a few times.

In the late '70s, when the stand-up community was still small, before the boom, the fear of being ostracized was a deterrent to thievery. When I moved to New York City in 1979, I was so careful that I dropped bits if someone had a similar one. The great Larry Miller had a nice long piece about partying as a teen and coming home to his parents' house. Soon as I heard his, I dropped mine. It didn't matter that our jokes were different; the premise was just too similar.

Unfortunately, there is no legal protection for a joke, and no recourse. It's not like music. Comics can't copyright a joke. Thirty years ago, Tom Dreesen floated the idea of creating a court to decide the ownership of disputed material. It was a noble effort to deal with an age-old problem, but not nearly practical. "Your honor, my client first did that joke in his bar mitzvah." Other than physical violence the comic's only recourse was to spread the word in the vain hope the community ostracized the offender.

One week in 1981, I played the Comedy Nest in Montreal. Adam Leslie was the act the previous week. The whole staff was raving about Adam and all his new material. As they told me the jokes, it quickly became apparent that Adam had done Mark Schiff's entire act. Any reasonable comic knew to wait at least six months before returning to a club to allow for the time to generate a sufficient amount of new material. Adam got greedy and came back in six weeks with his friend's act. The real problem was that Mark was to appear the week after me. No matter how hard I argued with the staff that Adam stole Mark's act, when Mark showed they all thought he was doing Adam's act, as did some audience members. Adam was ostracized by the New York community and frozen out of the A-room circuit.

The comedy gold rush of the '80s, attracting thousands of joke pro spectors, made it impossible for the community to police itself. It became the Wild West, with comics left to defend their stake against claim jumpers.

I once heard someone say that they can steal your jokes but can't steal you. Maybe so, but my dealings one night with The Thief of My Gags Steal taught me that if they stole enough of your jokes, they had stolen you.

I was in the upstairs office of the Atlanta Punchline in 1988, watching TV, before the ninth and last show of the week. After a three-show Saturday night, the Sunday show always felt a bit anti-climactic and unnecessary. On the plus side, Sunday's audiences were usually relaxed, less demanding, and thus perfect for trying new material.

It wasn't important to pay close attention to the show. When headlining a comedy club, it was my practice to watch the opening acts for one or two shows, mostly to determine which of my jokes needed to be shelved for the week. It was a terrible feeling when one of your best bits died unexpectedly, the shocking autopsy quickly delivered by an audience member. "The other guy already did that joke."

My act mostly involved the differences between men and women. By then it was pretty well-plowed territory, so I was accustomed to a comic possibly coming away from an argument with his woman with a joke similar to mine.

I heard of headliners who approached this problem of overlapping acts by telling the openers to ditch certain jokes and even avoid certain subjects. It was a source of pride for me to have enough material to run around any comedy roadblock.

At some point, I took off my headphones to see how the show was progressing just as the middle act did one of my jokes. Then another. And another. I was paying attention now. Every other joke out of his mouth was one of mine.

My first instinct was to stop him. It just didn't seem possible to rush the stage, swat him with a broom and pull it off as hilarious slapstick. To the audience, possession of the joke was proof of ownership. All that matters to them is whether the joke was funny or not. If a thief performed a George Carlin routine an astute comedy fan might protest. But nobody this night was picking my jokes out of this comic's rapidly growing stash.

I looked to the club's employees. They were serving drinks and counting the door, oblivious to my dilemma. It was understandable that after eight straight shows, the steady onstage chatter and crowd laughter became comedic Muzak to the staff — only a long silence, or a crazy man rushing the stage with a broom, might get their attention.

Early in my career, in the heat of the stage, another comic's joke popped from my mouth. However, there's a difference between an accidental trespassing and a burglary, and it's the intent. After watching about 15 minutes of my material go out the door I decided this thief clearly knew what he was doing. A thief was ransacking my house and I was powerless.

My preshow jitters became rage. I always comforted myself with the belief that the thief never did the joke as well as the originator. The premise was that the joke thief's conscience caused a hiccup in the joke's delivery, a distracted facial twitch, or pulled the punch in some way. This guy crushed that theory. He was really selling my jokes, performing whole routines, exactly as I did them, with my cadence and gestures. Watching another comic killing — as me — was getting more bizarre with each joke. I was through the looking glass. My feeling of uniqueness was shrinking. This guy was messing with my comedy mojo.

Panic eclipsed my anger. I had no idea as to how many of my jokes he had already done before I started listening. Not only was I going to have to follow myself, but I was going to do so without knowing how much of me was still available. I never liked watching video of my performances, but this guy had me hating myself in a way I never thought possible.

The comic finished to a huge ovation. He bounced into the small dressing room to the side of the stage like a winning prizefighter. I grabbed him. While the MC made some announcements, I read him the charges, a full listing of the stolen jokes.

He went limp and dropped his head. "I'm sorry, man. I forgot you were here."

There were no excuses or explanations. The man admitted to being a kleptomaniac. Instead of punching him, I suddenly wanted to send him to treatment.

He kept saying "Sorry." My anger turned to resignation, and then pity with a surprising tinge of empathy. I felt like Jack Nicholson in *Easy Rider*. "No need to be sorry. We're all in the same cage here." His only punishment that night was a loss of stage buzz.

The MC, Roger Kleiss, introduced me. It was not an easy show. I spent an hour dancing through a minefield of my material, but considered myself lucky that only a handful of jokes met the deadly silence. I tried a lot of new material that night.

When I came offstage the varmint had skedaddled for the next henhouse in his two-year-old, 300,000-mile Honda Civic. I never heard of or saw him again.

He's probably on a cruise ship, in the safety of international waters, performing a Tribute to Richard Jeni.

# 65. "INTERCONNECTING PRINCIPLES …
ALMOST IMPERCEPTIBLE"

The phenomenal success of *The Cosby Show* had prompted the networks to hand out development deals to comics like Tic Tacs. Somewhere around 1987, I was getting a little heat in Hollywood. CBS wanted to create a sitcom based on my act, which was centered on the relationships between men and women.

Then Tim Allen blew into town. Suddenly I heard his name everywhere. Tim Allen was killing at the Ice House and Igby's. Tim Allen made one appearance on the *The Five O'Clock Funnies* segment on the KLOS radio show of Geno Michelini, and immediately became Geno's most requested act. Tim Allen quickly sold out theaters like the Wiltern in Los Angeles and the Celebrity in Anaheim.

It was a bit startling. The last time I saw Tim, a couple of years earlier at Mark Ridley's Comedy Castle in Detroit, he was a nondescript middle act.

One night at the Improv someone said those magic words, "Tim Allen is doing your act."

The comic didn't say, "stealing your jokes," but instead, "doing your act." The difference was monumental and the implications far more sinister than simple joke thievery. The biggest fear was the comic who not only took a few jokes but also copped your spirit, your point of view. Any shot at stardom depended to a large degree on the uniqueness of your persona. It was infinitely easier to write more material than to create a new you.

Toronto Yuk-Yuks marquee, 1982 (Photo by Rosanne Buemi Jarvis)

I temporarily lost my mind and looked for evidence to support this claim.

The bulk of Tim's act was material about men and women, and specifically men's lust for power as exemplified in things such as cars and tools. In 1982 I did a "Power Tool Tour" of the Midwest. It was nothing much, just a gimmick, something to put in the newspaper ads besides "As seen on *Evening at the Improv*." Maybe I was inspired by all the chainsaws and electric drills used in the psycho-killer movies popular at that time. I only had two jokes relating to the subject. One was, "I just got a new vacuum cleaner, and like any guy I wanted the best, so I got that new Sears riding vacuum cleaner." The other was, "I just put a 200-horse outboard motor on a 10-foot duck boat. I tell you something right now… you hook a bass at 90 miles an hour, takes the fight right out of him." This was enough to convince me that Tim was poaching.

One day I complained to a mutual friend, Mike Binder, that Tim ripped me off for his onstage character. Mike knew Tim from Detroit and cautioned me, "No. You're wrong. Tim really *is* that guy. He gets off on tools and cars and that kind of stuff."

Mike caused me to take a second look at Tim and his act.

I remembered hanging out with Tim in Detroit. He absolutely loved his high-performance Volkswagen GTI. I hadn't heard a guy go on about an engine like that since the gearheads in high school. My knowledge of cars started and ended with knowing how to drive.

Tim didn't steal anything from me. It was a case of parallel thought for the joke applied to the persona. We were two middle-class white guys born in the '50s, so it was no surprise that at times we sounded alike and came to the same comedic feeding grounds. On closer inspection the differences between our acts were obvious. We took on similar subjects from completely opposite directions: I mocked the male fascination with power. Tim Allen celebrated it.

For better or worse, I was more of a male apologist, raised to blame the man and defend the woman. Tim did not ask forgiveness for his masculinity.

Like all the star comics, Tim had excellent "career timing," reflecting his times perfectly. By the late 1980s, many men felt battered from two decades of feminism. Tim Allen championed the virtues of testosterone and a legion of men rose to greet their standard bearer.

I was so close, but he was right on it.

"There's a fine line between stupid and clever," Michael McKean, as rocker David St. Hubbins, said in the 1984 movie *Spinal Tap*.

In 1990, Tim and I both had development deals at ABC. A year later, Tim's stand-up character and his point of view were reflected perfectly in his hit series, *Home Improvement*. I have a pilot script from that year in a storage box somewhere.

# 66. "TONGUE-TIED AND TWISTED, JUST AN EARTHBOUND MISFIT"

On Oct. 17, 1989, a major earthquake damaged a San Francisco theater where 12 comedians were scheduled to record their HBO half-hour specials, *One Night Stand*. The Vic Theater in Chicago was quickly chosen as a replacement.

An HBO special was important to me, as my agent and manager both said repeatedly. I flew to Chicago on a mission.

This was to be my longest television shot. A year or so earlier I did 15 minutes on Ken Weinstock's *Triple Crown of Comedy* for Showtime with Richard Jeni and Margaret Smith. This was to be twice that length but still nowhere near the hour-and-a-half sets I was typically doing in the clubs. The problem was, live shows and television appearances were not comparable. A TV shot was always a little surreal. First of all, it was a little greatest hits package, with jokes pulled from all over the act and stitched together with awkward segues to form a Frankengag. Then there was the vague feeling of somehow auditioning for the President of Show Business. Even the studio audience reacted differently than a live crowd, instinctively knowing that they, too, were on camera, and on trial. A TV audience applauded for jokes, which never happened in a live show, as if to say, "We, the audience, found that last joke to be particularly clever, and now signify that we are doing our job by delivering this verdict."

The stress to be perfect on TV was always intense. This HBO special

An earthquake moves a one-night stand 2,127 miles, 1990

was six times a normal five-minute talk show shot. That meant six times as many places to screw up.

I prepared for a *Carson* or *Letterman* appearance by practicing the five minutes every night for a couple of weeks. If headlining on the road, I opened with it. In LA, I made the circuit of the Store, Improv, and Comedy and Magic Club, juicing that odd little joke creature until it moved smoothly and sounded natural. I worked the HBO half-hour every night, two times on Friday and three on Saturday, for more than a month, trying to make it part of my DNA.

HBO scheduled two comics for two shows a night for six consecutive days at the 1,400-seat Vic. Tom Parks, a very nice and clever fellow, and I were to share the two audiences. Two straight white guys working clean for half an hour. Neither of us was going to have a problem following the other guy.

The first show, I opened. Five minutes into my act the unthinkable happened, I drew a blank. There wasn't a thought in my head, just a howling wind and a single tumbleweed rolling across an empty desert. For the first time in my career I forgot my act. I stood onstage and stared at the audience until finally blurting, "I don't know what to do next." The audience laughed. I stared at them vacantly. The audience didn't laugh.

Twelve years of performing stand-up practically every night, and a month of practicing that particular hunk of material, did not prevent my worst nightmare from coming true. I was suddenly a pimply, skinny 12-year-old entering a classroom without any pants to take a test for which I had not studied.

In the past, audience members sometimes asked after a show, "How did you remember all that?" I always said, "I don't know." Turned out I wasn't being modest. I didn't know.

It was a bizarre, temporary loss of memory. My act returned before the director reached the stage. In the nicest, most reassuring tone she reminded me that HBO always intended to use the best shots from both shows. It didn't help. I was embarrassed, still standing in front of a theater full of witnesses to my failure. My confidence was always easily shaken; it never had taken much. I finished the set, but it was not a great performance.

In my mind everything rode on the second show. Even though it went smoothly, there was an unfamiliar tightness in my performance. There was not enough time between tapings to recover the trust with my mind. The fear of blanking again was a ghost in the machine.

In the days and months following the Chicago calamity, I replayed the scene in my head countless times, studying the blanking like a personal Zapruder film, looking for a second shooter. I was 4½ years sober, so that excuse was out. Besides, I had been on stage drunk, coked and even tripping, and never forgot my act. There was no heckling or the distraction of a woman giving birth in the front row. In the end it came down to a single assassin, the pressure from the importance I placed on the moment.

To me, this half-hour special represented another step on the stairway to stardom. That was the cracked logic I fell into. There was no show business ladder of success. Everyone waited face-down in an open sewage ditch hoping for their name to be called. You never knew what might be the thing that yanked you out of the ditch, so none of it meant more than anything else. Equating show business to any other industry was always a dangerous trap. The thought of moving forward in some sort of orderly fashion with recognizable achievement markers created a false sense of status. Any feeling of entitlement led to resentment and bitterness when someone inevitably came out of nowhere and blew past.

One thing's for sure, that gaffe forever tainted my HBO *One Night*

*Stand*. If anyone complimented me on it, I had to hold back from blurting, "But you don't understand. I screwed up." That part actually wasn't difficult, having already learned that lesson from years of club appearances. Too many times I responded to a simple "good show" with a detailed analysis of the flaws in that show. Then I got to watch the smile dropping from their face and the lights going out in their eyes. The audience never needed to know what I thought of my performance, especially if it only served to diminish their experience.

Anytime I thought of the Chicago Blanking I remember the words of the 19th century German statesman Otto von Bismarck: "Those who love war, sausage, and comedy should not see how they are made." Okay, I added the comedy part.

# 67. "TALKING FUNNY AND LOOKING FUNNY AND TALKING ABOUT NOBODY JUDGE ME"

In the early days of stand-up, I experimented with stage wear as much as my act. I started performing with whatever I wore off-stage, mostly T-shirts, blue jeans or bib overalls, then for a short period a shirt and tie. I favored baggy pants, and not just for the freedom of movement they allowed. One night after a show my girlfriend, Alice, remarked that my jeans were a bit too tight, making even my tiny package a big distraction. The jeans were out. Alice stayed until she became a distraction. Nothing got in the way of the pursuit of the funny.

Around 1980, my stage costume became bowling shirts and shoes, suits from the '50s and '60s, and clip-on bowties. Putting on the stage clothes signaled it was time to go to work, time to be funny.

I once asked Rodney Dangerfield why he always wore the dark suit, white shirt, and red tie. He said, "What do I know. I'm lazy. I don't know. It's one less thing I gotta think about." For a comic, one less thing to think is always a good thing, but especially before a show.

Generally a stand-up comedian didn't hide behind the clown's mask, but some used very effective stage costumes. Steve Martin's white suit was a brilliant choice, making the pompous, self-important stage character seem even more ridiculous ... and funnier. It was much the same with Foster Brooks, who did a perfect parody of a drunk. That he came on-stage perfectly put together — a clean suit, neat beard, and

Nipples are flashed one last time in Montreal, 1989

coiffed hair — made his inability to put together a cogent thought so much funnier than if he dressed like a bowery bum. In my generation, Emo Philips' calculated eccentric look — pageboy haircut, cardboard belt, flood pants — underscored his oddball material.

I remembered hearing a few older comics, of the suit-and-tux dinner club era, laying down one of those showbiz dictums, "Always dress better than the audience." But our audience was moving from the rock concert to the comedy club, so the bar was lower. Stand-up comics are teenagers in so many ways. Teens feel the need to talk, dress and act differently than their parents, while conforming with their peers. So as much as young comics strive to carve out a comedic identity different from the previous age group, most eventually sound and look the same. The T-shirt under a suit vest, jeans and sneakers or the sport jacket pushed up on the forearms became our generational cliché. As I settled into being just another white guy doing observational material, my stage wear became the standard jacket and tie. Whether vintage or new, that was all it was, one less thing to think about.

As the MC for the New York Improv's audition night in 1979, I introduced a guy who took the stage wearing a total scuba outfit: fins, tank, mask, and wet suit. His opening line got a big laugh: "Which way is the Hudson?" Unfortunately, he didn't have any more scuba material and was stuck with the suit for the rest of his set. The sound of those flippers smacking the floor as he walked off to dead silence was very sad.

Don't let the stage clothes get in the way of joke. I experienced that a few years later.

I was performing in England in 1990 when my agent called me with an offer to do the Letterman show on the same day of my return. Before leaving, I visited London's Portobello Market and bought two articles of vintage clothing, a suit and a bright, shiny blue shirt.

Near the end of my five-minute set was a bit about how difficult it was for women to initially know whether they are premenstrual or pregnant because the symptoms were so similar. The punch line had God helping out by causing a woman's hair to shoot straight up in the air at the moment of conception. The man celebrated by signaling for a touchdown. "It's good."

When I raised my arms to signal for the touchdown, instead of getting the expected bump in laughter, it all stopped dead. I never really recovered from that loss of the momentum; the set ended kind of flat. The joke's failure to launch was puzzling.

My post-set call to my wife solved the mystery. The material for my vintage shirt was very thin. When I raised my arms on the TV show, the shirt drew tight against my chest, the bright stage lights highlighting my nipples. As the studio audience reminded me, man nipples are not functional, sexy, or funny.

The flap over the shirt caused a shake-up within my organization. I kept the jobs of performer, writer, director, and editor, but my wife became the new head of the costume department. She retired the shirt on my return to Los Angeles. Before that happened, I went directly from that Letterman appearance to the Montreal comedy festival, Just For Laughs. Of course, I wore the shirt one last time, because I'm a rebel.

# 68. "GOT TO FIND A WAY TO BRING SOME UNDERSTANDING HERE TODAY"

The term "comedy condo" was first used at either the Comedy Store in Pacific Beach in 1976 and/or the Fort Lauderdale Comic Strip in 1980. In both cases a condominium was rented for the comics, and someone named it "the comedy condo." By applying the comedy principle of "parallel thought," it was easily possible that comics on both coasts, operating independently and without knowledge of each other, possessed sufficient creativity to brand a condo they occupied on a regular basis the comedy condo. Regardless the origin, in the ensuing comedy boom of the '80s, whether the place was a house, apartment or tent, it was called the comedy condo.

That initial Comic Strip comedy condo was first-rate, with a nice TV and unblocked telephone. In an era before cellphones or even calling cards, this was important. One night, a drunken Mark Schiff dialed countries all over the world. After the club owners got the bill, the comics were forced to hike to a gas station pay phone with a pocket full of change. In the same fashion, the condos were initially cleaned by a maid service. Eventually the job went to the club manager's girlfriend, who performed a weekly walk-through, looking more for fire damage and dead bodies than things to clean.

In the summer of 1989 I worked at the Comedy Corner in West Palm Beach, Fla. The club was managed by the beloved comedy aficionado Colleen McGarr. Unfortunately, her reach didn't extend to the comedy condo. The club owner, a concert promoter, housed the comics as you might a pack of hound dogs — with just enough shelter to keep the rain off them until you need them.

My ride from the airport unlocked the front door of the old clapboard house and sprinted to his car. The slanting floors and mismatched doors gave the place a whimsical, funhouse feel. The grimy kitchen, with blackened tin pots on an ancient stove, was probably last used to brew Prohibition beer. I flushed the toilet and thought I heard the sound of water hitting dirt.

No big deal, because at this point in my career I no longer viewed the road as a path to stardom. There was a check nailed to a tree. My job was travel to the tree, pull out the nail and bring home the check. Some nails took longer to remove than others. I could survive a week in this moldy, smelly pile of kindling.

The neighborhood streets were fairly empty when I left for the 8 o'clock show. On my return a few hours later, the block was alive with commerce. A steady stream of cars crawled through a gantlet of unlicensed pharmaceutical sales reps.

I went into the house, stripped down to my undershorts and sat in front of the house's cooling device, a vintage swamp cooler constructed from B-29 bomber scraps. It blew musty 90-degree air into my face, a relief from the 95-degree stench of raw sewage percolating through the house's floorboards.

I was adjusting the antenna on the black-and-white TV, which somehow managed to still display the ghostly images of Milton Berle's Texaco Theater, when someone pounded on the front door, yelling, "Help! Let me in! Help!"

I opened the door and a young white guy with a bleeding head wound pushed past me. He was dressed in Southern Yuppie (chino pants, a button-down blue Oxford shirt and tasseled loafers). His amateurish cursing was the perfect comedic complement to his outfit.

"Motherfucker! Cocksucker motherfucker. Fucking ball-peen hammer. Ass-fucking, shit-fuck."

He paced frantically about the tiny living room in a tight circle, almost as if one foot was nailed to the floor.

I interrupted with the obvious, "What happened?"

"The fuckers hit me with a ball-peen hammer. A fucking ball-peen hammer!"

I shared his surprise. A ball-peen hammer seemed more of a weapon of opportunity than of choice. The tool's funny name certainly added humiliation to the victim's physical pain.

"I need a phone. The fucker took my money and hit me with a fucking ball-peen hammer." The more he said "ball-peen hammer" the more I had to check myself from laughing out loud. I was beginning to see the genius of the use of the ball-peen hammer.

He was looking around the room. "Where's your fucking phone?"

While digging out one of my T-shirts to staunch the bleeding, I explained that this was a comedy condo, and even gave him a history of the long-distance calling abuses that led to our loss of phone privileges. My nervous babbling didn't distract or inform him.

Holding the T-shirt to his head, he moved into the open front doorway and began yelling into the street. "Motherfuckers! You motherfucking shit-fuckers!"

At first the response from the street was composed. "You know what you did."

There was more to his ball-peen hammering than my bleeding guest was telling.

Despite nursing a head wound, the Bleeder became threatening. "I'm gonna get you, ass-wipe. I'll fuck-up all you low-life, shit-bag motherfuckers!!"

The street responded quickly. "Yeah, Cracker? Come on."

I was familiar with the term, "Cracker." It dawned on me that sharing the doorway with this angry Cracker might not be good for my community standing.

"Somebody is going to pay for this shit. I know people. Motherfuckers."

This brought laughter from the street, a mocking laughter that enraged the Bleeder. He let loose with a long, continuous barrage of cursing, screaming for all he was worth. "Motherfuckers! Cocksucking motherfuckers!! ..." He might have tossed out a few n----- bombs.

The approaching police sirens gave me as much relief as depicted in any movie, except the cops just walked the guy to his car, without saying anything to anyone. After he drove away, they did the same. I was left alone, standing on the porch, and loudly proclaiming to anyone who might be listening, "I don't know the guy."

The road was getting narrow, rough and lined with tollbooths. It was time to look for an exit ramp.

# 69. "NOTHING TO DO AND ALL DAY TO DO IT"

The first comic I saw sell merch was Jackie Martling, who recorded, edited, and pressed his first comedy album in 1979. I bought one for $5. Jackie quickly moved into making cassettes that he and other comics could sell. He made one for me in 1980 titled *Itchy Schneider Live Somewhere*. He even told me where to get copies mass-produced, but I never did. Everyone laughed at Jackie's post-show hustling, but he was pocketing an extra $30 to $80 a night, basically doubling his pay. Jackie produced two more LPs: *Goin' Ape* (1980), and *Normal People Are People You Don't Know That Well* (1980). He then hustled them over to a rising New York City radio personality, Howard Stern, and made some real money.

To be fair to myself, all my effort went into writing new material and working that material onstage. My confidence was show-to-show. I really didn't want to risk evaluating whether I had enough decent material to fill an album. Jackie's act was old jokes, great old jokes the crowds loved, so supply was not his problem.

The comedy explosion in the early 1980s raised the pay for comics so fast and so high that no one felt the need to sell product. Besides, I'm sure in the back of everyone's minds was the notion that we were all going to be stars in a day or two, so why go through all the trouble of financing and producing an album when a big record company was sure to do it for you.

Comedy CD, back and front covers, 1993

The next comic I noticed selling stuff was James Gregory, who was based out of Atlanta. He started selling T-shirts in 1986, when he was still only a feature. Like Jackie, his merchandise sales earned James more money than what the club paid him to tell jokes. When he became a headliner, the increase in pay didn't cause James to drop the merchandise. The prestige that came with closing enabled him to offer more items after the show. In the early '90s, I visited his office in the little complex adjoining the Atlanta Punchline. He had a gift catalog with not only the expected T-shirts, bumper stickers, CDs, and tapes, but also tire gauges, pens, and rain hats. He also bought about a couple hundred lottery tickets a week with the vow that if he hit big he was retiring from showbiz. Apparently, running a catalog company is exhausting.

James Gregory was the Pied Piper of Merch. Many acts were inspired by his success with post-show merch sales and followed his lead. A young merch-selling comic once told me that his merch income had enabled him to lower his asking price to the clubs, thus ensuring more work. "James Gregory says you can't sell if you're not booked."

Jeff Foxworthy sold his first redneck books after his comedy club shows. Initially, he was reluctant to do so but James Gregory told him, "You're there anyway." James should have put that phrase on a bumper sticker and sold it to comics.

Like a great joke, the merch idea eventually filtered down to the opening acts. One night, I got offstage in a club in Nebraska and wandered to the back of the room where the middle act stood at a merch table brimming with T-shirts, bumper stickers, hats, and tapes, all emblazoned with his catchphrase, "Hell, yeah." He even sold a few things unrelated to his act, a few old music CDs and magazines. He saw me eyeballing his stall's offerings and quoted the master. "James Gregory says 'You're there anyway.'" I thought, "Yeah, but I don't think he meant you have to run a flea market."

It didn't take long before acts started using stage time to promote their merch. I hated these commercials during a comedy show more than the ones in movie theaters. It wasn't just headliners, but the middle acts and openers were selling. I would stand in the back and mutter, "Work on your act." It boggled my mind that an opener or middle would waste precious stage time selling merch rather than using it to develop their stand-up. I have seen acts barely get laughs and then stand proudly at their merch table as the crowd hurried by, trying to avoid making eye contact. They might have been better off selling timeshares. They were there anyway.

Once, a comic asked if he could do five minutes in front of me, "to work on some new material." Classic line. Of course he did five minutes of stuff he had done for years, and then promoted his T-shirt, which was why he wanted the time in the first place. He then walked offstage and put a pile of T-shirts on a table by the door. He was standing there with a clueless smile on his face as I passed him on my way to the stage. I snatched one of the T-shirts and spent my first five minutes onstage mocking it. As usual, I saw a douchebag move and raised it to total asshole. He was gone when I got offstage with the intention of apologizing.

In 1991, Mark Anderson, my tireless promoter, convinced me I should produce a comedy album, more specifically a cassette. He paid to record eight of my shows at his San Diego Improv. I recorded every bit of material I had, including any bits I could remember from my first years. I dumped my notebook on that stage. Editing the tapes was painful; it amazed me how embarrassed I was by some of the material I did when I was first starting out. We did manage to fill three 90-minute tapes. No record company was interested, but Mark gave me two boxes of cassettes to sell. Actually I paid the opener to sell them for me, and stood by for any signing requests. Even that was too painful. One night I emptied the last box by tossing tapes into the crowd. A couple came flying back, so at least I got a few laughs out of it.

The late, great Vic Dunlop had one of the best-selling pieces of merch. He would put on a pair of plastic bulging bloodshot eyes. Just putting them on got some laughs, of course. Vic then added a few more jokes on how to use them in public to prank strangers. He sold the crazy eyes after the show for $5 a pair. And he sold them like crazy. Vic would drive down to some place in Tijuana where he got them for 5 cents a pair and bring back a trunk-load.

One night, watching him struggling to make change while handing the customers the eyes, I jumped onstage to help, casually telling Vic he should get one of those hawker trays with the strap around the neck like vendors used at the ballpark. The next time I saw him at Igby's, Vic showed me his new hawker tray. I said something like, "You're ready to clean up now." Vic shook his head. "Ah, man, I messed up. The other night I pulled out the eyes and some heckler yelled, 'You're not going to sell those stupid eyeballs again, are you?' I got my ass all in the air and said, 'Let me tell you about these stupid eyeballs, man. I made $80,000 with these stupid eyeballs.' There was an IRS agent in the audience and now I'm getting audited."

Come to think of it, maybe I would have sold a bumper sticker if I could have written a decent dick joke that ended with the line, "You're there anyway."

## 70. "IF I HAD MY CHANCE, I COULD MAKE THOSE PEOPLE DANCE"

The road chewed up a few comics. Away from family, friends, agents, and managers, comics on the road were lacking their usual support system. As much as comics liked to complain about club owners, sometimes they were the only person that kept the joker from a bad end in a strange town. The relationship between comic and club owner is ancient and symbiotic, necessary and antagonistic. It's the scorpion and the frog story. The scorpion begs the frog for a ride across a stream, promising not to sting him. Halfway across, the scorpion stings the frog. The dying frog asks the scorpion why he would do that knowing he will now drown. The scorpion replies, "You had to know I would. It's my nature." When it came to the club owner and the comic, who was the frog and who was the scorpion was a matter of perception.

Bill Heard at the Childe Harold in D.C. was my first club owner. He introduced me to the extremes inherent in the relationship. After I braved The Ramones crowd he treated me like a victorious gladiator. We partied till dawn on his dime. A week or two later, I opened for some local band and managed to get through my whole 15 minutes. Wild Bill screamed to everyone in the bar that his club was my new home. The next weekend, five minutes into my first performance in my new home, Bill marched to the stage waving his arms and yelling, "This is the same shit you did last week. I ain't paying for the same shit." I stood there like an idiot before

Harry Monocrusos on Bank Street, NYC, 1981

amateurishly restarting the joke he had interrupted and limping through the rest of the same act that had set him off. It was hard to be angry at him since I had only learned about a month earlier that comics didn't have to do an entirely new act every time they went onstage. Still, every time I came back to drink with friends, Bill looked at me as if I had cheated him for the fifty bucks that night.

Early on in D.C., I did a lot of opening-act work for Cellar Door Productions, run by Dave Williams. Some nights after I finished battling 600 rock fans at the legendary Bayou nightclub, Dave would hand me a shot and a beer and challenge me to a game of pinball. "Double or nothing for your pay." He'd tilt, first ball, every time, peel me off a hundred, and go back to his work. Later I saw it as his way of giving me a bonus.

I will always thank Paul Brookman for having the vision to put stand-up comedy at El Brookman's, his parents' bar, in the summer of '77. I learned a lot, met some great people, and had big laughs. But Paul was as new to being a comedy club owner as I was to being a stand-up comedian. We were both flying blind so it was not a surprise that we suffered a mid-air collision. When Garvin's, a restaurant in D.C., announced it would soon feature professional comics from New York and LA, I saw it as a personal opportunity and more possible stage time for all the local comics. Paul only saw my interest in Garvin's as disloyalty. It was my first experience with a phenomenon that has bedeviled comics forever: "If you work that club you can't work mine." There was no crazy like showbiz crazy, especially when there was money involved.

Harry Monocrusos, the owner of Garvin's, drove a new Cadillac and always carried a wad of cash, a black book filled with powerful names, a bag of white powder, and a loaded gun. To paraphrase Slim Pickens in *Dr. Strangelove*: "A fella could have a pretty good time in the nation's capital with all that." More important, Harry understood the importance of stage time for a comic's development and did all he could to get it for me. If someone called Garvin's looking to book a comic, most of the time I got the job. If the job looked dicey, Harry drove me there and made sure I got paid. He was my first real champion. He wasn't an effusive, back-slapper type, but when Harry nodded his head and said, "You got 'em," I knew in my bones that I had. There was nothing I needed more than praise. Even after Harry got out of the business, any time I came to D.C., no matter where the gig or who I was working for, Harry showed up. That meant a lot to me.

I was on the road in the summer of 1981 when Budd Friedman came to the New York Improv to scout comics for his new TV show, *An Evening at the Improv*. His ex-wife, Silver, convinced him to include me, sight unseen. That was a huge gift from a very nice woman.

Budd became part of my career. We met for the first time at a pretaping meeting in the fall of '81. Budd looked at my stage outfit of baggy pants, rental bowling shoes, and bowling shirt topped by a shiny '50s jacket and asked, "Are you Polish?"

I hung out at the Melrose Improv every night I was in town from 1982 to 1989. If you ask any comic to do an impression of Budd Friedman, they will invariably intone, mimicking his impresario's drawl: *"Cleear the aiiisle."* Eventually my goal dropped from becoming one of his favorites, to him one day saying to me, "That is a good place to stand."

A lot has been said and written about Budd, but a couple of experiences I had with him stand out.

Around 1990, I sat next to Budd during a taping of *An Evening at the*

*Improv* at the Santa Monica club. Budd was laughing like crazy at the comic onstage. It surprised me that after 30 years around comics, he still had that kind of enthusiasm. I blurted out, "You ever get tired of this?" He looked at me as if I had just asked if he ever thought of accepting Jesus Christ as his personal savior. "No. Never."

In 1985, I quit drinking and drugging. The transition to working sober was not an easy one. I was angry, and very unfunny. Night after night I tossed the mic and stormed offstage in frustration. Budd always knew everything that happened in his showroom, and certainly was aware I was bombing. Yet he kept giving me prime-time spots and words of encouragement as I stomped out of the club. "Go straight home. See you tomorrow night."

So when comedian Robert Schimmel's lawyer asked me to join a lawsuit against Budd for unauthorized use of my material on cassette tapes being sold in supermarkets, I declined. An agitated Schimmel called minutes after I hung up with his lawyer. After I told him why I would never sue Budd, to his credit Schimmel said, "That fucking Budd. I love him ... but I'm still gonna sue him."

I have to mention club manager Arthur Chichese, who made many friends during his reign at the Austin Comedy Workshop in the 1980s. Those friends got together to perform a benefit for Arthur when his health went south in 1985. It was the greatest comedy show and scene of backstage debauchery I ever witnessed, all for the love of Arthur.

There were tons of stories about club owners or promoters stiffing comics. Surprisingly, only one bounced a check off my head, for $350, and 30 years later he settled the debt. Even more surprising was the fact that Giggles owner John Cochran, the most coked-out owner in stand-up's Dead Nose Era, never even tried to rip me off.

I have to mention one club manager, Arthur Chichese, who made many friends during his reign at the Austin Comedy Workshop in the 1980s. Those friends got together to perform a benefit when his health went south in 1985. It was the greatest combination of onstage comedy and backstage debauchery I ever witnessed, all for the love of Arthur.

The original owners of the Punchline in Atlanta — Ron DiNunzio, Dave Montesanto, and Chris DiPetta — set the standard in the '80s. Everybody looked forward to working a week at the Punchline. They set a tone conducive to a great show, from the ticket booth to policing the room. But where they really excelled was in how they treated the comics. These guys made every comic feel as if he or she were their favorite. Nobody could party as hard and still take care of the business side.

The funniest club owner was the Chicago Funny Firm's Len Austervich, a former stand-up who enjoyed doubling over the comics the way they liked rocking his packed houses. He paid the comics top dollar, put them in a top hotel and never sweated the small stuff. Around 1990, a new club, Chaplin's, was opening near Wrigley Field. They offered Rich Jeni and I about three times our rate to jump ship. Len said, "Go ahead. Take the money. They don't have any parking. You'll be back in my club in a month." We did and we were.

The scariest club owner I ever met had a share of the Cleveland Comedy Club. One night after the show he invited us to a party at his house with the added bonus of seeing his collection of "World War II memorabilia." I was into history, especially if it included free alcohol. In his basement museum was a collection, but not a very wide-ranging one — not a single American or British artifact. Everything was Nazi — pistols, medals, flags, helmets, and a big, framed picture of Hitler. "Oh, jeez, look at the time. I just remembered I gotta get up early to iron my clothes for tomorrow night's show."

My favorite club owner, Mark Anderson, was also a close friend. The first time I worked for him was in 1984 at the San Diego Improv. Mark was so humble that it was a couple of years before I learned that he was a former stand-up himself. Never once did he say, "When I was doing it ..." He was just a big supporter with the deepest, most sincere laugh. I always felt funnier and looser with Mark in the room. Not long after I got sober in 1985, I got a big Las Vegas booking. While chatting with Mark, I mentioned the upcoming gig, and that the thought of playing Vegas sober made me nervous. He rented a Cadillac and let me drive it across the desert at a hundred miles an hour, laughing with me the whole time. By the time we drove into Vegas I felt as funny as Buddy Hackett. He was always trying to find a way to help me succeed, putting his money where my comedy was. We both helped each other through good times and dark times. Mark died suddenly in 2012. I will miss his friendship and laughter till the day I die.

Mark Anderson, San Diego, CA, 1988

# 71. "A MAN HEARS WHAT HE WANTS TO HEAR AND DISREGARDS THE REST"

In the summer of 1986, I traveled to British Columbia to play a small part in the film *Roxanne*, a modern-day take on *Cyrano de Bergerac*, starring Steve Martin as the lovelorn hero cursed with an unfortunate nose. The audition was just a meet-and-greet with the director Fred Schepesi – "Hi. How are you? Where are you from? New Jersey? That's great. Well, see you on the set." Since my role was Drunk No. 1, Fred probably just wanted to see if I could find my way to his office. My scene partner, Drunk No. 2, was fellow stand-up Kevin Nealon. This would be the first and only time I received top billing over Kevin. There were five other stand-ups in the movie: Steve Mittleman, Max Alexander, Maureen Murphy, Damon Wayans, and Tom Curly, one half of the comedy team Edmonds and Curly. This was at the height of the stand-up craze, and maybe Steve Martin was just trying to help a few newcomers from his former profession.

With not much else to do in the small town of Nelson but hang around the set, I took advantage of every opportunity to talk with Steve.

I first saw him at the Kennedy Center in Washington D.C., in 1977, maybe 2,000 seats. A year or so later, I saw him at the Capital Centre, an 18,000-seat basketball and hockey arena. People were yelling the punchline to nearly every one of his bits, like a sing-along at a Springsteen concert. Every great stand-up mirrors the zeitgeist perfectly. The late '70s was an era of incredible self-indulgence littered with self-

Kevin Nealon, Steve Martin, me, and unidentified photo bomber,
set of *Roxanne*, 1986

help books, and a best-selling toy called "the pet rock," a companion requiring no effort or commitment. Steve's self-absorbed, fatuous stand-up
character parodied the era perfectly.

He was the first comedy rock star, and a huge inspiration to me when
I finally picked up the mic. I didn't emulate the content or style of his act
in any way, but did try to duplicate the amount of energy he gave every
show to get maximum laughter.

On the set of *Roxanne*, I just had to ask the biggest stand-up of the
1970s why he'd retired at the height of his popularity. He said the money
was great but by the time of his arena touring he was no longer performing stand-up but merely orchestrating the crowd's recitations of his act.
Additionally, it had taken him more than 10 years to build that first act,
and instead of trying to scale Mount Everest again, he preferred to do
movies. And maybe he instinctively knew his self-centered stand-up persona was, for better or worse, forever tied to the Me Decade.

Of course, the whole experience of working with Steve was unfor-
gettable, but two events particularly stand out. During my five weeks on

location, I had been itching to get onstage and perform. I got the opportunity when I overheard two local firefighters complain that they were short of funds for a much-needed piece of equipment. In no time, it was decided — the six stand-ups would do a benefit show. Steve even agreed to MC, as long as his name wasn't used in any advertising. Ticket sales were sluggish until a local radio guy mentioned that Steve Martin would also be on the show, and then people flew private planes in from Idaho and Washington. They jammed about a thousand people into the 600-seat theater.

Even more of a thrill than sharing a stage with Steve was when he asked me to review the 20 put-downs he would be using about his character's long nose. To do a little punch-up with Steve was an indescribable high. Come on. I was writing dick jokes with *Steve Martin*, one of the greatest and most creative stand-ups ever.

Kevin Nealon and I rehearsed for a month to do our little fight scene with Steve to open the movie. It's not that we were that incompetent, but the script called for the outdoor fight to take place at dusk. They had to wait for a cloudy August day, without rain ... apparently the white rhino of Canadian summer weather. No matter. We bought mountain bikes and explored the area as highly paid tourists, a perk of working on location. Kevin is a great guy and fun to be around. He even tried to teach me golf.

The day of the shoot, I got a lesson in stardom. Steve showed up early to rehearse the fight. After walking through the choreography once or twice, we started shooting. There is one sequence where I try to jump Steve from behind and without looking he snaps his tennis racquet up and catches me full in the face, and I drop like a rock. On the first take, Steve stepped back a bit too far and his racquet caught me in the temple. I dropped like a rock, for real.

When I awoke on the ground, all I could see were a dozen people surrounding Steve. "How's your wrist, Steve?" "Maybe we should get X-rays." I lay there with a head wound, wondering if I would get fired for hurting the star.

To stay in shape while we waited that month to shoot our one scene, Kevin and I worked out every morning. Since 1979, when Kevin and I first saw the body-building documentary, *Pumping Iron*, I narrated a workout with a half-assed version of Rooney's Arnold Schwarzenegger impression, "Are you willing to throw up?" or "Let's get pumped up."

*Conan the Barbarian* had catapulted Schwarzenegger from cult figure into stardom, so people had started getting who I was doing. Kevin got a kick out of it.

A short time later Kevin became a new cast member of *Saturday Night Live*, along with his good friend Dana Carvey. I went back on the road.

Sometime later, I was backstage preparing to perform at Harrah's Casino in Lake Tahoe, psyching myself up with the Schwarzenegger impression, "I'm going to pump this crowd up." One of the stagehands, laughed, not at me, but in recognition of something else, "Ha. You're doing Hans and Franz."

Later that night I watched *Saturday Night Live* for the first time in years. Kevin and Dana were doing their weightlifting characters. I surprised myself by not getting angry.

I might have inspired the bit, but in no way did I view this as thievery. I wasn't an impressionist and my lousy Schwarzenegger was not part of my act. In fact, all I was doing was an impression of my dear friend Kevin Rooney's Schwarzenegger. Whatever words or phrases I was doing came from *Pumping Iron*, and Rooney had turned me on to that.

A few months later I bumped into Kevin at the Beachwood Café in LA. We were both happy to see each other. As we were parting, Kevin said, "I want to buy you a vacation in Hawaii." I could see he meant the offer. I said, "You don't owe me anything." I meant that, too.

# 72. "EAGLE FLEW OUT OF THE NIGHT"

Bill Gross, my agent, called me in the spring of 1987 with an interesting offer: morning DJ at a Washington, D.C., radio station. The radio station's manager, Andy Bloom, wanted to prepare the D.C. audience for Howard Stern's entrance into the second market outside his New York home base by switching formats from classic rock to comedy a few weeks before Howard's D.C. launch date. Andy thought it would be easier to put a comedian behind the mic (with a radio technician to work the controls) than to teach a music DJ to be funny. I was one of the comics chosen to do a week.

It was exciting to return to D.C., where I had started my stand-up journey. I had so much fun those five mornings that Andy hired me for a second week. Then he gave a bigger bonus: three weeks at WYSP in Philadelphia while Howard took his summer vacation.

Philly was the big city when I was an adolescent — a half-hour, or "two roadies," car ride from my hometown of Pennsville, N.J. It's where we saw the Rolling Stones and *Clockwork Orange* and bought the paraphernalia to fuel those teenage daydreams. Never did I fantasize that 20 years later I'd be blasting jokes from the same radio station that turned us on to Cheech and Chong.

I didn't quit my night job for my new day job. Being able to announce my stand-up appearance on the radio in the morning filled seats at night. Every night, I performed at one of the many comedy clubs

303

Valley Forge Music Fair, 1987 (Top and bottom)

in the tri-state area before getting up at 4 a.m. to drive from my parents' house to the station for a four-hour shift behind a different mic. Having to be on the radio at 6 a.m. helped me to duck the nightly post-show pressure to party, but even so, there was no way I could have kept that schedule for more than three weeks. Sobriety, caffeine and Mom's home cooking could only patch up so many mental leaks from sleep deprivation. By the end of my stint, my voice was as shot as my brain. I had respect for Howard's discipline to go to bed early enough every night to maintain his talent.

I had listened to Howard Stern when I was in D.C. in the late '70s and again in New York City. He was the genius who figured out that most people listened to morning radio alone, either at home or in their cars. He could take his humor over the edge of what was permissible in mixed company.

Attempting to be interesting and funny for four hours a day on the radio convinced me of his talent, toughness and work ethic. I blew through all my stand-up material the first day and every story I knew the second. As I babbled, one eye was always on lights of the phone lines, hoping a listener would call in to provide me with a crowd to work. Half of the callers were Howard fans who simply shouted "Where's Howard?" or "You suck," before hanging up. I didn't even deserve a "Baba Booey."

One regular caller was my high school friend Joe Mullin, who created so many different characters for me to play off of. One of my favorites was when he described, "Live from Memphis," the annual Elvis Presley Memorial Parade, including The Dr. Nick Drill Team tossing bottles of pills to the crowd.

The biggest adjustment was the lack of audience laughter in the studio. Even though 10 years of sharpening my sense of the funny all over the country gave me confidence, without the constant calibration of laughter my performance felt a little off-balance.

Occasionally, I broke up my on-air partner, legendary Philly rock DJ Debbi Calton, but she was not there to be my audience. Debbi ran the board, answered listeners' phone calls, and flipped through newspapers and magazines to find comedy fodder, all while keeping up a steady banter with me.

As station manager, Andy Bloom was very supportive and knew his business. Every time we'd talk sex on the air, he'd pop his head into the studio and say, "I smell ratings."

Filling in for the hugely popular Howard gave me a little taste of the perks of celebrity.

One morning on my pre-dawn commute to work I got pulled over by a Jersey state trooper while I was doing about 90. As usual, the cop asked, "What's your hurry?" (One of my earliest jokes was a response to this question: "Godzilla's heading this way!" Yes, I was heavily influenced by *Mad* magazine's "Snappy Answers to Stupid Questions.") This day I told the cop that I was filling in for Howard Stern. He laughed and said, "I love Howard. Try to keep it to 80. I'll clear the road ahead for you."

There were other celebrity perks. I co-hosted the annual summer WYSP picnic with Debbi. The theme was the '60s, with lots of wacky tobacky, air guitar, and tie-dye. One of the guest celebrities was '60s radical Abbie Hoffman who, 20 years after the revolution, still had an edge. I opened things awkwardly by mentioning that I had read his manifesto *Steal This Book* in high school. He probably felt the way I do now when some 30-year-old comes up to me after a show and says, "My mom is a big fan of yours." Abbie hit the autodial button: "Did you steal it?" I solidified my lameness by telling him I had borrowed it from my best friend. He then asked where I was during the Vietnam war. Quickly thrown in a defensive position, and attempting to get on the right side of Abbie's history, I proudly stated that I had attended the May 1970 protest in Washington, without mentioning that I was there mostly due to a case of senior-itis, and promise of unlimited marijuana. That admission got me a taste of his celebrated wit when he shot back, "Yeah, a lot of fucking good you did." Abbie then lived up to the legend and earned his appearance fee by getting his microphone cut when his diatribe against power companies went overboard.

The best thing about the Stern job was the experience of being a draw. A local promoter who heard me on the radio talking about my nightly gigs called me and asked if I wanted to make some real money.

His first date for me was the Broadway Theater in Pittman, N.J., about 20 minutes from Pennsville. In 1987, the Broadway was a 1,000-seat, freshly refurbished vaudeville theater. After just two days of promoting the show on the air it was a sellout. I even brought a special guest, the legendary 1950s Philadelphia Cowgirl television personality Sally Starr. When I was a kid, Sally and her white horse, Star, appeared at my hometown's amusement park, Riverview Beach. Afterward she put on a different show for the adults at the local honky-tonk, the Musical Bar. Sally got a standing ovation from the crowd that night in Pittman. I was so awestruck that I made the rookie mistake of handing her the microphone. A half hour later it was all I could do to wrestle the mic back from "Our Gal Sal."

The second theater date was the 3,000-seat in-the-round Valley Forge Music Fair. I told the promoter it was my last week filling in for Howard, and there was no way to sell that many tickets in that little time. It sold out in three days.

The first day I mentioned the date on the air, a young comic, Ralph Harris, called in to ask if he could be my opening act. He said he was fairly new to stand-up but was certain he could do the job. I agreed to see him that night at the Comedy Works in Philly. Ralph didn't lie. He was raw, but he was very talented and got big laughs.

After it was over, Andy Bloom offered me a job hosting the afternoon drive-time slot. It was tempting to come home, but I had my eye on television. Video Killed the Radio Star.

# 73. "TURNING CARTWHEELS ACROSS THE FLOOR"

By the late 1980s, stand-up comedy had seeped into all the cracks and crevices of show business. Every mid-sized city had a comedy club; bigger cities had two and three. On cable television, comic shows were cheap and simple to produce; point a camera at a fake brick wall, grab a handful of squirming comics from the bucket and bait the ratings hook. One night, in the Comedy and Magic Club green room, we came across about a half-dozen of these shows. They were getting the same ratings as motocross with about the same number of fatalities. Stand-up comics popped up as characters in stories on TV dramas. It was not a total surprise when my agent called with a booking on *American Bandstand*.

Looking back, it was easy to see that this was an obvious mistake. *American Bandstand* had been on the air since 1952 as a teen dance show. For 37 years, new music was rated by a teenager and each one said the same thing, "It's a good beat and you can dance to it."

My experience with MTV a year or two earlier might have led me to believe that making the kids on *American Bandstand* laugh was doable. While doing publicity for the Steve Martin movie *Roxanne* at Daytona Beach's Spring Break, a couple of MTV execs asked me to do some stand-up for their channel. They then gave me a camera crew, a giant gray brick cellphone and turned me loose. We taped everywhere, near-naked beach scenes, drunken nightclub wet T-shirt contests and debauched hotel room parties and hung-over breakfasts. Half the stuff we filmed couldn't be aired because of the cursing, drug usage, and sex. The execs were so happy with the usable footage they crowned me their favorite comedian. To be honest, I think I was the top vote-getter in a field of one. The execs asked if I might be interested in hosting a game show they were developing. In my mind, game shows were something to be suffered on sick days in grade school. I couldn't envision the funny show that Ken Ober later made his star vehicle. Instead, I pitched them a show about a hard-drinking preacher in a trailer park. What better to go with all those Poison and Whitesnake videos. Shockingly, they gave me enough money to shoot a half-dozen scenes in Austin, Texas, with great local talent like Kerry Awn, Michael Emody and Chris Bono. We sent these weird little Pink-Flamingo-goes-Honky-Tonk videos to the MTV offices in New York City and never heard from them again. Someone had gone to rehab between green-lighting my videos and watching them.

I grew up watching some of my favorite bands on *American Bandstand* so it was a bit surreal being introduced by Dick Clark, who stayed behind his clear plastic lectern, when I joined him on the stage.

First of all, the teenagers were standing. I didn't have any proof that people laughed better when seated, but it was strange to see them standing.

The crowd meandering about the dance floor did underscore the importance of fixing audience members into seats pointed in the direction of the comic. Aim the head, immobilize the body, and the brain can concentrate on the jokes.

These kids, jacked up on adrenaline and hormones, were still sweating and vibrating from their last dance number. They checked their hair, makeup, and each other, not really hearing a thing I said. Some looked bewildered as to why I was up there at all.

Two failed jokes into my act, Dick acted quickly to defuse a potential bomb. In the nicest tone, he interrupted my next silence and addressed the dancers. "Excuse me. All right, kids. Maybe you didn't hear what I said. This fella here is a comedian. He's very funny, so laugh at him. Take it from the top, Ritch. And kids, go ahead and laugh. And laugh hard."

America's most-popular music impresario then smiled warmly at me, winked, and pointed. I picked up where I left off. The kids obeyed their boss to the letter. As soon as I opened my mouth, some of them started in with fake laughter. "HA-HA-HA!"

This started an avalanche, the other teens joining piecemeal. Phony laughter followed my set-up all the way to the punchline, past it, and into the next set-up. For five minutes these kids pushed out one unholy cackle after another; inhaling, confusedly looking to their neighbors for a cue, and then laughing without ever finding one. Their laughter wasn't in unison, or continuous, but a spastic rhythm. An audience's laughter is the GPS for the comedian, telling us where and when to go. I was completely lost. My timing was all over the place, veering from nursery-rhyming to a reggae beat.

Creating fake laughter is insanely difficult on the body and soul. Most people could only force out about three fake laughs in a row before showing signs of serious mental illness. Who knows what kind of damage was done to those young minds that day.

After my last joke, I made a clear signal that it was time for them to stop laughing by letting loose with my best rock star closing, "Thank you! Good night!!"

Dick was very nice after the show. I got a check, a goodies basket, and the satisfaction of being able to say that just like Chuck Berry, the Beach Boys and Talking Heads, I once played *American Bandstand*.

# 74. "I'LL TRY NOT TO SING OUT OF KEY"

I never was much of an attack comic. I had no problem pounding hecklers, but even early on, I generally didn't bash celebrities. For purely personal reasons, I've always felt that if I couldn't do a joke to someone's face, then I shouldn't do it from the stage.

In the late '80s I did a few jokes on the wine cooler craze — how it was the perfect drink for fans of big-hair metal bands. The piece went along the lines of how it looked like bong water to me, repackaged Boone's Farm with bubbles, but that every generation needed an entry-level alcoholic drink for their young women. In the late '60s, a typical teenage girl of my generation would drink sloe gin fizzes, a mixture of sweet-syrupy cherry-flavored liqueur and 7-Up, in order to get drunk enough to forget that she wasn't really sexually attracted to the guy fumbling with her bra in the back seat of his dad's car. The last joke in the riff concerned a TV commercial for wine coolers featuring Ringo Starr that was running at the time: "I saw Ringo Starr in a wine-cooler commercial with a polar bear. Ringo, did you spend all the money?"

One night I came offstage at the Melrose Improv and a comic/club employee told me that Ringo was at Budd's table. Not only that, but someone from his party had poked their head in the showroom just as I was doing my wine-cooler bit, and told Ringo my joke about him. I waited a beat for the comic to finish the story, specifically whether Ringo laughed or not. And he just smiled at me with the same silly grin he gave the audience when his jokes inevitably fizzled. A lot of comics would have shrugged and forgotten about the whole thing before they reached their car. I'm not one of them. There's room in my ointment for a whole lot of flies.

I'm sure I was agitated when I asked, "Did Ringo laugh?'

He didn't break character, smiling blandly as he said, "I don't know."

Agitation is always a short gearshift into my cruising speed of anger. "You were there, right? You saw this whole thing happen, right?"

"Yeah." His smile never dropped a millimeter.

"How could you not know whether Ringo laughed or not?"

"I don't know. What does it matter?"

There was no real comeback for that boulder of truth. Not that any of this mattered — it was all just jokes in the wind. And really … after he convinced me he didn't know the answer, what was the point? With any other comic I would have considered the possibility he was busting my balls, but this guy didn't have the chops to even attempt a high school level prank of that sort. The fact that he didn't understand why it was important for me to know whether Ringo had laughed was just a tiny bit sadder than my need to know.

I never did the bit again. It was just a TV commercial joke, easy pickings of low-hanging fruit. Anyway, I bet Ringo laughed. Yeah, he must have laughed.

# 75. "YOU HAVE YOU TO COMPLETE AND THERE IS NO DEAL"

"You gotta quit this racket. You can dish it out, but you got so you can't take it no more." — *Edward G. Robinson in* Little Caesar

I never considered myself a provocative or particularly daring co-median. It didn't take long for me to understand that working the edge meant you occasionally had to cross the line, and maybe even roll the clown car. The line can only be found by crossing it ... especially in stand-up, where the line moves from show to show, from audience to audience. It's not like I didn't veer off the pave-ment and kick up a little dirt once in a while. I even had a saver for get-ting a largely negative reaction from the crowd. I'd draw an imaginary line on the stage, and say, "The line." Then I'd hop over it, and quickly hop back, smile and say, "I'm back." Half the audience probably didn't know what I was talking about, but probably found the hopping funny. I just wasn't built for a lot of off-roading.

In the early '80s, I got into some religious material. Combine anger over my youthful church experiences with generous amounts of alcohol and drugs, and jokes about God were bound to happen. Hanging out with fellow biblical stone-throwers Sam Kinison and Bill Hicks made it inevi-table I was going to make fun of religion and some audience somewhere was not going to get the joke.

In 1985, after a two-day party to celebrate the one-year anniversary of the Columbia Punchline, I was thrown in the back seat of a car and driven across South Carolina to the new Punchline in Greenville.

The first night was Tuesday, with the expected half-house of the half-hearted. I did my religious material and quickly reminded more than a few that the Devil can take many forms, even a stand-up comedian. They made sure to boo while fleeing, lest they become collateral damage when God ended my reign of blasphemy with an indoor lightning bolt.

After the show, I went straight to the comedy condo, since I was still detoxing from the weekend's Columbia binge. While watching TV with the middle act, the same guy who had suffered through a week of me in Atlanta, he casually asked if I was going to keep doing the Jesus jokes. It seemed like a stupid question. He just saw the bits work in Atlanta. My response was something along the lines of, "Why the fuck wouldn't I?"

"Well … Bob Jones University is right up the road. This place is the buckle of the Bible Belt."

"Then they need to hear it more than anyone."

"You got some balls, man."

More like stupidity and fear masked as righteous indignation, but whatever the reason, I did every religious bit I had in Wednesday night's show. My attitude was that anyone can do Jesus jokes in liberal places like New York City or Los Angeles to mock religion, because it was just preaching to the choir. After all, I had worked with Hicks in Oklahoma City and Tulsa, and night after night he mocked Pat Robertson, right in the guy's back yard.

Wednesday night, the crowd was bigger and so was the reaction when I did the religious material. The groans equaled the laughter and there were a few yelps of protest. And for the first time in my career I noticed quite a few walkouts. It was all I could do to whip out my dick jokes and finish with decent applause from whomever hadn't protested with their feet. That is pretty much the way it went for the rest of the week. I didn't back down, and neither did they. I had a few confrontations at the bar after the show, but didn't have Hicks' wit, who once famously told similarly offended angry Christians, "Then forgive me."

It was not a typical week on the road for me back then. I was miserable. Of course, I was getting what I was giving. I'm sure there were a few people who liked my Bible stomping, but all I noticed were the people who didn't. Bottom line, it just wasn't in my nature as a stand-up to put anything before the achievement of maximum laughter. Making my point didn't satisfy me as much as getting the Big Laugh — and that was challenging enough to do without deliberately ratcheting up the degree of difficulty.

I have nothing but admiration for comics who dedicate their careers to striking at the status quo. Watching someone ridiculing cherished political or religious beliefs sure can be entertaining, as long as the comic remembers to be funny.

Regularly working that edge takes dedication and an all-out commitment. It means being prepared to receive blowback from audience members who don't appreciate their most sacred tenets being dissected and held up for public ridicule. It also means being prepared to take a financial hit when you lose bookings from club owners who don't want the hassle.

I have no tolerance for comics whining when people are offended by their controversial material. If you want to be Lenny Bruce or Bill Hicks, then you need to have the stomach to watch the whole audience walk. Those high-wire acts who eventually made it had the rock-solid belief to spend years in the desert until their following finally found them.

A comic won't change a person's deeply held religious or political values, but instead exposes the truth behind those shared beliefs. Put the funniest liberal comedian in front of a conservative audience and see how well it goes.

I did once see an audience change their collective mind on a subject. It really was one of the most remarkable stand-up performances I ever witnessed.

At the height of the 1990-91 Persian Gulf War, I went to the short-lived Santa Monica Improv to watch my friend Randy Credico do a set. Randy was not only a deadly accurate impressionist, but one of a handful of stand-ups from my generation whose act consisted mainly of political material. The others included Barry Crimmins, Will Durst, and Bill Maher. Randy was as committed offstage as on, traveling to Nicaragua to support the Sandinistas in their civil war.

That night, comic after comic did jokes about the inept Iraqi army, and led the audience in cheers for the advancing U.S. forces. It was in no way clever or incisive political material they were doing, nor did it need to be to excite the crowd. Yelling "Fuck Saddam Hussein" into the mic was enough to get a standing ovation. I had never seen patriotic fever so high.

Credico took the stage and immediately stated he was against the war. Following about six comics who had led the giddy crowd through countless cheers for the war, Credico got mostly stunned silence, and a few boos.

He then deftly acknowledged how out of step he was and launched into a bit about his agent shaming him for it. "Randy, I can't get you work with that attitude. People love the war." He was self-deprecating about his career, while slyly taking digs at the war, and he started to get some laughs.

I'm probably not doing any of his material justice, but it was mostly improvised. He did a devastating impression of President Bush the Elder rehearsing to sell the war to the American people. "We are doing this for oil … No, you can't use that. Okay, we're doing it to protect our way of life … Just as bad. Bring back democracy to Kuwait … I just made my- self laugh with that one. Oh I got it … He's like Hitler. Let's get Hitler before he goes into Czechoslovakia. They even have the same mous- tache."

He kept hammering with the Bush impression: "We are not at war with the people of Iraq, we are at war with the Iraqi people. We must go in before they come out, otherwise we lose our pretext."

He started getting more and more laughs and fewer boos. He went darker. "Bush thought he was Churchill when it was over." As Bush: "Never have so few killed so many for so few who have so much." He even mocked our military victory: "We were outmatched. There were 300,000 Iraqi troops against only 299,000 fighter planes and bombers."

The highlight was when some guy near the stage stood and proudly pointed to his Gulf War T-shirt. Credico said, "Yeah, I see a lot of guys like you wearing Gulf War T-shirts. Last summer it was a Batman T- shirt." It brought the house down. Granted, this was the People's Repub- lic of Santa Monica and the crowd was probably mostly liberals tripping out from round-the-clock CNN war reports. Credico's set was a shot of Thorazine to bring them back to reality. If Credico had done that set in a club in, say, Fayetteville, N.C., the crowd probably would have dragged him to the town square, unstoppered the Civil War cannon and shot him to back to New York City.

The next day I was talking on the phone to Bill Hicks, and told him about Credico not just swimming against the tide the previous night, but changing it. At a New York comedy club a few days later, Credico saw Hicks preparing for an upcoming *Letterman* appearance. Bill profusely complimented Randy for his Santa Monica set and added that his own anti-war material didn't match Randy's. Credico gave Hicks the Batman T-shirt line to do on *Letterman,* with the logic that the joke deserved a bigger audience. Being combative, angry, and controversial doesn't mean you can't also be generous.

# 76. "I GOT A BEGGAR'S BRAIN AND AN OLD MAN'S HEART"

Exposure to the New York comics early in my career taught me about the ancient stand-up policy of making fun of any group not in the room. Its roots lie in the late 19<sup>th</sup> century vaudeville stage, where comics mocked the wave of new immigrants, until those Germans, Italians, and Jews became paying customers who knew enough English to understand the putdowns. Volleys of rotten vegetables convinced the comics to target someone else. Virtually every minority found protected status from public ridicule, except for one: homosexuals, who in the 1970s seemed eternally tied to the comedic whipping post.

In the stand-up world there were jokes poking fun at gay sex and stories featuring lisping, limp-wristed caricatures, but the abuse was most prevalent in crowd work, especially heckler put-downs. A '70s George Carlin heckler retort, "Do I come to your job and knock the shovel out of your hand?' had naturally degenerated in the '80s to match the societal manners. "Do I come to your job and knock the dick out of your ass?' If the comic knew his mother was in the audience, he might replace the word "ass" with "mouth."

One night at Garvin's Comedy Club in Washington, D.C., I saw a visiting New York comic use that line on a heckler. The crowd roared with laughter. After the laughter died, and before the comic could begin talking again, a man yelled, "That was homophobic." He was with three other smartly dressed men who cheered their companion's heckle. The comic had earlier baited their table with another gay slander. "Four guys … where are the women, parking the car?" That line too got a loud, we-are-laughing-at-you laugh from the crowd, no doubt boosted by the comic delivering it with a mincing voice and limp wristed posture. Not surprisingly, the comic hit the gas instead of the brakes. "It's only homophobic to the gays who take it in the ass." Naturally the comic went for the laugh from the hetero audience — playing to the majority of the people in the room is a formula for success. The last I saw of the four gay men, they were complaining to the owner. Owner Harry Monocrusos politely listened before offering them free tickets and drinks for another abuse-filled show. Being a little drunk, they happily accepted.

The gay-bashing stand-up was, of course, worse on the road. Stock lines were included with every new comedy club starter kit. Countless middle acts accepted the microphone from the opener with this bit of brilliance: "How about a hand for Nutty Nutson, one of the finest homosexuals working the business today … he just got back from Cleveland, where he got two blowjobs. He was nice enough to bring me one."

Like most comics, my sense of humor and my standards were formed long before I took the microphone for the first time. My parents didn't judge people by skin color or religious beliefs. One of my dad's favorite sayings was, "There are just good people and bad people." My comedic compass naturally pointed toward the idiosyncrasies of human behavior. Without any conscious effort, I didn't do jokes about things people can't change, such as race, gender, age, and sexuality. Besides, I felt powerless growing up and always identified with the underdog.

My reasons for any enlightenment in this area were personal. Clyde Collier was a high school friend in our small town in the mid '60s. Of course he wasn't out, but he didn't need to be. I knew Clyde was gay before I knew what gay was. Clyde was beautiful and artistic, and encouraged me to write when we were in the third grade. Harry Bolich, one of my college professors, was as out as any man could be in 1972. Harry was the first adult who said I was funny and encouraged me to explore my funny nature, exposing me to the art of comedy.

Arriving in LA, I noticed more gay jokes coming from stand-ups than in New York City, despite the fact, or maybe because of the fact, that the two comedy clubs, the Improvisation and Comedy Store, were located in famously gay West Hollywood. Predictably, the San Francisco comics were sometimes even worse. Even though the gay-rights movement had only started a decade before with the 1969 Stonewall riots, "homo jokes," no matter how they were gussied up, seemed kind of clueless in 1982. It bothered me.

As usual, my frustration resulted in new material. The added appeal was the fact that no one was doing jokes about homophobia. Nothing got me more excited to hit the stage than doing it with new jokes in a fresh area.

I decided to do three of the jokes on my next *An Evening at the Improv* appearance. The best joke, and longest, was inspired by a visit from the East Coast by a friend. He stayed with my wife and I in our rented West Hollywood house. The number of openly gay men and their open physical affection for each other disturbed him. Over and over he'd say, "Look at them. They're everywhere." In the car, he treated the whole thing like an African safari, keeping the windows up and doors locked at all times.

Late one night we went shopping at the Ralph's on Santa Monica Boulevard. As I got out of the car, he panicked, pointing to the store. "I'm not going in there with you. They'll think we're a couple."

"What? I'm not good enough for you?"

"I'm not kidding around, Shydner."

"All right, wait in the car."

"No, give me the car keys. I'll come back and get you. If I sit here, they'll hit on me."

"Yeah, like gay men are so desperate they're waiting in ambush."

I then completed the bit by using a mincing voice for my friend's fictional gay predator: "There he is ... get down! You boys circle behind the shopping carts, and I'll sneak up on the driver's side. Remember, he's mine."

The night of the taping it got a big laugh, and I left the stage for the bar and my natural reward at that time: a bottle of Heineken and a shot of Jack Daniel's.

A few minutes later, a man approached to say he liked my show. After buying me a beer, he brought up my homophobia material, and as a gay man how much he liked it. Basking in his reflection of my genius almost warmed me as much as the alcohol. Then he brought up my gay characterization in the last joke. He said he understood my intention, but politely asked if I thought the audience was laughing at my friend's homophobia or at my over-the-top portrayal of the gay stereotype. Of course I hadn't considered the possibility that my great joke was getting laughter under false pretenses, and probably excused myself to go the bathroom and pack my nose. When I finally did return the man was gone. He didn't leave a silver bullet, but he did leave another beer and shot for me.

His words wormed into my brain. My actions had not matched my intentions. The next time I did the final joke in my normal voice. The drop-off in laughter was noticeable. I did it a few more times with similar results. The shine was off that bit. I dropped those jokes from the rotation before their expiration date. Besides, other comics had jumped my claim and started doing homophobia material, two of them even getting laughs with a mincing gay character.

Since that time, I've been interested in who gets the short end of the joke. Every joke puts a pie in someone's face. Every joke gives someone a kick in the ass.

The comic is responsible for why the audience is laughing. I grew tired of comics doing racist, anti-Semitic, sexist or homophobic jokes or making fun of some disadvantaged group that's not in the room, and hiding behind "It's just a joke, man." I heard comics defend those jokes as only words, even using the stupid childhood rhyme, "Sticks and stones may break my bones, but words will never hurt me." Words can wound deeply, especially when they create labels that trigger institutional powers to exclude and discriminate.

Twain said, "Against the assault of laughter nothing can stand." If ridicule can help bring down the president of the United States, as Johnny Carson's nightly jokes about Richard Nixon did, then it certainly can kick the downtrodden into the gutter.

I understand the importance of freedom of speech in stand-up comedy. The First Amendment is probably one of the main reasons why stand-up comedy originated and flourished in America. Comics had the freedom to say whatever they wanted, and the audience always had the freedom to laugh or not.

Everyone in the room had First Amendment rights, not just the person holding the microphone. If a comic wanted to be a shit-thrower, then he'd better wear a raincoat. I defended a comic's right to be an asshole up there, but no perverted sense of professional courtesy caused me to defend racist or bigoted cruelty passing as comedy.

Around 1990, I was part of a benefit at the Dallas Improv. A white comic from San Francisco did a few hack "Chinese can't drive" jokes. Chinese driver jokes surely had plenty of traction in his home base of San Francisco, with its sizable Chinese population. Dallas had very few Chinese citizens, but this audience laughed anyway. He then did a long bit built around the word "nigger." After the show I got in his face about his racist material. He claimed the "nigger" bit was hip and ironic, and that the audience's laughter was proof. I told him an all-white crowd in a Dallas comedy club wasn't howling at his ironic use of "nigger." They were laughing at all the cruel stereotypes that word conjured. Luckily it was the last time I ever had to watch that guy perform.

My job was to make the audience laugh, plain and simple. Nothing in the rulebook said you had to do controversial subjects. As more and more comics poured onto the playing field, the urge to do something shocking to stand out became greater. If a straight white guy wanted to go to the edge by talking about race or rape, it just seemed like he should know who the joke was going to land on before he launched.

In 1991, I read a book about how women choose their mates, just trying to sneak a peek at my opponent's playbook. A passage on rape inspired this joke: "Rape is not really about sex, but violence and power. If rape were sexual, women could rape men, but I tell you right now, if a woman puts a gun to my head, the last thing she's gonna get is an erection. My leg will be twitching like crazy, if she wants to hop on that." The joke got a decent laugh, but one night a woman friend and I couldn't really decide where the pie landed, so even though my intent was clearly to mock the rapist, I dropped the joke.

Picking on the less fortunate, we-can-feel-better-we-are-not-them comedy came into play during the late '80s. If stand-up comedy is an art form, then jokes mocking the homeless or mentally handicapped are velvet paintings of dogs playing poker.

It was around then that I first heard complaints about "politically correct" audience reactions. Being politically incorrect became a badge of honor for some conservatives, before Bill Maher turned that meaning inside out. Most of the derision for PC behavior was aimed at traditionally liberal targets — gays, feminists, minority groups. The fact was, every group practiced groupthink and political correctness. The tighter the group's demographic, the tighter the PC controls. Any comic who mocked gun ownership in front of an NRA convention would get a taste of the gun enthusiast's particular brand of political correctness.

Society progressed and some people were left behind. There were always comics staring, slack-jawed, at a suddenly sullen audience — dinosaurs staring at a cloud-filled sky wondering why the sun no longer shines on their former killer bit of ignorance. Whenever a comic complained, "Everything is so politically correct you can't say anything," what they really meant was, "Why can't I do sexist, bigoted material like in the good ol' days." The old rag peddlers kept pushing their carts until they found an evolutionary-challenged outpost that still bought their cheap material.

Even the most skilled high-wire acts can take a misstep. A couple of years ago, I heard a story from several witnesses about a performance by one of the greatest comics of all time in front of an audience of people recovering from alcoholism and addiction. He was famous for working the edge. They knew that, and expected him to do so. However, when the comic mocked bulimia and anorexia as "bullshit conditions," the audience turned on him.

Show business offers great freedom and rewards risk-takers. In the same way that some commercial pilots might fantasize about flying an air show stunt plane, watching some great comedians soar with risky material tempted me to ignore my limitations. I may not have been the edgiest comic, but by sticking to my standards, I was able to safely land a lot of jokes.

# 77. "LET ME PLAY AMONG THE STARS"

From 1984 to 1991, I was on *The Tonight Show* about a dozen times. Even after getting to panel on my fourth appearance I wasn't a lock to be called to the couch. That was okay. I wanted his approval but never felt as comfortable with Johnny Carson as I did with David Letterman. This was strictly my problem. Plenty of comics my age rolled with Johnny, but to me he was a father figure. Growing up, my Dad and I had an adversarial and sometimes violent relationship. Later he felt my choice of a career in comedy was a mistake. I just couldn't get loose with Johnny.

My dad saw me perform a few times early in my career and never had anything to say. One night, I did the whole show about him and he left without saying a word. He never called after any of my *Tonight Show* shots. The only thing he ever said about my chosen profession was, "What you do is tough. If they don't buy the insurance I sell, I can say they didn't like that insurance, but if they don't laugh, they didn't buy you." Not really a ringing endorsement, but in my family, acknowledging your existence was as close as you might ever get to a compliment.

I got sober in 1985 and made amends to my dad for a lot of things, including wrecking his cars, the fistfights, and shooting at him while hunting. Three years later he got sober and came to California to clean up his side of the street. Afterward, we hugged and cried but there remained a gap between us.

Johnny Carson, 1988

During a 1989 *Tonight Show* appearance, I was told right before walking onto the soundstage that there wasn't enough time for panel. I tossed the disappointment and did my job. Feeling loose, I walked out and did a quick gunfighter pose before I started my set. It's something I did in the clubs from time to time. Three people might get it, but that was fine. I guess it was my version of Don Rickles' metaphor of the stand-up comic as bullfighter. The gunfighter, confrontational and suspicious, covered my relationship with the audience and the world at large.

After finishing my set, instead of acknowledging Johnny and walking for the curtain, I did a little more of the gunfighter. I pulled my jacket back with my right hand, assumed a gunfighter stance and backed slowly to the curtain, while scanning the audience for trouble.

A baffled Ed McMahon asked Johnny, "What's he doing?"

Johnny laughed. He said, "He's doing a gunfighter."

The next day my dad called me. "That gunfighter thing you did really cracked Johnny up. You know what? You're really good at this."

No call ever meant more to me. There's this old Southern expression, "You're not a man until your daddy says you're one." When I was young, I saw my dad making people laugh and my friends even said he was funny, but I didn't get it. He closed the gap that night. We've been laughing together ever since.

# 78. "EVERYBODY WANTS A BOX OF CHOCOLATES"

The title of Steve Martin's excellent autobiography is *Born Standing Up*. I don't take that literally, because people aren't born funny. A person may be born with certain capabilities useful for performing comedy (intelligence, goofy looks, a good ear, or physical and vocal abilities) but funny is not written into the genetic code. The sports and music fields abound with tales of parents passing on their great talents to their children. A stand-up can't be bred. Children of professional comedians are far more likely to pursue careers in mental health to treat the conditions that cause stand-up.

A sense of humor is learned at an early age. One or both of the professional stand-up's parents probably had an elevated sense of humor. The comic grows up in a home where comedy is valued as a diversionary tactic or for the cleverness it represents. Even with early training, it takes time for a sense of humor to develop. Nobody is looking to find comedic genius in a child as they might musical or athletic talent. The Disney Channel is filled with precocious child singers but not one 8-year-old stand-up.

Stand-up comedy is an extreme career choice, an unstable profession filled with high risk and high reward. Even with that in mind, for those who choose that path, there doesn't seem to be much choice at all. I have heard people call it a disease, an affliction. We don't do it because we can, but because we must. Something drove me to stand-up. For years I could barely talk to my family, but every night was eager to please people I had never met, and likely would never see again. No one walks out of their cubicle every night at the State Farm office to wild applause from their co-workers. Stand-ups simply need more attention and acclaim than any straight job can provide.

The process required to forge such an outrageous personality must be excessive. My theory is the young comic exists in the family as either a Prince or a Prisoner of War.

The stand-up raised as a Prince is the star of the family, to at least one of the parents; every bit of progress, from potty training to passing his driver's test, is applauded and celebrated as a mark of brilliance. When the Prince leaves home, pretty much the only jobs handing out that kind of unadulterated love and wild approval are in show business. The Prince's stand-up is a gleeful performance. Every night onstage is like the first time riding a two-wheeled bicycle in front of beaming parents. By the end of the show it's, "Look, Mom. No hands!"

The POW grows up feeling tortured, emotionally and/or physically. The stage is the only place the POW might get the positive attention and warm recognition missing from childhood. The POW's performance is a desperate plea for reparations, one last chance for the world to make it right. The POW grabs the mic as if holding a loaded gun to his or her head and screaming to invisible parents in the back of the room, "Can you see me now?"

There's no finger-pointing here. Either you're a duck or a goose; no amount of therapy, prayer or stage time can change your feathers. It's no secret. Look around. Play the game yourself. Jerry Seinfeld, Prince. Ellen DeGeneres, Princess. Eddie Murphy, Prince. Richard Pryor, POW. Sam Kinison, POW.

The nature of the beast is usually revealed in the way he or she handles the ovation at the end of the show. The Prince lingers on the stage, soaking in every last bit of that love and approval. There isn't enough possible. The Prince basks in the applause as a birthright, bowing and blowing kisses to encourage more. The POW quickly leaves the stage, fearing the audience might change its mind.

A key element in stand-up comedy is vulnerability, inherent or expressed. Openness requires trust, a scarce commodity for the POW. The

Prince easily projects likability. It's not that the Prince doesn't have demons, but he or she doesn't have to wrestle with them onstage. Those on the business side of the show can attest that at times it isn't any easier dealing with a Prince than a POW.

Most Americans gravitate toward the joyful performance of the adorable over the thinly disguised anger of the damaged. Stand-up comedy is a performing art. Connecting with the audience is priority one, and therein lies the unidentifiable "it" factor, which the audience, genius that it is, picks up on every time.

The Prince is the more likely candidate for sitcom or movie stardom. The POW peaks as a cult hero. The POW can fill a theater. There are just more Princes filling bigger theaters for a longer period of time. There is a burnout factor with a lot of POWs.

Of course, in the race to the top, there are other factors such as talent, ambition and career timing. Nonetheless, all things being equal, bet on royalty.

# 79. "SOMEDAY YOU'LL NEED SOMEONE LIKE THEY DO, LOOKING FOR WHAT YOU KNEW"

One thing has become clear to me after 39 years in the showbiz asylum; make as many friends as you can and at least flash a little respect at those who are strangers. It is a lesson I have practiced imperfectly, but there have been a lot of great teachers along the way.

Henny Youngman played the Cellar Door in Washington, D.C., in 1977. New to the game and desperate for information, I stopped Henny on his way from the stage to his dressing room. Henny was a 70-year old man looking to get back to his hotel room, but he still gave me a few minutes. He said, "Write, write, write." This from the guy who lived for six decades off the same 50 jokes, but Henny was right. More than the advice, I was impressed that Henny Youngman took the time to speak to me.

About a year later Franklyn Ajaye appeared at the Door. Fellow comic Andy Evans and I were in the audience to see one of the brightest and funniest young comics at that time. When Franklyn left the stage, we followed him outside. This was a 28-year-old guy probably looking for some kind of post-show action that didn't include a sidewalk interview with two neophytes. Still, Franklyn treated us kindly. He advised we steal some of Henny's old jokes. Actually, I don't remember anything Franklyn said. He had some great pot. What I do recall was that he made Andy and I laugh a lot, and we walked away happy.

Laugh at . . . Central Ohio's Premier Comedy Night Club

**giggles**

Big Apple Comedy in the Capitol City!

. . AND . . .

**MICHAEL RAPPORT**          **RITCH SHYDNER**

Also . . . ED DRISCOLL & KEN SONKIN (Magic Mime)

―――――Coming―――――
**Feb. 11 thru Feb. 14 James Wesley Jackson**

**AUDITION NIGHT—Every Sunday Night 8:30**
SUNDAY NIGHT ONLY — SPECIAL $2.00 Cover per person

8:30 p.m. Weds. and Thurs.
2 Shows on Fri. and Sat., 8:30 p.m. & 10:45 p.m.
Rt. 161 and Huntley Rd. . . . entrance behind
The Blarney Stone Inn
Valet Parking * Reservations Recommended
888-5909

Are you an aspiring comic? Come
and compete for a talent contract
**ON SUNDAY AUDITION NIGHT**
at Giggles with your host and M.C.
— Fritz the Night Owl. Call us at
888-5909 for information.

Somebody will be there and be funny, 1980

One night in 1981 at New York's Catch a Rising Star, David Brenner arrived in a limo, wearing a full-length fur coat and accompanied by a beautiful young woman, but when he hit the stage he was all business. I didn't get to fully enjoy his performance because I had to follow him. When I left the stage, David was still in the room. He stopped me as I passed, smiled, and said, "Young pups snapping at my heels." I felt accepted by a big brother.

In those early, sometimes shaky, days of a stand-up's career, any recognition from someone higher up the food chain was important. At one time or another, in one way or another, Robert Klein, Rodney Dangerfield, and Jay Leno showed kindness and support to a lot of novice comics, myself included.

Sometime in 1981 or '82, I stepped offstage at Tickles, the original Pittsburgh Comedy Club, and Garry Shandling introduced himself. Naturally I knew who he was, having watched him do a *Tonight Show* or two. He reminded me physically of David Brenner; both could flash big, toothy grins, but Garry's held a hint of pathos. The fact that his grand smile seemed so close to collapsing into a grimace made him funnier and kind of vulnerable. He wrote the best bad-date and break-up jokes ever.

I can't remember why he was in town, but he joined me at the bar and produced some notes he had taken during my show. That was a friendly sign of respect among comics. Another act might give you a cocktail napkin with a suggestion for a punchline or a tag or two. Garry handed me a piece of paper filled with tags, alternative punchlines, even ones for places I didn't even know lacked a punchline. He then asked to do a guest set in the second show. When he finished, he mentioned my name as the next act and included the word "funny." It felt like a slap on the back from one of the stars on the team.

One older comic even took a chance and gave some unsolicited advice. One night at the Melrose Improv in late 1984, I came offstage and headed for the bathroom to enjoy a post-show toot. I failed to latch the stall door. It opened just as I brought the coke spoon to my nose. Suddenly, I was face-to-face with Shelley Berman. The Shelley Berman who helped lead the stand-up revolution of the late '50s and early '60s. The Shelley Berman who had the first gold comedy album. The Shelley Berman whose contemporary, Lenny Bruce, died of a drug overdose. He held the door open and looked at me for a second, probably considering what to say. "You're funny, kid, but that's not all there is. I've seen a lot of talent wasted." My only response was some mumbled nonsense, "I got all your albums." I squeezed past him and never saw Shelley again, but his words stayed with me. That night, a legend in comedy cared enough to point out the obvious, and it was one of the things that led to me to sobriety and a whole new life.

Only one comic treated me harshly in those early years. This guy happened to be one of the rare LA acts to appear at Garvin's in 1979, its first year of operation. To him, I was a lowly house MC. He had such a condescending attitude, speaking to me as if I were an ignorant child. Everything I did irritated him — my crowd work, my announcements, and especially my introductions. He was one of those guys with a long, detailed introduction. For one show, I forgot to state the hotel casino in the "Opened for Engelbert Humperdinck in Las Vegas" part of his intro. He later lectured me about my lack of professionalism and understanding of showbiz subtleties.

He rode me hard the whole weekend, badgering me before and after I came offstage. He told me what jokes to drop, saying, "I do a joke about driving. Don't do yours." Fine. He told me how long to stay onstage. "If you get them laughing like three times in a row, that's enough. Bring me right up." Fine. He told me what wasn't funny in my act. "I don't get why you do that rock concert thing." Fine. He moved to No. 1 on my resentment list.

A year or so later, after a set at the New York Improv, John Cochran approached me about playing his new comedy club, Giggles, in Columbus, Ohio. He asked if I might middle the first time because an LA act was already booked as the headliner.

A couple weeks later, I was in the back of Giggles, watching the MC and in my preshow ritual of bouncing around with a Sony Walkman blasting in my ears when I got a tap on the shoulder. I turned to face the LA comic from Garvin's. As the headliner, he reminded me of my time limitation, "Don't do a minute over the 25." I didn't. What I did do was to put every fiber of my being into that set, easily plugging into a very hot crowd. I left on a big peak of laughter, probably with some classic encore baiting, "That's all the time I have, folks. I'd love to stay but I gotta go. Good night!"

The LA comic had a tough set.

The next night he approached me in the bar and said, "Hey, go easy on me out there, okay?"

I don't know if it was possible for me to dial it back in those days. A hot house was blood in the water. Maybe it would have been possible if we were friends. If he had been a little civil to me, at least I would feel bad for him. Instead I slammed him to the mat again the next night.

The next afternoon, John Cochran called us into his office to announce a switch in the lineup. He bumped my pay, but didn't cut the former headliner's. That didn't appease the LA comic. "You can't do this to me. They're looking at me for a TV show. If this gets back to LA, I'm screwed." John smoothly assured him this would be our little Ohio secret, laid down two long lines of cocaine and handed the straw to him. The guy was still protesting as he leaned over the mirror. "What am I going to tell my fiancé?" He took a long snort and rose, wide-eyed, with a new attitude. "Actually this works out for me. I can work on my *Carson* set." Nothing fueled bullshit like a little White Line Fever.

Show business is tough enough without being in someone's crosshairs.

On the other end of the spectrum, some of my best gigs were provided by other comics, like Mike Binder, Roseanne Barr, Jeff Foxworthy, Christopher Titus, Ron White, and Jay Leno. A comic sharing the crappy condo and 500-mile car ride one day might next day hand you a six-figure studio job with a dental plan and a parking spot.

It wasn't about sucking up for work opportunities, or rolling over for powerful assholes. It was just about simple courtesy. In that space, respectful associations and some deep friendships grew, and that has to be a baseline for any job.

I came to enjoy befriending young comics, and passing along whatever experience and knowledge I might have. Their passion and dedication always inspired me.

# 80. "PAINT-BY-NUMBER DREAMS"

In the 1980s, the move from performing in the comedy clubs to the theaters was the Snake River jump of stand-up. That was the only way to truly determine if you were a draw, the simplest method of certification as a stand-up star.

Most of us felt that the surest launch vehicle into theaters was the TV sitcom. There were, however, plenty of acts who did it with far less, like Sam Kinison and Emo Philips. I had a long list of television appearances, including *The Tonight Show, Late Night With David Letterman*, HBO and Showtime specials *An Evening at the Improv, Comic Strip Live*, and *Sunday Funnies*, and I was still banging away in the comedy clubs. Steven Wright did two *Tonight* shows in 1983, and became an instant draw.

By the late '80s, I was feeling the love in the packed comedy clubs. Most of the clubs I played were nine-show weeks — one show each on Tuesday, Wednesday, Thursday, and Sunday, two shows on Friday, and the death-defying three-show Saturday night, where the main goal was to avoid repeating a joke.

I experienced that sudden and total eclipse of the laugh at the Atlanta Punchline in 1984. Given my alcohol and drug intake at the time, it was more surprising that it, or much worse, didn't happen more frequently. I was whipping the third show to the finish when I followed a joke with the exact same joke. A huge laugh was followed by a sudden stillness, broken briefly by a single voice, almost offering an apology for the

```
      GENERAL
     ADMISSION
  TKT. NO.    655
  **************

      RITCH
      SHYDNER
     LAUGH TIL
    I DROP TOUR
   PRESENTED BY
      IMPROV
  CONCERT PROD.
      AUSTIN
   OPERA HOUSE
   200 ACADEMY
  AUSTIN, TEXAS
      $10.00
    SUBJECT TO
   SERVICE CHG.
  SAT.8:00 P.M.

  APR.30,1988
  **************
  TKT. NO.    655
     GENERAL
    ADMISSION
```

crowd's silence, "You just did that joke." It was a pretty abrupt shift in mood for everyone — the crowd went from the pleasure of laughter to the anguish of confusion; the comic went from boisterous confidence to thumb-sucking fear. I knew of no stock savers to dance out of that grave, and can't remember what I said to get them going again. Theorizing that it was the repetition that had caused me to nod off on the assembly line, I avoided that ever happening again by doing as much different material as possible in each of the three shows. It would be another year before I realized that cleaning the gunk from my brain box might help a little, too.

A week of packed houses was seductive in so many ways. The money kept going up. The smart club owners were very willing to pay a premium for acts that sent 300 rave reviews into the night. Sometimes, extra shows were added on a Sunday or Thursday night. Comics were getting door deals – from a hefty percentage to a guarantee and bonus. There was even extra cash for mentioning the club's name on *Carson* or *Letterman*.

All those packed houses, big ovations, and post-show back-slapping made it easy to think that those people came to see you specifically, that you had fans.

Such was my state of mind when Mark Anderson approached me about transitioning to theaters in 1988. Mark opened the first Improvisation franchise in San Diego's Pacific Beach in 1984. It's not that he didn't have enough going on, tending to his far-flung empire of comedy clubs, but Mark was always restless, and I had become a pet project. He was determined to help me reach the next level, and he put his money where my mouth was.

After running some numbers, Mark thought my strongest market was Austin, Texas. I had played there since 1983, and in the last two years the comedy club had added extra shows and always sold out. Mark pointed to my success the year before, when I sold out two theaters in Philly after filling in for Howard Stern at local radio station WYSP for three weeks. He thought my time had come, but I had seen other popular road comics attempt the jump, only to crash and burn, suffering not just a hit to their pride, but their swagger and mojo.

Mark booked a night at the 1,200-seat Austin Opry House, figuring I had sold far more tickets during a 10-show week at the local comedy club at that time, the Laff Stop. That bit of simple math I understood. What didn't make sense to me was headlining the same venue as Willie Nelson.

It's not like I was going to be able to do a couple of radio phone-ins, fly into town the day of the show, and then go home the next day. On Monday morning, Mark and I were already banging the drum for the Saturday night show. We did every morning, noon and night radio show that would have me as many times as they would have me. We did local TV. Every newspaper and local magazine did an article about the show. Walt Whitman said, "The public is a thick-hided beast and you must pound it constantly to let it know you are there." I whacked that beast nonstop for a week. When I finally stepped onto the Opry House stage, there were 300 paying customers — not enough to stop the Persians at Thermopylae and certainly not enough to elevate me from comedy club barnacle to theater draw.

Three-hundred people jammed into a 300-seat club buzz with the shared excitement of being in the right place. Three-hundred people in a 1,200-seat theater look at all the empty seats surrounding them and question their entertainment choice for the night. Maybe that was as much a part of the difficulty in leaping from club to theater as the difference in ticket price. The comedy club was more part of the drinking rotation, with the bowling alley, sports bar, and karaoke. When someone buys a theater ticket, they are first and foremost paying to see that act, not to see something as an excuse for knocking back that night's quota of alcohol.

Mark wanted to try other markets, like San Diego and Dallas, but I had no taste for further humiliating myself or wasting more of his money, so it was back to being a liquor pimp.

By the early '90s, the comedy boom was clearly on the decline. Club owners saw the empty seats on the weekdays and lowered the cover charge. Finally they papered the room: giving away free tickets with the justification that empty seats don't buy drinks.

The Funny Firm in Chicago set up a boiler room where young people got valuable experience they later used to sell printer toner over the phone. "Hello sir, you just won 19 tickets to a comedy show." "How did I win?" "You answered the phone, didn't you?"

The comics paid the price when the ticket winners invariably talked to each other during the show as if they were at the corner bar and you were a baseball game playing on a snowy black-and-white TV. A cover charge had always sharpened the crowd's focus.

The '90s also saw a new horde of freshly ordained comedians who were pushing up through the clubs, blocked by my g-g-g-generation. In 1991, I went back to a club I had played since it opened in 1983, and for the first time in years didn't get a pay raise. The club owner looked at a half-full house on Tuesday and almost apologized to me: "Sorry, Ritch, but I can get a younger guy to do your act for less." He didn't mean my act, per se, just a guy who could hold the crowd for that hour ... and he was warning me that the next offer was going to be less.

About that time, a new hope appeared on the horizon: the one-man show. Rick Reynolds had become a theatrical hit in San Francisco. Then Rob Becker scored in Dallas with his one-man show. Suddenly there were a lot of old-guard club comics looking for ways to retool their acts into these vehicles. The formula quickly became: Concoct a title *(Ghost Dog)*, and add a bit of pathos ("My dog was hit by a car when I was a kid and that's why I decided to never ever have kids. But I'm a terrific uncle to my sister's kids and here's a bunch of jokes about them."). Most of us just slapped a new hood ornament on our old rides, hoping to spark some interest.

Mark Anderson told me to focus on male-female relationship material, which had been the core of my act since 1980. I placed a bunch of props onstage I never even made reference to, and added a few "insights" that only served to drop the time between laughs.

I did one-man shows at nearly all of Mark's Improvs. The titles changed from *True Love Confessions, The Male-Female Dictionary, The Life and Times of Canton Man,* and *The Adventures of Canyon Man.* The half houses didn't change. Brad Greenberg then gave me long runs of basically the same show in a few of his Comedy Zones with a new title,

*Man Is a Hero*, inexplicably changed to *Man Be the Hero*. It didn't matter what I called the show; the people weren't buying it. It was like that scene in *Tootsie* where Dustin Hoffman's character tells the casting director, "I can be taller, or shorter, or …" The casting director cuts Hoffman off with a curt, "We don't want you."

The last time I did a one-man show was at the Hiccups comedy club in Rochester, N.Y. I think the title of that fizzler was "Somebody Please Come Watch Me." Two weeks into that run, I understood why Evel Knievel pulled the parachute handle on his Snake River rocket cycle.

# 81. "SUSPENDED FROM A ROPE INSIDE A BUCKET DOWN A HOLE"

I n 1993, the last of my five network development deals ended with the death of the sitcom pilot, *Buddies*, co-starring Rick Ducommun. It was my bad luck that ABC decided not to put any unfunny sitcoms on their fall schedule for the first time in years.

I asked my agent for our next move. He explained his was searching for new talent and he presented me with a parting gift, a booking in Charleston, S.C. "There's nothing for you here (Hollywood)." I thanked him for believing in me until the network money stopped flowing, and walked through the William Morris hallways unrecognized for the last time.

I happily got on the Big Airliner. Getting laughs as a liquor pimp in the nightclub of a mid-sized American city was always a good salve for fresh Hollywood wounds.

My airport ride, the comedy club's assistant manager, a recent college graduate with a degree in Food and Beverages, and a minor in Microwavable Nachos, excitedly detailed the situation. This new club was located in a sports bar across the street from the North Charleston Coliseum, home to a minor-league hockey team and on this night, the Eagles, in the midst of their massive Hell Freezes Over reunion tour. They expected a big crowd as the Eagles concert was a sellout and frustrated rock fans without tickets were sure to straggle into the next available entertainment option.

I hit the stage prepared to face some serious "Play Freebird" heckling. Sure enough, a heckler appeared early in my set, but a really good heckler. This type of heckler, who never jumped into a routine, but popped up between bits, was always a gift from the gods of Mount Shecky. Nothing convulsed an audience like a great heckler exchange. The audience loved well-honed bits but nothing fixed them like in-the-moment improvisation. I had never met the man before and still hadn't really. He was just a voice from the dark. Despite this, or maybe because of it, the heckler and I quickly got into a rhythm, as if we were an old vaudeville duo. He heckled. I responded and then hit a vein of material. He disappeared while I dug every bit of comedy from that mine and bit of breath from the audience. Taking a drink of water somehow became the signal for him to reappear, leading me to a fresh motherlode. At this time in my career, I had so much material that no matter where he led, I had jokes stashed, so even my prepared material appeared to be coming off the top of my head.

It became one of those sets where even stray, punchless premises worming through my brain got a try-out. "All these new antidepressants might not be good for creating art. What if Ernest Hemingway was on Prozac? The Sun Also Rises, and it Sets too. Who cares?" The heckler added, "For Whom the Pill Tolls." Both our lines totaled maybe three laughs, and two of them were his, but it didn't matter to me.

This was one of those shows where I was so free, in the moment, and in sync with the crowd that finding the strength and sense to say "good night" became the challenge. I finally left the stage and the assistant manager bumped up my already considerable performance high, saying, "That was Sean Penn heckling you, man. He's waiting for you in the office."

Sure enough, there on the manager's stained convertible couch was a certified movie star. Sean praised my talent and then launched into a four-hour monologue of poetry, song lyrics and what sounded like a mental house-cleaning of unused movie dialogue. He was still dynamic, intelligent and blazing at 5 in the morning. Whenever I started to fade, I simply reminded myself of my new film career as Sean Penn's comedic sidekick.

The sun was rising when Sean finished his impressions of Sam Kinison with this line: "You have to move out to LA. All the good comics are there."

It suddenly dawned on me that he didn't know who I was. My Ego had convinced my Massive Insecurities that Sean had seen me perform at the Improv, or the Comedy Store or on a TV talk show. Finding himself in Charleston, S.C. with nothing to do, Sean came to see one of his favorite stand-ups. If I wasn't so laugh-drunk I would have realized that was not my career. Sean Penn simply thought he found a funny guy from South Carolina.

By the time I reached my hotel room, my mind was careening on two wheels into the dreaded pre-sleep curve of Heavy Thoughts with the fresh information that after 12 years of giving my life to making it in Los Angeles, I was still an unknown. I had been out riding fences for too long. Comedy stardom was not in my DNA, not in my future. I faced the choice confronting any comic who found themselves at my particular juncture: either continue squeaking out a living in the carnival sideshow, or go into writing for a shot at the Big Top.

# 82. "YOU'RE SO AFRAID OF BEING SOMEBODY'S FOOL"

I returned from the chance encounter with Sean Penn in Charleston, with a brand new fear: that my stand-up career was stalled. I had a wife and a 3-year-old daughter. As difficult as it was for me to be truly present with anyone, I wanted to be in their presence as much as possible. I would be out of town half of each month. By the time I recovered from the road and began to feel comfortable with my family it would be time to pack the bags again.

Rick Rogers, my friend and one-time manager, had an idea. He thought I should write for TV. I wrote funny for my act, so why not write funny for a sitcom? Stand-up to writer is a time-honored transformation.

It was February. I knew the TV series were staffed, but I called everyone I knew who had a show, hoping to plant a seed for a job in the fall. About an hour later, Roseanne called. "You want a job? You got it." The next morning I drove on the CBS Radford Lot in Studio City, filled out some tax forms, and took my place at the writers table for a hit television show.

The *Roseanne* staff was loaded with former stand-ups: Allan Stephan, Lois Bromfield, Dave Tyree, Carrie Snow, Cathy Ladman, Monica Piper, Stevie Ray Fromstein, Ed Yeager, Pat Bullard, Sid Youngers, Matt Berry, and Bob Nickman. Some had been there for a few years while others, like me, had only recently received our notice that stardom wasn't happening.

Immediately I detected a separation between the writer/producers and the stand-up/writers. The writer/producers kept the mystical job of breaking down the story and relegated the stand-up/writers to joke punch-up. And there was a lot of joke punch-up. Here's basically how it went: A line that got a big laugh during the read-through Monday morning got no laugh during the first rehearsal that afternoon because the production crew had already heard the joke during the read-through. So the word would come back that we needed to "beat" that line, *i.e.*, replace the proven joke with a new one. That's the way it went all week, beating the same line over and over, so by the taping that one line might have seen five or six jokes pass through it. Then the line wouldn't get a laugh from the studio audience during the first take, so the head writer brought out a book filled with jokes that might work for that line. Usually, Roseanne would choose the new line, usually the first joke, the one that scored in the read-through before four long days and nights of rewriting.

So that was my job, writing jokes and pitching them to writer/producers who decided if they were funny or not. Although every aspect of transitioning from a free-range stand-up to a caged TV writer was difficult, this might have been the hardest part. A stand-up is in control of everything, from the creation of the joke to when, where, and how to use it. The audience decides which jokes stay in the act, and since they generally have no other agenda but an honest desire to laugh, it's a symbiotic relationship that works brilliantly. The stand-up/writer creates a joke and the writer/producer decides which jokes get in the script. It is a boss-employee relationship filled with opposing agendas, jealousy and mistrust. I would see jokes get a laugh from a roomful of comedy writers and then some boss would kill them. There was nothing you could do but pitch another joke. Dave Tyree would lose his mind sometimes. "I know that shit is funny. Put it in the script, dammit." It was fun to watch Tyree go off, but it didn't get the joke in the script.

There is a certain satisfaction to sitcom writing; it was a thrill to hear one of the characters get a big laugh with a line I wrote. It can't compete with the rush of hearing the laughter from a club crowd, but bigger checks and sleeping in my own bed helped grease that transition. There is no stage high in a writers room.

I never knew that writers resented the performers so much. There were constant jokes between some of the writer/producers about the actors. As a former performer, I didn't think the actors' demands were so out of line ... after all, they were the ones who had to face the audience. It became apparent that those writers who complained the most about the actors were themselves frustrated performers. Jealousy is a toxic drug. These writer/producers used the writing room as their stage and the rest of the staff as a captive audience. They performed sketches they did in high school, sang entire Broadway musicals. The amount of time wasted by writers performing for each other was insane.

That was another difficult aspect of the transition from stand-up to writing — the hours spent with 20 other people in a few small rooms. One of the main reasons I chose stand-up for a profession was that I worked alone. I'm not a herd animal. A typical teacher comment on my grade-school report cards was, "Ritchie does not play well with others." I came from a dysfunctional household — put me in a room with strangers for a prolonged period of time and I start assigning old roles to new faces, "There's Dad. That one, he's Uncle Lou ..."

I found myself reverting to my high school days, staring out the windows more and more. There was no escape, not if I wanted that paycheck. For the first time in my life I became a true-blue American worker, and started overeating. There's a lot of free food in a writers room. My idea of dieting was to alternate snacks between salt and sugar. I gained a pound for every one of my jokes they rejected, and was up to 230 by the end of the season.

I was told that a young Norm Macdonald was briefly on the *Roseanne* staff before I arrived. One day he excused himself from the writers room for a smoke break. Several hours had passed when someone noted that Norm had never returned. Later, the entire writing staff was enjoying their daily ritual of a leisurely group walk around the studio lot when they spotted Norm sitting on the bank of the LA River at the edge of the lot. He spotted them, jumped up and ran away. Hearing this made me think of a story about the Battle of Gettysburg. As Confederate soldiers massed in the woods waiting to begin Pickett's Charge, a rabbit ran away. One of the soldiers yelled, "Run, rabbit. Run. I'd run too, if I could."

The more time I spent in a writers room, the less I spent onstage. I sold most of my old act and recoiled from taking the microphone to create a new one.

I used to joke, "I didn't get into this for the fame and money ... and that's been working out real well." The frustration that was the seed of that joke became a bitter snicker. My 25 years with a microphone had given me a sense of entitlement, which is a death knell in showbiz. Failing to score a sitcom caused me to feel like a failure in stand-up. I wanted to be where I thought I should be, completely ignoring that I was already where I ought to be, onstage making people laugh. The stage, once my sanctuary, became an imposing gallows, the audience, my former saviors, now a lynch mob. I completely lost sight of why I walked on the stage in the first place.

I felt double-crossed by stand-up when all it had ever promised was the chance to hear laughter. The paradox that fueled my drive to the stage — striving to be more than I was to keep from feeling less than everyone else — was spent. The perpetual motion machine stalled, leaving me lost in a dark fog of remorse and self-pity. I was consumed with self. My lack of spiritual growth was shrinking my life.

It's fine to be at war with the facts of life when you're a comic with a bully pulpit, but I found that without a microphone I didn't have much to say. My anger fermented to bitterness.

For years, my job as a comic had been to turn problems, angst, and sorrow into laughter. My instincts were to find drama, twist it maniacally, and present the audience a fresh piece of comic origami. I was always on the hunt for fresh trouble, never noticing what I was killing.

When I slammed the brakes on my stand-up career, all the troubles that I had so carelessly been tossing into the back seat came flying forward. I was suddenly buried under a pile of regret, bad memories, and guilt. I was right back to where I was when I first took the stage in 1977, without the alcohol and drugs.

One night I saw John Hiatt perform in San Francisco. At one point he told a little story of being in his basement working on a piece of music. He could not shake the feeling that he was alone and unloved, always was, and always would be. All the while he could hear his wife and children laughing and playing in the room above his head. People around me laughed. Tears popped out of my eyes.

I had been in that same room in my house, with those same feelings of isolation and despair, listening to my wife and daughter play in the next room. I know all I had to do was walk into the next room and they would greet me with hugs and smiles, pure love and total acceptance. Salvation was 10 steps away but I couldn't move.

Every day I went to the writers room and did the best I could but, unlike all my years doing stand-up, this felt like a job. At age 40, I found myself doing what I had so easily avoided, grinding it out for a paycheck. Sure it was a cushy, high-paying Hollywood job, but in stand-up I never once felt like I worked. This was a shock to my self-centered, entitled system. All those songs, *Take This Job and Shove It, Welcome to the Working Week, Blue Collar Man,* and *Factory,* suddenly had meaning beyond a catchy tune.

Then I would go home and try to be a husband and father. I felt unworthy of love, no matter how much love was offered me. I felt separate and apart from people not just on the street, but in my house. The urge to run was stronger than ever, the obligation to stay non-negotiable.

Within weeks of entering the writers room I was seeing a therapist for depression. Then came a series of psychiatrists, with their evaluations, and diagnoses of clinical depression, bipolar disorder, and PTSD. I started taking a mixture of psychotropic medications: antidepressants and antipsychotics.

The comedy boom of the 1980s was soon just another memory.

I left stand-up, and all that stand-up was, left me. I became a writer. That's making funny without the laughter.

Other comics kept joking, and hearing that sweet laughter, but I couldn't hear the music.

All my high-flying dreams were now unmarked crash sites.

I stopped imagining possibilities and went to bed.

Late in the show someone in the crowd yelled out "Condors!", and after a few seconds, Shydner began churning out an elaborate imaginary scenario about condor hunting, and how the pioneers had to first clean up the skies "that were black with condors" so they could get on to the important business of massacring the buffalo. Thanksgiving Day, he explained, was once Condor Day. In point of fact, there were once Condor Weekends, days devoted entirely to ridding the country of this winged pestilence. He was so close to saying "Three Days of the Condor," I almost yelled it out myself. But that's the magic Shydner works: Everybody wants to get into the act.

'88

'88

Early in his more than hourlong set, he took off the top of his iridescent gray sharkskin suit, revealing sweat-soaked underarms. As he paced around the microphone, his thinning blond hair began to mat against his head. Unlike a young comic who gets flop sweat, Shydner oozes confidence but not arrogance.

'82

Ritch Shydner, currently star of the show at Tickles in the Holiday House, is about five minutes into his act before he turns the evening into a party.

In his show last week at the Pittsburgh Comedy Club, he threw out lines about Pittsburgh and moved into the audience as soon as he heard a ringsider make a remark. The conversation wasn't too exciting until the fellow said he was a student at Grove City. This brought on a steady flow of college situations: blue books, fraternities, hazing — and the crowd made contributions.

When the subject wore out after 10 minutes, Shydner directed his humor toward the settling of the football strike, I.C. Light Beer and the Pitt-Penn State game. The laugh level remained high, and Shydner switched gears whenever a new customer contributed to the act.

'87

A tense Rich Scheider followed—he looks like a tall, thin Pat Haden with jump-started nerves—with fairly conventional club material on dating and marriage ("You get home late, you better have a medical excuse").

'88

The two-hour performance was not as structured as a Jay Leno gig (more on that later). Shydner left themes and returned as the mood struck him — or as the audience prompted him.

'84

Unless you are a comedy aficionado, it is possible you aren't familiar with the name Ritch Shydner. You may not know that he has been called "the Bruce Springsteen of comedy" for his intensity, intelligence, good-naturedness and his marathon performances. You may not have heard that comedians like Jay Leno and Jery Seinfeld lavish praise on him. You may be unaware of his appearances on the Tonight Show and on Mike Nesmith's new TV show, Television Parts. And you may not have been aware of his reputation for improvisation. Now that you know, wouldn't you like to look back someday and impress a friend by casually saying you saw him when? Ritch

348

# Stand-up Comedy Glossary of Terms

## A

**Act** — The total performance, all the jokes and ad-libs of the stand-up.

**Act out** — To take on a persona or create another situation onstage.

**Ad-lib** — To make up a joke within a scripted show; a spontaneous bit of humor.

**Alternative comedy** — A 1990s shift to other venues by comics rebelling against the staid and conservative format of the comedy clubs.

**Anthropomorphic humor** — Jokes where human characteristics are given to animals. Usually the comic acts out the talking animal.

## B

**Beat** — A pause; to take a break for the purpose of comic timing.

**Behavioral jokes** — Jokes constructed with the nonverbal connectors of character, emotions/state of mind, body language/actions, and sound effects.

**Bit** — A section of a stand-up comedy show or routine; also a short routine or a section of a routine.

**Blue material** — Jokes using graphic sexual overtones, scatological (toilet) references, and swear words. Derived from the practice of the Queen's censors marking out offensive line and words with a blue pencil.

**Bomb** — To perform a comedy show that gets little or very few laughs. Also: to die, go down the tubes, to tank, or eat it.

**Booker** — A person who hires and/or pays comedians to work in nightclubs.

**Borscht Belt** — Hotels and resorts in New York's Catskill Mountains known for developing and employing stand-up comedians.

**Bringer** — Amateur night show where the comics are required to bring a certain number of patrons for their stage time.

**C**

**Callback** — A joke that refers back to another joke performed earlier in the show, often presented in a different context.

**Callback** — To recall a bit again later in the show, sometimes more than once.

**Capper** — An antiquated term for the final joke in a series of jokes on the same subject matter, which ends the routine with the biggest laugh.

**Catchphrase** — A line from a comic's act that seems to neatly sum up his or her comedic voice as to become the trademark of a particular comedian. For example, Rodney Dangerfield's "I don't get no respect"; Steve Martin's "Excuse me"; Larry the Cable Guy's "Git 'er done." Sometimes called a "Hook Line."

**Character POV** — The perceptual position achieved when pretending to be someone or something else.

**Check spot** — That point during a nightclub performance when the wait staff drops the checks on their customers, thus diverting their attention and making it rough going for the comedian for that period of time.

**Closer** — A bit or hunk of material strong enough to close the show and leave the audience howling with laughter, usually the comedian's signature piece.

**Closing line** — The final joke of a stand-up comedy show, which should get a huge laugh.

**Clown** — A comic who uses anything to get a laugh, such as jokes, slapstick, or props. Also called a "wet comic."

**Comedian** — Someone who makes his or her living being funny by means of an amusing character. Someone who says things in a funny way.

**Comedic voice** — The stand-up's point of view. The essence of the stand-up's comedic character.

**Comedy condo** — Where the comedy club cages the performing monkeys between shows, usually stained with the bodily fluids of thousands of festering comics.

**Comedy explosion** — A 10-year period from the early 1980s until the early 1990s when stand-up comedy reached never-before heights of popularity and general acceptance as an art form.

**Comic** — Someone who makes his or her living being funny by telling jokes. Someone who says funny things.

**Cracker barrel** — Applied to comedians who talk to audiences in a way that resembles "just plain common sense," or folk wisdom.

# D

**Deadpan** — To keep a straight, impassive face while delivering comedic material, derived from the 1920s slang for face.

**Dick joke** — Usually referring to material that is strictly sexual in nature without any insight into the human condition or other artistic merit. Sometimes it is used to suggest any sexual joke.

**Double take** — To react twice with a shocked facial expression for comedic effect.

**Dry humor** — The use of irony and deadpan to score laughs.

**E**

**Emcee** — The comic who starts the show, makes the stage announcements, and brings up the other comics. Also called the MC or master of ceremonies.

**F**

**Feature** — The middle act in the show, going on between the opener and the headliner.

**Flop sweat** — The overabundance of perspiration one experiences from a panicked reaction to bombing.

**Flopping** — Bombing; not getting laughs.

**G**

**Gag** — A joke.

**Gag file** — A joke file.

**Gasp** — The collective reaction of the audience indicating they are shocked and affronted and that the comedian has lost them.

**Gig** — A show business job, implying a length of employment as short as the word. Derived from a phrase used by entertainers to signify that any job is a blessing, "God Is Good."

**Graphing** — A scaling device with dots on paper for evaluating the effectiveness of jokes to determine their proper placement within a routine or show.

# H

**Hack** — Material that is overused and thus cheapened and trite. Also a term used to describe a comedian who does other acts' material or does old bits that have been done to death. Generally a person who approaches stand-up without the passion of an artist but with the soul of a grocer: Are they buying airline jokes? Then let's fill the shelves with airline jokes.

**Hammer** — To pound the audience with a strong performance.

**Headliner** — The third and final comedian, considered the star of a standard stand-up comedy show. Also called the closer.

**Heckle** — An intentional interruption of the show by an audience member.

**Heckler** — An audience member who talks and interrupts a show, usually by exchanging insults with the comedian.

**Hell gig** — A low-paying job, with bad accommodations and otherwise tough working conditions, usually meaning a tough crowd.

# I

**Illegal spritz** — A comic's attempt to slip a proven bit of his or her act into conversation.

**Impressionists** — Comedians who do imitations of other people for the majority of their act.

**Improvisation** — Similar to an ad-lib, but usually refers to the spontaneous invention of an entire bit, or the continual comedic conversing with audience members.

**Inside joke** — A joke referring to information only a select group of people have.

# J

**Joke** — A device for expressing humor that employs a setup, which contains a decoy assumption to misdirect the audience into accepting a bogus first story; and a punch, which contains a reinterpretation that creates a second story, thus shattering the decoy assumption.

**Jokey** — A term used to describe such obvious jokes that one would expect to hear a rimshot following them.

# K

**Kick-around** — A joke or premise, passed around the comedy scene, used by many comics.

**Kicker** — The punchline to a joke, or last joke in a string of similar jokes or a story.

**Kill** — To give an excellent comedy performance, leaving the audience breathless and their faces sore from laughter. Similar to "Laid them out," "Did some damage."

# L

**Lineup** — A list of the comics in the order they are slated to perform.

**LPM** (laughs per minute) — A measurement for counting the number of laughs in a show. It is a meaningless statistic, as it does not account for the length of the laugh or its relative intensity. Its only purpose is to provide some club bookers and agents with a false sense that they understand comedy.

# M

**Malaprops** — Jokes that depend on word scrambling, or the improper use of words(s). Norm Crosby is its greatest modern practitioner: "Speak louder. I can't extinguish your voice."

**Material** — The jokes that make up the stand-up's performance.

**Memory laugh** — Getting a laugh from the audience by tapping into their collective reminiscence or their nostalgia, usually most effective with something they haven't thought about in years. Also called "nostalgia humor."

**Merch** — Short for "merchandise," or the things sold by the comic after the show. These items can range from DVDs and CDs to props from the act and T-shirts with a catchphrase.

**Mic (mike)** — An abbreviation for the microphone.

**Middle** — The second comedian in the standard three-comedian stand-up comedy show lineup. Also called the "feature."

**Mimic** — Copying the tone and language of another person.

**Momentum laugh** — Scoring with a joke because of the success of the previous joke rather than strength of the current one. It sounds like a joke, so the audience reacts as if it were one. Also called a "rhythm laugh."

**Monologist** — A comic whose act is comprised of verbal jokes and stories.

**Monologue** — A speech for one person; in comedy, a stand-up comedy script for a solo comedian.

**N**

**Necklace comic** — A stand-up who strings together a series of unrelated one-liners (Rodney Dangerfield, Steven Wright, Mitch Hedberg).

**Nostalgia humor** — See "Memory laugh."

**O**

**Observational comics** — Comics who gather material by watching and examining everyday life.

**On a roll** — Delivering a string of jokes so that the audience continues laughing for an extended period without interruption.

**On the road** — Continually working in places requiring overnight stays, away from the stand-up's home.

**One-liner** — A quick joke made up of only one or two sentences. One of the shortest ever was Henny Youngman's four-word classic, "Take my wife, please."

**Open-mike** — A policy to allow anyone to get onstage and try to be funny.

**One-nighter** — A one-night gig, usually in a smaller venue, or small town.

**Opener** — The first of three comedians in a standard comedy club line-up who also typically emcees the rest of the show. Also the first joke said by the stand-up.

**P**

**Pacing** — The speed or flow of the jokes over the entire show by the comic.

**Parody** — To imitate the distinctive style of an author or work for comedic effect or ridicule.

**Pause** — To stop talking in a show to enhance the timing of a joke.

**Physical comics** — Comedians who use physical movements (slapstick) throughout their act.

**POV** — Point of view.

**Pratfall** — An intentional fall to the ground by the comedian for the purpose of getting a laugh.

**Premise** — The central concept from which a series of jokes or a routine is based and written.

**Prop** — Using a created or ordinary device to get a laugh.

**Prop comics** — Comedians who use props throughout the majority of their act.

**Pun joke** — A play on words, either on different senses of the same word or a similar sound of different words. The expected audience response is usually a collective moan.

**Punchline** — The pay-off to the setup. A reinterpretation that creates a second story that shatters the setup's decoy assumption.

# R

**Regulars** — Comedians who appear frequently at a particular nightclub.

**Riffing** — Improving within the framework of a particular subject, or verbally bantering with the audience.

**Rip into** — To attack, insult, or verbally tear into an audience member or comic who has heckled or otherwise deserves the abuse.

**Routine** — The comedian's act, jokes, and stories that can be repeated on a regular basis.

**Running gag** — Multiple callbacks; a recurring joke within the same show.

# S

**Satire** – Human folly attacked through irony, derision, or wit.

**Saver** — To get a laugh by recognizing the failure of the previous joke. "I wasn't born here, but it looks like I'm going to die here." Jack E. Leonard was the King of Savers, and was rumored to have intentionally tanked jokes as a setup for his funnier savers. Johnny Carson took it to an art form.

**Segue** — A transitional sentence for purposes of leading from one joke or routine to another.

**Set** — A stand-up comedy show of any length.

**Set-up** — The first and unfunny part of the joke laying out the premise, which contains a decoy assumption.

**Shade tree comic** — An amateur approaching stand-up as a hobby, who usually has a straight job that he or she never intends to leave. Sometimes identified by using "comedian" or "comic" in his or her Facebook profile.

**Shaggy dog story** — A seemingly plausible (usually) story of varying length. As the story progresses, the listener/reader should become more and more intrigued, even if they know it's a shaggy dog story. The last line is always an absolutely hideous pun. A long, rambling joke whose humor derives from its pointlessness. As with shorter jokes, it plays on an audience's preconceived options on the art of storytelling, so the ending has nothing to do with build.

**Shock joke** — The use of language or a premise so outrageous as to cause the audience to laugh at the sheer audacity of the stand-up.

**Shot** – The material used by the stand-up in a television appearance.

**Showcase** — To perform a stand-up comedy show for little or no compensation for the purposes of getting experience, or being seen by a potential employer.

**Showcase club** — A comedy club offering little pay but exposure to comics. Usually the show is a continuous line of comics doing 15- to 20-minute sets.

**Shtick** — A Yiddish word meaning a comic scene or piece of business; often implying physical comedy.

**Sight gag** — A physical joke meant to be watched.

**Stage time** — The duration, in minutes, a comedian spends in front of an audience making them laugh.

**Stock joke** — A joke done so long and by so many comedians that the original author is anonymous. Usually it is a heckler retort. See also "kick-around."

**Stretch sign** — The emcee or club owner gives a signal of the hands pulling apart to let a comic onstage know to do more time.

**Sweater comics** – General 1980s stagewear favored by safe, TV comics.

**Switch** — Restructuring the gist and premise of a joke to make it seem like an original. Also called a "twist."

**T**

**Tag line** — An additional punchline that immediately follows a punch that does not require a new setup.

**Take** — A comedic facial reaction. Like the long pause and eye roll that Jack Benny would take before an audience.

**The hook** — Or some method to get a bombing comedian off the stage, whether it is a light, hand signal, cutting off of mic, or physical removal.

**The light** — The blinking or red light in the back of the room meant to notify the comedian it is time to wrap it up and get off the stage.

**Throw away** — To put little emphasis on a point usually considered important.

**Time slot** — The specific spot a comedian occupies within a showcase club lineup.

**Timing** — The use of tempo, rhythm, pause, etc., to enhance a joke, or tailor it to an individual performing situation.

**Toomler** — A comedian working in a Catskills resort who is expected to entertain the guests all day long, by any means necessary. Also a "clown" or "wet comic."

**Topic** — The single and overall subject of a routine.

**Topical comics** — Comedians whose material is based mostly on current events.

**Topical jokes** — About current events, politics or pop culture.

**Topper** — An antiquated term referring to a joke playing off a previous joke; same as a "kicker."

# W

**Wrap-it-up sign** — The club owner or emcee draws the hand or finger across the throat to let the comic know it is time to get off the stage.

Mainstreet's less than silent partner, Kirkland Teeple, put it simply when he said, "This guy was so overwhelming his first time through that we decided he was the *only* act we wanted for art fair week. He is truly a one-man show."

**Friedman emcees; he could skip the jokes...Marty Pollio could have easily been the closer; his mine bits are first-rate...Tommy Sledge has a good "Philip Marlowe" hook; Bobby Slayton and Rich Shydner work too much alike to be in sequence.**

Ritch Shydner's first area appearance in five years was a special one. Flowing through over an hour of strong material, the truly amazing part of his four shows over the weekend was his massive turnover of bits from set to set. He killed with his views, particularly an extended look at how mates "train each other." Shydner

It helps to be in good physical condition to see Ritch Shydner at the Comedy Workshop. This active, brilliantly improvisational comic had a Wednesday night audience limp with satisfied exhaustion.

The California-based comic's two-hour routine sparkled with quickness, sharpness, savagery. Using only about 45 minutes of prepared material, he bounced off a roudy audience like a nervous racquetball in a heated match.

**Hiccup's,** 207 Rideau St. ... **Rich Shydner** is a comedian who should have stayed in his native New Jersey. But it seems he's been making it big on the North American comedy circuit these days selling comedic contraceptives.

You know the kind of guy ... talks dirty to be funny, but he's not really.

MTV recently put Shydner at the top of the charts by naming him their "favorite comic," quite a kudo for a man who once jumped from bridges and flagpoles to make his college cronies laugh.

Shydner's ace-up-the-sleeve, however, is his ability to improvise. Improv is a dangerous game. If a comic isn't quick enough, he looks pitiful. If he resorts to insults, he comes off witlessly cruel. But when it works, the show is made more intimate and electric. Shydner calls improv "the comedy mine field." He ventures into it often. Normally, he returns not first unscathed, but with above-and-beyond-the-call-of commendations. Because of improv's spontaneous nature, it doesn't translate well to paper.

The few spontaneous moments of the evening were confined to the stand-up comedy of Ritch Shydner. A young inventive comic, Shydner took control of the audience early in his act and never let go. He could teach Le Roux a few things about pacing.

Emcee Elvis DeGroot summed it all up. "Some people think that five minutes on this stage is the longest time in the world," he said.

If I only have one life, let me live it as an audience member when Ritch Shydner's onstage. Comedian extraordinaire, he's a one-man blockbuster, a marathon comic. If or they lay, laughing is internal jogging, you'll know why so many people felt exhausted at the end of his near two-hour combination of set pieces intertwined with ad libs with the audience including a hilarious opening-night bit involving the "Variations" column of the Chronicle personals. The beauty of Shydner's comedy is that no one is the brunt. No one is ridiculed except himself, his lingering masochism. He is never hurtful, nasty or lewd.

Saturday at the Austin Opera House, comedian Ritch Shydner plowed through a wealth of prepared material, but that only took the first hour and a half. His second set of the night was reserved for woodshedding, with Shyder taking requests for the most bizarre joke topics the audience could conjure.

But Shydner regards the T more as a second wind than as a signal to wind down. "He has endless energy," says Silver Friedman, founder and owner of The Improvisation in New York City, the nation's most influential comedy club. "He can do very long sets. He's bottomless. Constant."

But everyone I talk to says his strengths outweigh his weaknesses. "He probably has more material than anybody I know," says Monocrusos. "He epitomizes the good comedian. He writes constantly and he is constantly learning." Jerry Seinfeld, a young comic who has made several appearances on the "Tonight Show" and "Late Night," says, "He takes some of the most interesting chances of any of the new comics. And he's one of the most committed. He always gives 100 percent onstage. I don't see any major weaknesses. I think he has the chance to go very far."

In the opening set, comedian Rich Shydner was right on target with his parodies of an arena rock group, a hillbilly musician, a stoned driver and a lawyer's TV commercial. Hunter and Shydner return to the Cellar Door tonight.

# Index

**A**

Abbate, Andrea, 151
Abelson, Gabe, 61
Addota, Kip, 133
Ajaye, Franklyn, 48, 330
Albano, Lou "Captain," 105
Albrecht, Chris, 52–53, 54
Aleck, Jimmy, 41, 134
Alexander, Max, 61, 299
Allen, Byron, 134
Allen, Fred, 198, 225, 263
Allen, Jeff, 41
Allen, Jerry, 61, 84
Allen, Tim, 43, 274–276
Allison, Mose, 34
Altman, Robert "Uncle Dirty,"
48, 61, 77–79, *78*, 223
Alto, Bobby, 61
Amsterdam, Morey, 262–265
Ancis, Joe, 27, 68
Andelman, Bob, 373
Anderson, Dave, 44
Anderson, Louie, 43, 96, 133
Anderson, Mark, 146, 163, 291,
297, *298*, 336–337, 338
Anderson, Vic, xiii
Anzalone, Tom, 43
Archibald, Dottie, 133, 151
Arthur, Irvin, 220
Asparagus, Freddie, 133
Astrow, Joanne, 134
Austervich, Len, 127, 297
Avon, Alan, 61
Awn, Kerry, 309
Ayers, Bob, 41

**B**

Baby Man. *see* Baum, Bruce
"Baby Man"

Bales, Peter, 61, 72, 75
Barber, Riley, 43
Barkley, Paul, 41–42
Barr, Leonard, 146
Barr, Roseanne, 151, 197, 236,
334, 343–344
Bartlett, Rob, 43
Baum, Bruce "Baby Man," 134,
147, 149
Bear, Richard T., 60
Beck, Basil D., 12–15, *13*, 44,
51
Becker, Rob, 338
Beezer, Larry, 134
Behar, Joy, 151
Belle, Craig, 15
Belmondo, Buzz, 40
Belzer, Richard, 41, 48, 60, 62,
63, 133, 150, 152
Benatar, Pat, 60
Benny, Jack, 149, 198, 225, 260
Benvenuti, Leo, 41
Bergeron, Teddy, 42, 133
Berle, Milton, 66, 225, 264, 286
Berman, Shelley, 158, 268,
332–333
Bernhard, Sandra, 133, 150
Bernstein, Craig, 13
Berry, Barry, 61
Berry, Matt, 343
Bias, Len, 249
Binder, Mike, 43, 133, 147, 274,
334
Bismark, Otto von, 280
Black, Lewis, 23, 27, 197
Blakeman, Scott, 61
Blassie, Freddie, 105
Bloom, Andy, 303, 306, 307
Bluestone, Ed, 133

Bobcat. *see* Goldthwait, Bob "Bobcat"

Bolich, Harry, 3, 319

Bolster, Joe, 48, 61, 86, *87*

Bono, Chris, 309

Boosler, Elayne, 48, 59, 70, 134, 150

Bower, Bill, 43, 96

Bradley, Brian, 133

Brady, Bill, 41

Brady, Jordan, xiii

Braverman, Marvin, 59

Brenner, David, 59, 60, 332

Breslin, Mark, 88, 89, 92, 95, 147

Brogan, Jimmy, 48, 61, 62, 134

Bromfield, Lois, 133, 343

Brookman, Paul, 23, 25, 46, 294–295

Brooks, Albert, 39, 89

Brooks, Foster, 281, 283

Brown, A. Whitney, 40

Brown, Julie, 134

Browne, Jackson, 26, 256

Bruce, Lenny, 20, 26, 27, 40, 41, 81, 100, 105, 129, 141, 150, 158, 197, 214, 224, 225, 229, 266, 315, 332

Buckles, Pat, 125

Bullard, Pat, 343

Bullard, Ronnie, 167

Burg, Lenny. *see* Shydner, Ritch

Burns, Butch, 49

Burns, George, xvi

Bursky, Alan, xiii

Burton, Irv, 133

Bush, George H.W., 316

Butler, Brett, 43, 204

Butler, Ernie, 88

**C**

Cagney, James, 90

Cain, Mike, 61, 178

Calfa, George, 61

Calley, Mike, 152

Callie, Michael, 45

Calton, Debbi, 305, 306

Camen, Joey, 133

Campbell, Bill, 42

Cannon, Dyan, 209

Cantone, Mario, 61

Caponera, John, 41

Captain. *see* Albano, Lou "Captain"

Carlin, George, 3, 26, 39–40, 81, 151, 197, 198, 223, 224, 233, 254, 257, 318

Carrey, Jim, 90

Carroll, Jean, 213

Carson, Johnny, 126, 132, 138, 191 194, 211, 227, 321, 324, *325*

Carter, Scott, 61

Carvey, Dana, 40, 134, 302

Centor, Mark, 61

Cesario, Jeff, 43, 96

Chappelle, Dave, 49

Charles, Jimmy, 61

Chase, Chevy, 113

Cherry, Donna, 133

Chichese, Arthur, 296

Ciarrochi, Bob, 18

Clark, Barney, 193–194

Clark, Blake, 133

Clark, Dick, 309–310

Clarke, Lenny, 42, 152

Clay, Andrew Dice, 133, 148, 198, 236–238

Cochran, John, 120, 122, 177, 296, 333, 334

Cohen, David, 23

Cole, Alex, 43, 96

Coleman, Fritz, 134

Collier, Clyde, 319

Colmes, Alan, 61
Conrad, Donnie, 5–6
Conrad, Joanne, 5
Cooper, Alice, 102
Corey, Irwin, 1
Corey, Jeff, 241
Coronel, Billiam, 61
Cosby, Norm, 147
Coulier, Dave, 43, 133
Cowan, Andy, 42
Craig, Ricky, Jr., 263
Credico, Randy, 149, 315–317
Crick, Ron, 43
Crimmins, Barry, 42, 149, 226, 315
Crystal, Billy, 39, 134, 141
Curly, Tom, 299

**D**
Dangerfield, Rodney, 26, 27, 48–49, 59, 60, 66–68, *67*, 75, 125–126, 148, 173, 197, 199, 205–206, 212, 217, 281, 332
Danko, Rick, 36–37
Darian, Ron, 61
Dark, Johnny, 133
Daugherty, Frank, 42
David, Larry, 61
Davies, Dave, 118
Davies, Ray, 118
Davis, Evan, 44
Davis, Michael, 40
Davis, Sammy, Jr., 168
De Niro, Robert, 268
Dearing, JoAnne, 134
DeBellis, John, 48, *57*, 61, 72
DeGeneres, Ellen, 328
DeGroot, Elvis. *see* Shydner, Ritch
Delia, Tony, 133
Dengrove, Lois, 61
DePaul, Tony, 38–39, 40

Diamond, Barry, 61, 133
The Dice Man. *see* Clay, Andrew Dice
Diller, Phyllis, 150, 212–214
DiMaggio, Lou, 61
Diner, Jerry, 61
DiNunzio, Ron, 164, 217–218, 296–297
DiPetta, Chris, 296–297
Dixon, Richard M., 42–43, 74
Dobler, Bruce, 43
Dolcelli, Max, 61
Donovan, Mike, 42
Downes, Bill, 41–42
Dreesen, Tom, 41, 134, 270–271
Drew, Allen, xvi, 263
Ducommun, Rick, 44, 134, 340
Dufor, Leo, 43
Dunlop, Vic, 133, 147, 184–188, *185*, 292
Durst, Will, 41, 149, 315
Duvall, Robert, 91
Dye, Jerry, 41
Dylan, Bob, 261

**E**
Edison, Dave, 61
Edwards, Tony, 134
Ehrlich, Paul, 256
Elmer, Bill, 43
Emody, Michael, 309
Epstein, Steve, 43
Eubanks, Bob, 161
Evans, Andy, 48, 49, 330

**F**
Farneti, John, 43
The Fat Doctor, 49
Faulkenberry, Carl, 43
Fay, Frank, 49, 63, 195
Federman, Wayne, 61

Felder, Lou, 40
Fiala, Ed, 41
Fisher, Bob, 45
Flack, Roberta, 17
Fleischer, Charlie, 134
Foster, Phil, 263
Fox, Ann, 41
Fox, John, 41, 133, 151, 164, *165*, 166
Foxworthy, Jeff, 170, 236, 238, 290, 334
Francis of Assisi, St., 15
Freud, Sigmund, 80–81
Friedman, Budd, 59, 132, 134, 137, 146, 207, 263, 295–296
Friedman, Silver, 59, 295
Fromstein, Stevie Ray, 343
Frye, David, 68

**G**
Gagen & Fine, 61
Gallagher, Jack, 42
Gari, Brian, 60
Garofalo, Janeane, 43
Gavin, Don, 42
Gayle, Jackie, 68
Gaynor, Joey, 133
George, Melvin, 61
Gerardi, Vince, 61
Gerbino, Jeff, 43
Giovanni, Jim, 40
Gleason, Jackie, 64
Gold, Richie, 54, 60, 61
Goldberg, Karen, 49
Goldberg, Whoopi, 240
Goldman, William, 235
Goldthwait, Bob "Bobcat," 42, 197, 198
Gottfried, Gilbert, 48, 54–55, 61, 63–64, 70–71, 102, 150, 225
Graham, Bill, 41, 45
Grainey, Bob, 24, 26

Green, Steven Alan, 133
Greenberg, Brad, 147, 338–339
Greenfield, Sam, 61
Greenlee, Fred, 43
Gregory, Dick, 163, 233, 255
Gregory, James, 290–291
Griffin, Merv, 181, *182*, 209–210
Gross, Bill, 58, 244, 303
Gross, Marjorie, 60, 151
Grushecky, Joe, 35

**H**
Hall, Arsenio, 41, 133, 149, 238
Hall, Jerry, 244
Hall, Rich, 42, 48, 50, 61, 70, 102, 134, 177
Hamilton, Argus, 133, 134, 152
Hansen, Scott, 43, 96
Harris, Dan, 58
Harris, Ralph, 307
Hartnett, Will, 120, 122–124
Havey, Allan, 61
Hawthorne, Dave, 43
Hayes, Tony, 43
Hayman, Jon, 23–24, 27, 61
Heard, Bill, 32, 37, 293–294
Heenan, Dave, 61
Heery, Clay, 42
Hertzog, Gilbert. *see* Prater, Ollie Joe
Hiatt, John, 346
Hicks, Bill, 43, 153, 200, 229, 231–234, 238, 313, 314, 315, 317
Hill, Charlie, 133
Himmel, Larry, 152
Hirsch, Glenn, 48, 50, 52, 61, 72
Hockstein, Ed, 61
Hoffman, Abbie, 306
Hoffman, Dustin, 27, 339

Holiday, Billie, 174
Hollis, Sam, 42
Holum, Ted, 41
Hope, Bob, 63, 225
Hoyman, Bill, 3
Huggins, Andy, 43
Hunter, Robert, 35, 174

**I**
Irrera, Dom, 61, 270
Isaris, Mike, 7
Ivy, Mike, 61

**J**
Jacobs, Neal, 100
Jagger, Mick, 244
Jane, Martha, 133
Jeni, Richard, 238, 277, 297
Jessel, Georgie, 48
Jimmy Pineapple. *see* Ladmirault, Jimmy Pineapple
Johnson, Paula, 23
Johnson, Rick, 43
Johnston, Denny, 133, 147
The Jokeman. *see* Martling, Jackie "The Jokeman"
Jones, Tim, 133
Jordan, Brent, 133

**K**
Kalenick, Sandy, 45, 56, *57*, 58
Kasten, Hiram, 61, 62
Kaufman, Andy, 39, 105–108, 134, 232
Keaton, Michael, 134
Keller, Bill, 61
Kelly, David, 61
Kelly, Paul, 41
Kelton, Bobby, 134
Kenney, Ron, 133
King, Mark, 61
Kinison, Sam, 43, 82, 133, 135,

148, 149–150, 172–173, 193, 195–200, 238, 313, 328, 335, 341–342
Kirchenbauer, Bill, 149
Klein, Howie, 52–53, 54–55
Klein, Robert, 26, 59, 81, 148, 171, 191, 198, 224, 332
Knapp, Dan, 23
Kolinsky, Sue, 61
Kozak, Paul, 178
Kramer, Kenny, 48, 53
Krenn, Jim, 43
Krug, Art, 44
Kubach, Gerald, 146
Kurland, Ben, 42

**L**
LaBove, Carl, 43, 133
Lacy, Mike, 45, 137, 258
Ladman, Cathy, 60, 151, 343
Ladmirault, Jimmy Pineapple, 43
LaMarche, Maurice, 134
Landesberg, Steve, 59, 133–134
Langston, Murray, 134
Langton, Chance, 42
Langworthy, Mike, 61
Lapides, Howard, 93
Lawrence, Martin, 49
Leary, Denis, 233
Leavett, Ron, 243, 244
Lee, London, 146
The Legendary Wid, 104
Leifer, Carol, 48, 61, 81, 86, *87*, 94, 129, 131, 134, 151, 167, 170, *216*, 220–221, 226, 238
Lennon, John, 129
Leno, Jay, 48, 59, 134, 136–138, 149, 197, 258, 332, 334
Leonard, Jack E., 260
Leslie, Adam, 271
Letterman, David, 138, 147,

251–252, 268, 324
Levine, Emily, 151
Lewis, Jerry, 236
Lewis, Joe E., 134, 265
Lewis, Richard, 59, 134
Liebman, Wendy, 151
Linde, J.P., 44
Lord, Robert, 134
Lubas, Randy, 43
Lunch, Bud. *see* Shydner, Ritch
Lynch, Ken, 42

**M**
Mabley, Moms, 1, 162–163
Mac & Jamie, 61, 134
MacDonald, Bonnie, 93
MacDonald, Mike, 89–93, *90*, 199
Macdonald, Norm, 90, 345
Madison, Joel, 43
Mae, Etta, 134
Maher, Bill, xiii, 48, 60, 62, 134, 149, 178, 315, 322
Mahler, Bruce, 134
Mandel, Howie, 134, 149
Manetti, Howard, 24
Mantia, Buddy, 61
Marc, Franz, 94
Marder, Barry, 134
Marley, Bob, 177
Mars, Kenneth, 264
Martin, Billy, 43
Martin, Steve, 26, 37, 39, 102, 149, 247, 281, 299–302, *300*, 327
Martling, Jackie "The Jokeman," 43, 74, 110–111, 144, 289
Marty and Seth, 75
Masada, Jamie, 134
Mason, Jackie, 66, 68–69, 86, 151

Mason, James, 64
Masters, Bill, 23–24, 61
Matawaran, Lorenzo. *see* Belmondo, Buzz
Matteson, Pam, 134, 151
Mayberry, Jack, 43
Maynard, Bif, 134
McCarty, Bill, 61
McCauley, Jim, 191–194, 208, 211, 227–228
McDonald, Mike, 42
McDonald, Rushion, 43
McDonnell, John, 41
McGarr, Colleen, 285–286
McGrew, Steve, 43
McKean, Michael, 276
McMahon, Ed, 148, 325
Meader, Vaughn, 129
Meaney, Kevin, 42
Melchiorre, Camillo, 15
Mendoza, John, 61
Menzel, Paul, 43
Menzel, Sharon, 43
Michaels, Felicia, 81–82, 151
Michelini, Geno, 274
Mickens, Beverly, 151
Miller, Bill, 134
Miller, Dennis, 43, 63, 150, 179–180, 238
Miller, Jimmy, 141, 179–180
Miller, Joe, 265
Miller, Larry, 48, 61, 70, 84, 134, 270
Miller, Will, 61
Minervini, Richie, 42–43, 74, 144
Mittleman, Steve, 48, 61, 70, 226, 237, 299
Monocrusos, Harry, 45, 48, 49–50, 55, 56, 58, *294*, 295, 319
Montesanto, Dave, 164, 217, 296–297

Montgomery, Carol, 151
Mooney, Paul, 134
Moore, Steve, 43, 134
Morey, Sean, 41–42
Morris, Richard, 60
Morton, Robert, 252
Moto, Mike, 61
Moye, Michael, 243–244
Mukai, Arnold, 44
Mule Deer, Gary, 134, 147
Mull, Martin, 26
Mullin, Joe, 21, 51, 305
Mulrooney, TP, 23, 27
Murphy, Eddie, 61, 144, 149, 226, 238, 328
Murphy, Maureen, 299
Myers, Bob, 42
Myers, Jim, 43

**N**
Nadler, Marty, 134
Nealon, Kevin, 134, 299, *300*, 301–302
Neil, Julian, xiii
Nelson, Bob, 43, 144
Nelson, Willie, 337
Newhart, Bob, 3, 224–225, 268
Newman, Rick, 59
Nichols, Diane, 134, 151
Nicholson, Jack, 152, 240, 270, 271
Nickman, Bob, 42, 225–226, 343
Nipote, Joe, 134
Nixon, Richard M., 42, 321
Norton, Henry, 41

**O**
Ober, Ken, 61, 309
O'Connor, Des, 109
Odes, Carey, 134
O'Neill, Ed, 244

Orbach, Judy, 60
Orbach, Ron, 241
Orion, David, 41
Osmond, Donny, 240
Otsuki, Tamayo, 134
Overton, Rick, 50, 52, 61, 70, 84, 134, 141, 226

**P**
Pachtman, Bruce, 61
Palmer, Robert, 239
Pappas, Valery, 134
Parker, Nancy, 60
Parks, Tom, 278
Parson, Wild Willy, 134
Pate, John, 134, 227–228
Patterson, Jim, 43
Paulson, Pat, 100
Peet, Harris, 134
Penn, Jeff, 58
Penn, Sean, 341–342
Perdue, Jackson, 134
Petsas, Greg, 7
Philips, Emo, 41, 149, 238, 283, 335
Phillips, Ken, 147
Pickens, Slim, 295
Pike, Dailey, 41
Piper, Monica, 134, 151, 343
Piper & Tucker, 134
Piscopo, Joe, 48, 61, 62
Platt, Peggy, 44
Pollak, Kevin, 40
Poole, Greg, 49
Poundstone, Paula, 151
Prater, Ollie Joe, 134, 154, *155*, 156
Presley, Elvis, 232
Provenza, Paul, 61
Pryor, Richard, 26, 39, 81, 132, 134, 149, 206, 223, 224, 328
Pully, B.S., 81

**R**

Rafferty, Bill, 40
Ragland, Larry, 60
Raitt, Bonnie, 256
Raleigh, Steve, 1
Ramey, Rahn, 222
Ramirez, J.J., 61
Rapport, Michael, 134, *331*
Reagan, Ronald, 148–149, 197
Record, Scott, 205–206
Red Buttons, xv, 66
Reeb, Larry, 41
Reid, Peggy, 230
Reiner, Carl, 262, 263–264
Reiser, Paul, 48, 61, 134, 144
Reitzel, Roger, 41
Reyes, Orlando, 41
Reynolds, Mike, 61
Reynolds, Rick, 44, 338
Rhodes, Tom, 24
Richards, Michael, 134
Richards, Ron, 61, 72, 134
Richardson, Gary, 43
Rickles, Don, 138, 325
Ridley, Mark, 43, 45, 147, 274
Rivers, Joan, 73, 148, 191
Roberston, Ron, 43
Robertson, Pat, 227–228
Robinson, Edward G., 313
Rockwell, Rick, 43
Rodriquez, Paul, 134
Rogers, Kelley, 48, *57*, 60, 62, 86, 87, *87*
Rogers, Rick, 343
Rogers, Will, 225, 264
Rogerson, Kenny, 41, 42
Rooney, Kevin, 23–24, 27, 61, 120, *121*, 122–124, 301–302
Root Boy Slim, 32–33
Rowe, Mike, 61
Rudner, Rita, 60, 61
Rudnick, Steve, 41

Rush, Chris, 48
Russ T Nailz, 152
Rutkowsi, Bill, 61

**S**

Saget, Bob, 134
Sahl, Mort, 40, 48, 141, 150, 195, 214, 225, 266
Salazar, Angel, 134
Sanders, Brad, 41
Savage, Bill, 230, 232
Sayh, David, 48, 60
Scheft, Bill, 61, 62
Schepesi, Fred, 299
Schiff, Mark, 48, 61, 86, *87*, 134, 226, 271, 285
Schimmel, Robert, 134, 148, 198, 296
Schmock, Jonathan, 60
Schneider, Jeff, 146
Schneider, Leonard, 229
Schrader, Paul, 56
Schultz, George, 60, 75
Schultz, Lenny, 60, 134
Schwarzenegger, Arnold, 301–302
Scott, Angela, 61
Seinfeld, Jerry, 38, 48, 61, 70, 82–83, 134, 144, 149, 171, 192, 197, 227, 238, 260–261, 328
Sergio, Mike, 60
Severa, Ken, 41
Shaffer, Steve, 61
Shakes, Ronnie, 48, 60–61, 125–126, *126*, 259–260
Shandling, Garry, 147, 149, 332
Sharkey, Joe, 40
Shaw, Bob, 61, 134
Shidner, Frances Lois Hartley, xii–xiv, 1
Shidner, James Thomas, xii–xiv, 1, 3, 324, 325–326

Shidner, Robbie, 139–140
Shock, Ron, 43
Shore, Mitzi, 45, 132–133, 134, 147, 152
Shriner, Wil, 134
Shultz, Lenny, 104
Shurtleff, Michael, 241
Shydner, Kay, 234, 244
Shydner, Ritch, *18, 20, 39, 46–47, 52, 60, 85, 87, 103, 110, 115, 121, 128, 169, 175–176, 182, 185, 192, 202, 209, 216, 224, 242, 267, 282, 290, 298, 300, 304, 325, 331, 372-373*
Silcox, Grover, 42
Silva, Bill, 43
Simon, Jose, 40
Sinbad, 149, 152, 203–204
Sinclair, Les, 181, 208–210
Siskind, Carol, 61, 151
Skrovan, Steve, 61
Slayton, Bobby, 40–41, 134
Slim, 8–9
Smirnoff, Yakov, 134, 149
Smith, Jan, 45
Smith, Margaret, 151, 277
Smothers, Dick, 100
Smothers, Tom, 100
Snow, Carrie, 40, 134, 151, 343
Sobel, Tom, 147
Solomon, Jonathan, 61
Soltanek, Phil. *see* Philips, Emo
Southern, Terry, 129
Spade, David, 150
Spanky, 152
Springsteen, Bruce, 26, 35
Staley, Dee, 41
Stanley, Jerry, 55, 72–74, *73,* 82, 152–153, 257
Starr, George. *see* Schultz, George
Starr, Ringo, 311–312

Starr, Sally, 307
Steger, Robert, 40
Stein, Abby, 61, 151
Stephan, Allan, 134, 343
Stern, Howard, 198, 289, 303, 305, 306, 337
Stevenson, Skip, 134
Stoller, Fred, 61, 268–269
Storts, Danny, 41
Strassman, David, 61, 129, 134, 184
Sweedler, D.F., 61
Sweeney, Steve, 42

**T**

Tam, Jim, 24
Tannen, Julius, 268
Taylor, Howard, 134
Tenuta, Judy, 41, 150, 238
Thomas, Bill, 23, 24, 43
Thomerson, Tim, 134
Thompson, Robbin, 35
Thornton, James J., 163
Tic Tacs, 274
Tienken, Richie, 59, 63, 86
Tingle, Jimmy, 149
Tiny. *see* Weeks, Dave "Tiny"
Titus, Christopher, 334
Toll, Judy, 42, 151
Tolsch, Adrianne, 48, 61, 62
Tomlin, Lily, 150
Torres, Johnny, 185
Torres, Liz, 151
Tosh, Daniel, 150
Tosh, Peter, 177
Touisaunt, Maurice, 60
Townsend, Robert, 149
Townshend, Dave, 16
Townshend, Pete, 34
Travis, Greg, 134
Tribble, David, 147
Trivax, Stu, 61

Tubby Boots, *254*, 257–258
Twain, Mark, 206, 229, 233, 253–254, 257, 258, 268, 321
Tyler, Robin, 151
Tyree, Dave, 134, 343, 344

**U**
Uncle Dirty. *see* Altman, Robert "Uncle Dirty"

**V**
Vallely, Jim, 60
Valli, Frankie, 236
Van Dyke, Dick, 262
Vance, Mike, 43
Vega, Joey, 61
Vernon, Jackie, 68
Vicich, Tony, 207
Vidale, Thea, 43
Vince, Dino, 45, 112–113
Vine, Howard, 17, 19
Von Hoffman, Brant, 48, 61, 72, 134

**W**
Wachs, Bob, 59, 86
Wachtel, Waddy, 34
Waddington, Dave "Waddo," 16
Waits, Tom, 264–265
Walker, Jimmy, 134
Wall, JJ, 48, 61
Wallace, George, 48, 61, 134, 149
Walrus. *see* Woods, Bob "Walrus"
Walters, Mitchell, 199–200
Ware, Don, 43
Warfield, Marsha, 41, 134, 151
Wayans, Damon, 149, 299
Wayans, Keenen Ivory, 48, 61, 134
Weeks, Dave "Tiny," 3
Weiner, Mark, 61
Weinstock, Ken, 277
Weinstock, Lotus, 134, 151
Weintraub, Barry, 61
Weiss, Anita, 61
Weiss, Barney, 42
Welles, Orson, 181
White, E.B., 91
White, Ron, 334
Whitman, Walt, 337
Williams, Bert, 265
Williams, Dave, 32, 36–37, 294
Williams, Robin, 40, 112, 134, 139–143, 198, 205, 246–247
Williams, Wendy O., 35–36
Wilson, Flip, 59
Wilson, Tom, 42
Windsor, Andy, 87–88
Wolfberg, Dennis, 48, 61
Wolfson, Carl, 134, 135
Wolinsky, Ed, 24
Woods, Bob "Walrus," 43, 74
Wright, Steven, 148, 191, 335
Wuhl, Robert, 48, 134

**Y**
Yeager, Ed, 343
Young, Bob, 42
Young, Steve, 42
Youngers, Sid, 43, 343
Youngman, Henny, 128, 330
Yume, Johnny, 134

**Z**
Zevon, Warren, 54
Zimmerman, Ron, 24, 61, 178
Zito, Chris, 43
Zucker, Charles, 61

# About The Author

In the 1980s, Ritch Shydner made numerous appearances on TV, including *Late Night with David Letterman* and *The Tonight Show with Johnny Carson* and *The Tonight Show with Jay Leno*. He did an HBO half-hour special, *One Night Stand*.

You may also recognize him as Al Bundy's co-worker on *Married with Children* and from guest appearances on many other TV shows, such as *Designing Women* and *Roseanne*. He wrote for sitcoms such as *Roseanne, The Jeff Foxworthy Show*, and HBO's *The Mind of the Married Man*.

Shydner translated his modest success on TV into an obscure film career, appearing in Steve Martin's *Roxanne* and Eddie Murphy's *Beverly Hills Cop II* before moving on to minor roles in smaller pictures.

He wrote material for Jeff Foxworthy's Grammy nominated comedy albums *Totally Committed* and *Big Fun*. He also wrote for Ron White and Jay Leno.

In 2006, Shydner was co-author with Mark Schiff of a book on stand-up, *I Killed: True Stories of the Road from America's Tom Comics*. Four years later, he produced and performed in Jordan Brady's award-winning documentary on the world of stand-up comedy, *I Am Comic*.

For more information, please visit http://www.RitchShydner.com
Twitter: @ritchshydner
Facebook: https://www.facebook.com/ritchs

*Get to know comedian **RITCH SHYDNER**,*
*author of* **KICKING THROUGH THE ASHES**
*and* **I KILLED***, in this Mr. Media® interview*
**https://youtu.be/ljXFh7OJJJI**

What is Mr. Media® Interviews? The calm of Charlie Rose, the curiosity of Terry Gross and the unpredictability of Howard Stern! Since February 2007, more than 1,000 exclusive Hollywood, celebrity, pop culture video and audio comedy podcast interviews by Mr. Media®, a.k.a., Bob Andelman, with newsmakers in TV, radio, movies, music, magazines, newspapers, books, websites, social media, politics, sports, graphic novels, and comics!

For more interviews like this one: http://MrMedia.com